EMOTIONAL MUSCLE

EMOTIONAL MUSCLE

Strong Parents, Strong Children

KERRY KELLY NOVICK & JACK NOVICK, PhD

Library of Congress Control Number: 2010914272
ISBN: Hardcover   978-1-4535-8475-0
                 Softcover   978-1-4535-8474-3
                 Ebook   978-1-4535-8476-7

This book was printed in the United States of America.

To order additional copies of this book, contact:
Xlibris Corporation
1-888-795-4274
www.Xlibris.com
Orders@Xlibris.com
86543

To our children and grandchildren and all the families at Allen Creek Preschool and beyond who have shared their lives with us and taught us the value of thoughtful parenting.

MORE PRAISE FOR EMOTIONAL MUSCLE

Parents write—
"I started reading it with much interest. After an hour, I realized I was filled with elation and hope. It made my day. The feeling has not worn off. It gave me the confidence and articulateness to challenge my kids on some chronic behaviors and amazingly, they have responded."

"I've read a lot of books about sleep and food and first aid, but I never know where to look when I have a question about my children's emotional development. In the heat of the parenting moment it's so hard to know what matters and what doesn't and what to insist on or let go. The ideas in this book really help me figure out what lesson I'm trying to teach and the kind of grown-up I'm trying to help my children become."

"**Emotional Muscle** opened up enjoyment of my job as a father. I now understand how much I have to offer my kids."

Grandparents write—
"I can't express how grateful I am for your putting my parenting values into words. I will give this profound and easy-to-read book to all my friends who are grandparents."

"I've read many parenting books over the years, but none that is so clear, precise and friendly. I'm grateful that **Emotional Muscle** gives me a common language to use with my daughter-in-law. That will reduce a lot of tension."

Educators write—
"The Novicks have captured the essence of early childhood in language both parents and teachers can appreciate. More than just another

exposition of the stages of child development, **Emotional Muscle** brings to life the challenges children face at various ages through vivid examples drawn from real experiences. The authors' expertise with living, breathing children comes through on every page."

Diane Manning, Ph.D., Former Chair of the Department of Education, Tulane University

"**Emotional Muscle** by Kerry Kelly Novick and Jack Novick is a must read for anyone committed to understanding how values are conveyed and how the development of character can be supported. Written in an easy to read, concrete, and informative way this book will surprise you with how it takes a very complex topic and makes it accessible and useful. At first I read it with the hopes of improving my work with young children and their families. I soon came to realize that it had a big impact on me personally and in my own interactions with my immediate family members. It is a book I will re-read and reference again and again."

Michelle Graves, Preschool Education Director, High Scope teacher trainer, Community Educator, Author of Educational Workbooks and parent.

"**Emotional Muscle** is a book that is needed, relevant and (should be) required reading for all parents and educators. The Novicks offer an inspiring blend of information with rich, real stories. They create not only a clear guide, but also a wealth of practical action steps to support adults in growing emotionally strong children in these challenging times."

Kathleen Kryza, International Educational Consultant and Author, University of Michigan School of Education.

Development Experts write—
"In this book Kerry and Jack Novick distill their years of experience with babies, young children, and parents. Walking their readers through the various developmental challenges that children and parents naturally face during the first five years, they do for these early years what Erik Erikson did on the broader canvas of the human life cycle in his classic Childhood and Society.

"The Novicks translate decades of clinical and developmental research into plain English, illustrating their points with examples that are easily accessible to any interested reader. Theirs is a practical psychoanalysis that is completely at home on the changing table, in the high chair, and on the playground.

"Their book will be a valuable resource to generations of parents, daycare workers, preschool teachers, and others caring for young children. What's more, the stories they tell make it clear how, as grownups help children to develop their emotional resources, everyone ends up feeling happier and stronger, better prepared for life's future challenges."

Paul M. Brinich, Ph.D, Clinical Professor, Departments of Psychology and Psychiatry, University of North Carolina at Chapel Hill, Psychoanalytic Education Center of the Carolinas

"We all want to know how to help children we care about to become kind, resilient, productive, and creative. **Emotional Muscle** is a rare gem that helps us, in practical ways, to accomplish this complex task. This book is a greatly needed contribution to the field of early childhood mental health, parenting, early childhood education.

"Based on their extensive life experience, their wisdom, and deep knowledge of what it is like to be a child or to parent children during their first formative five years, the Novicks, who are among the most innovative and dynamic contemporary child psychoanalysts, have provided us with a clear and engaging manual full of everyday examples of how to facilitate the emotional growth of children.

"Reading this book is not only very enjoyable, it is simply a must for everyone who works or lives with children, or for everyone who wants to understand themselves better."

Era Loewenstein, Ph.D Director of Preschool Consultation Program; Child, Adolescent and Adult Psychoanalyst

"It is a refreshing and welcome change when parents and professionals alike can be encouraged to notice strengths and to think in terms of building "emotional muscle" in both children and their parents. The Novicks and their work embody the idea that no one does anything reliably or well unless it brings with it a sense of pleasure.

"All who read this book will come away with an increased sense of appreciation for the behavior of young children as the vehicle through which they communicate. Recognition and acknowledgement of children's thoughts and feelings leads to celebration of understanding and feeling understood."
Thomas Barrett, Ph.D, Child and Adolescent Psychoanalyst and Psychologist;

Department Chair, Clinical Psy.D Program, Chicago School of Professional Psychology

CONTENTS

INTRODUCTION

When we first found out we were going to be parents, we were excited and scared and full of enthusiasm. We were busy making sure Kerry was healthy, preparing for the birth, organizing a cozy place for the baby to sleep, learning about feeding and diapering and how to keep our baby safe. But beyond this necessary focus on the physical, we were also busy figuring out together what kind of parents we wanted to be. There were parts of our own upbringings that we didn't want to repeat, and there were other things that we hoped to do as well as our parents had.

After a lot of talking about parenting, ranging from what we thought about allowances for children to how to celebrate family holidays (still only pregnant), we realized there was another area we hadn't even yet touched upon. What would our child be like? We knew we would love her. But how would we help her grow up to be a person we could admire and want to spend time with? How could we help her grow to be kind, creative, productive, and good?

Thus began a continuing fascination with how parents convey values, strength, and character to their children. We are child and adult psychoanalysts and psychologists. We talk to troubled families, consult with parents in our offices, at schools and businesses, and write articles, books, blogs, and newspaper columns about development. Our working life is filled with clinical experience of family situations that have gone awry in one way or another, and our experience is all too often the feeling of wishing to be able to intervene sooner, before the trouble starts. We see how hard parents and children struggle to cope with their life circumstances and the ordinary and extraordinary challenges they face. And we wish passionately to help them do this with more joy, confidence, success, and sense of purpose.

Through all the anxious nights and occasionally difficult days of our early parenting years, we also discovered the pleasure of figuring out what was going on with our own children. They gave us the great gift of sharing themselves with us. They told us what they were feeling and thinking and what they wanted and needed. Then we could either provide it or explain why we couldn't. The most wonderful discovery was how much fun it was! Parenting our three children opened new vistas for us as people and gave us access to parts of ourselves we didn't know were there. Plus, we got to know zoos, playgrounds, museums, and bathrooms in cities across the country and the world that we would never have seen without our children to lead us there.

Along the way, as we met our children's friends and their parents, we began to notice that some children were especially pleasant to be around; other children wanted to be friends with those kids; their parents were people we respected and enjoyed. Similarly, in our practices and our consultations, parents we worked with became more thoughtful and brave, more open and relaxed, happier and prouder of their children. All through those years, we did hundreds of consultations in preschools and day cares around our state, working with teachers and caregivers to help them understand what is important for young children and their families. We got to know wonderful teachers, devoted to being an important part of raising fine children to be good adults.

What were the qualities those friendly, interesting grown-ups and children were showing? They encompass many personal characteristics long considered desirable in all cultures throughout history. Whether we describe them as virtues, strengths, will, courage, character, grit, and so forth, one common thread is that they all imply effort, resolve, and strength. They all result in satisfaction and sturdy self-esteem.

What if everything you do with your child could include this extra dimension? What if each part of the day, no matter how you manage it, brought added value to your life and your child's development? What if you could build in a dimension that nurtures your child's character, offers wellsprings of happiness, promotes learning, and fosters friendships?

We call this dimension emotional muscle.[1] It can become part of everything you do with your child. And your children can build in the enjoyment of using sturdy emotional muscles, like trust and adaptability for babies, empathy and agency in one-year-olds, bounce-back and mastery in two-year-olds, assertion and persistence in three-year-olds, internal controls and realistic standards in four-year-olds, cooperation and competence in five-year-olds. This is what the book is about.

Everyone needs to develop and exercise physical muscles for health and well-being through their lives; without exercise, physical muscles will atrophy and you'll have lots of aches and pains. When people are in good physical shape, they are less tired at the end of their busy day. Similarly, emotional muscles make the ordinary interactions of daily life smoother. Emotional muscles promote happiness and sturdiness in the face of all life's challenges. Great athletes know this very well. Everyone tends to think of their amazing physical skills, but the athletes all state that mental factors make the crucial difference to their performance. And those mental skills come from training and practice as devoted as their physical drills.

No one gets in shape overnight. When should it start? How soon can children work out emotionally? Traditionally, people have talked about character development in children of school age and older. Our experience and modern research tell us something different: very young children are capable of much more than they are given credit for. As we will describe in the course of this book, emotional muscle can be fostered from birth on, and we continue to have opportunities to develop and exercise it until the end of life.

Consider, for instance, Toko, fifteen months old, who loved his toddler class and the children he saw there regularly with their parents. One day, he was busy with the garage at the far end of the room when he saw his friend Janie hesitating at the classroom doorway and clinging to her mother's leg. Toko went to the shelf and picked up the doll Janie usually liked to play with. He walked over to the door and handed it to her. Janie then came happily into the room and hung up her coat.

At this young age, Toko showed empathy—he was already able to see that Janie was having a different feeling from his and that she was worried. He could interrupt and defer his own play to address her need. He differentiated what she needed from what toy he would have wanted for comfort or distraction. His intervention was effective, and he registered this with a smile as he returned to his cars. As Toko and the many other children we will describe throughout the book show, emotional muscle can be fostered very early.

In 1994, we joined with colleagues and friends to create a nonprofit preschool as a laboratory to discover more concretely what is needed to raise children who will become kind, confident, productive, joyful, and creative members of the community. Toko was a student in one of the parent-toddler classes at Allen Creek Preschool.[2] The techniques developed by parents, teachers, and family consultants working together at Allen Creek are taken back out into the community to many other settings and situations. Much of the material for this book comes from putting together our personal and professional experiences about parenting with what we have learned as psychoanalytic family consultants. Throughout the book, we use discussions from Allen Creek parenting groups as examples of the challenges parents face and ways they can meet the challenges productively.

Parents and staff at Allen Creek and other such schools help each other to build emotional muscle. Their in-depth efforts give voice to many issues all parents face. But parents don't have to go to a special school or attend groups to become stronger and more confident. Everyone can use the insights and ideas generated at Allen Creek, whatever your circumstances. We hope in this book to offer suggestions from many sources that you can use to build your emotional muscles as parents. In turn, you will be able to help your child do the same.

Toko's emotional muscles did not come out of the blue; many fifteen-month-olds are not capable of doing as he did. He, with his parents and teachers, had practiced using his emotional muscles. We have learned from our model school that consistent and sustained effort makes a difference; parents need support and encouragement to help their children do the steady work needed to develop emotional muscle.

However, many parents and caretakers hesitate to demand work from children. Hard work has developed a bad reputation, and most people seem to think that "easy" is desirable. Along with the idealization of easy comes a fantasy that infancy and childhood are naturally magically idyllic and should unfold effortlessly. This can make parents think that their major goal is sparing their children any distress; if the child is upset, frustrated, angry, or disappointed, then parents worry they must have done something wrong.

All parents want their children to be happy. But it doesn't happen automatically. The most dependable happiness for children comes from a secure sense that they have the capacity to love and be loved. They need to feel confident that they can master frustration and distress. From that base, they can develop emotional muscles to be competent and effective in the world. There is almost nothing that feels as good as doing a job well and having that appreciated—the possibilities for pleasure, joy, and satisfaction are enormous.

In this book, we tell stories about parents and children, often in their own words, to describe practical techniques for parents and teachers to foster emotional muscle in everyday situations of living. The ideas for building emotional muscle draw on our long years of experience, the more than one hundred years of psychoanalytic understanding, and the revolution in child development research that has taken place over the past thirty years. Those ideas get tested in the laboratory of Allen Creek and other schools and then reexported to parents and teachers in the wider community.

Stories can sound quicker and easier than the real-life experience may be. For every kid who masters taking turns in a day, there are many who pitch a fit when asked to share. Life is messier than books, and different children may struggle, take a long time, or just not be ready for something. We hope to help you think about who your own child is and how you can best help him grow strong and happy. Any particular physical skill or emotional muscle develops in interaction with others, and each person's combination is his own. But eventually, we all need to build emotional muscles to live productive lives. Parents and children can use their emotional muscles as they negotiate the daily ups and downs of life.

One of our goals in this book is to help you do "thoughtful parenting." We don't expect you to agree with everything we say or suggest. Rather, we hope that our ideas help you realize that you can think about an issue and make a choice that feels good to you and builds emotional muscle. It will help you be a thoughtful parent if you think about your own goals for your child and reflect on your reactions rather than just reacting.

We are embarking on a journey together through the first six years of life with children, parents and grandparents, teachers and caregivers. There is a chapter for each age. But there are also consistent themes that run through development, spanning the years, which appear in all the chapters. You may find it interesting to trace the emotional muscles that grow over time within each theme. To help you do that, there are tables at the end of the book for parental emotional muscles and children's.

Each chapter contains

- characteristics and challenges of the particular age group,
- emotional muscles that parents and other adults work on to meet those challenges,
- emotional muscles that children can develop and suggestions for what parents and teachers can do to help children develop the strongest emotional muscles they are capable of at that age,
- endnotes that supply further research information or references to follow up.

Some emotional muscles relate most to only one age and may have only one component. Others are multifaceted and will have a longer description or several steps. Development is cumulative, so all the muscles from earlier years are contained in the later ones, even if we don't mention them specifically.

You can read this book in various ways; you may turn first to the chapter that relates to your kid's age. Each chapter can be read in that self-contained way. You may also find it interesting, though, to go back and start at the beginning as it's never too late to build those muscles that start at younger ages.

Have a good workout!

BABIES AND THEIR PARENTS BUILDING EMOTIONAL MUSCLE

Everyone knows that mothers need to prepare and take good care of themselves physically for pregnancy, childbirth, and the demands of infancy. People are less likely to recognize the psychological demands on new parents. All parents—biological, adoptive, foster parents and guardians—need emotional muscle to do the job, to master the challenges and enjoy the satisfactions of caring for babies. Knowledge is power—what you know about your baby will be a source of strength. If you are reading this book, you know that safety and physical care are essential, but they are not all that children need. From birth on, babies are complex, competent, and engaged people. To survive, babies need attachment to an adult who is tuned in. Then they can develop all their capacities. To be able to read your baby and be in tune, you will need emotional muscles and the strength that comes from using them.

What parents learn

BEARING THE UNCERTAINTY, FACING THE UNKNOWN

Meeting your new baby is like meeting a stranger. You don't know her well at first. So you are challenged to bear the uncertainty and excitement of a new venture.

The baby you've longed for, the baby you've imagined, is finally here. It takes courage for an adult to accept that the real baby is still unknown. From the very beginning, parents are challenged to acknowledge the separateness of their baby rather than taking an easy way out by putting on to the baby their own preconceived ideas or expectations. Only after digesting that idea can we turn our full selves to the task of getting to know *this* baby.

Harriet called for advice after her second baby, Joey, was born. Her mother-in-law was talking constantly about the way Joey was the image of his father, and she treated him as if he had the same personality. Many of the expectable challenges of the early months were explained by her mother-in-law as due to this similarity. Harriet was angry and felt helpless. Harriet said, "It's really hard to confront her, but I want to protect Joey. It feels like she's pushing him into a mold." We said that the really important thing was that Harriet knew Joey was his own person and that his own personality would emerge over time. Little by little, Harriet could share her perceptions of Joey, point out his signals, and maybe gradually her mother-in-law would appreciate him for himself.

Traditionally, we have all heard about teaching the baby to join us in understanding our world. In fact, that process will happen best if we first make the effort to understand babies, to enter their world with our feelings and thoughts.[3] To put ourselves in the baby's place, we have to imagine ourselves operating in an unfamiliar universe while limited by small size, untried physical and mental abilities, and lack of experience.

MAKING AN ALLIANCE WITH YOUR BABY

Your baby will be an active partner in the process of getting in tune. She has wishes, motives, and feelings of her own from the start.

The major challenge for new babies is to find an effective way to regulate themselves. But babies cannot do this alone—they need adults to help them. It is a shared and joint effort, separate people creating a partnership that ensures the survival of the baby and can provide deep satisfaction for the adult. Working from that premise, parents can then develop the emotional muscle to partner with their baby, who needs them to be as tuned in as they can be. Current infant research establishes what clinicians and many parents have long known—infants come into the world well equipped for relationships. Their main aim is to establish connections with others.[4] In what is called the new science of emotional competence,[5] researchers have demonstrated that infants are born able to recognize people as similar to them, be aware of their own and others' feelings, and recognize their caregiver's attunement.[6]

Babies can do a lot to help the partnership process; by one week old, they can exchange gazes, facial expressions, vocalizations, and movements with their mothers. They signal with their voices and whole bodies when something doesn't feel good; they let us know when they feel good by stretching, smiling, opening their eyes, falling asleep contentedly. When parents read their baby's signals accurately and do what's needed, babies feel competent and so do parents. These initial feelings of competence are a source of great joy for both parents and children and lay the foundation of emotional muscle. With this foundation, babies can gradually bear the inevitable little delays—they begin to develop the capacity to wait, to tolerate mild frustration. These demonstrate the beginning presence of emotional muscle. When you know that your investment helps your baby right away as she begins to organize her experience but will also lay the important foundation for her later character, it's an added incentive to you at a time of tiredness and conflicting demands.

Babies have their own rhythms and grown-ups have their own needs. It takes compromises from both to establish a general daily timetable that suits you both. But being able to predict and depend on the sequence of events helps babies feel secure and will strengthen the alliance between you. Baby and parents will both enjoy and rely on the routines. Once a routine is established, it takes emotional muscle to hold on to your knowledge that it's important. This can become especially difficult around times of holidays and family visits.

In all the schools we consult to, we recommend that parents think about holiday plans in the fall. This comes from our experience that holidays can be very stressful for young families. They may be visiting or being visited by relatives or in-laws, who often expect the family timetable to suit the grown-ups rather than the baby. New parents need support to be able to stand up to their own parents and enlist them as partners in maintaining the baby's harmonious balance. "Just this once" can sometimes lead to weeks of disrupted sleep, which can have far-reaching effects.[7] It takes courage to advocate for your own and your child's needs in your effort to support your baby's growing trust in your predictable activities. Knowing that this can have lifelong impact is an added incentive to resist pressures to sacrifice your baby's needs to other grown-ups' wishes.

CREATING SUPPORTIVE PARTNERSHIPS

*No parent can do the whole job alone. It takes effort to
seek, create, and maintain a support system.*

Being a parent is the most demanding job most of us will ever do, and it is the least supported. In our culture, there is a lot of talk about the importance of family and children, but very little institutional or public backup. To develop the necessary emotional muscle to be an effective parent, everyone needs the help of others. We all need someone to support our efforts, to help us think things through, to point out habits we may not be aware of, to spell us when we are worn out, to bring new ideas, and, in general, help us develop emotional muscle for this very challenging task. Few people would start an exercise program without consulting a physician or at least a trainer or coach. No one would think of running a marathon with no training or conditioning. Parenting is longer and more demanding than any marathon.

Partners or significant others are usually the first resource. There are many sources for the strong urge to bond with your baby. Biological mothers produce the hormone oxytocin in childbirth and breastfeeding; this primes them to bond with their babies. Adoptive mothers often make sure to have close physical contact to support this process. Fathers who are given the chance for close physical care of a newborn infant produce vasopressin, a neuromodulator that evokes protective and loving feelings of commitment to the baby and its mother.

Many fathers, who have not seemed particularly interested in infants, can become very involved parents if they are given the chance early on. This may include direct care but is most often seen in their devoted support of the mother. Mothers have to make sure that they don't deprive themselves of needed support by excluding their partner from the early stages of attunement. It takes emotional muscle to assert the legitimate need for help, to persist in maintaining the partner's bond with the baby, and to stay connected as grown-up partners.

Roxie's mother Jenny loved coming to Under Ones class at Allen Creek Preschool and talking about how much fun she was having watching her baby grow. She was staying home for the first few months, and breastfeeding. One day, she described an important experience with her husband the night before. She had greeted him with a heartfelt sigh, saying how tired she was, since Roxie had nursed extra and slept less that day. He said how that didn't sound like fun and maybe he was lucky to be at work after all even though he had been missing them both. She had a moment of feeling that he didn't deserve to be part of her fun with Roxie since she was the one doing all the work. This struck her as a pretty mean attitude and also as something that would deprive her of support she wanted and needed.

Jenny realized that she had been taking more and more satisfaction in feeling so essential to Roxie, and she was leaving her husband out of her overall pleasure and growing sense of accomplishment as she got to know Roxie. She then told him all about Roxie laughing when she had sung "This Little Piggie" to her on the changing pad; when Roxie woke up during their supper, her daddy went to change her and sang the song. Roxie gurgled with pleasure and her daddy did too. Jenny felt so good seeing her husband and Roxie having fun together. She realized that she had made that possible by sharing her own pleasure with him and that she had to make the effort to do so.

Sharing the pleasure helps to cement the caring relationship between spouses and with other family members and caregivers. It has another effect as well in promoting flexibility in the mother's ways of relating. Staying in tune demands focus and a huge effort to meet the baby where she is; to do this, a parent shifts into a particular gear. Relating to others involves switching gears, moving into a more grown-up state of mind. As the baby grows, and later, when there may be a child of a different age to engage with, parents are challenged to multitask, switching gears to the level of relating appropriate to each person. Practice from early on promotes this strength.

When a spouse is not most helpful or available, some seek advice from family members or friends; others ask the doctor or nurse for help in planning their baby's care; others may research issues of feeding, sleeping, equipment, and practices by reading books or searching the Internet. Being able to ask for help is an important ingredient of emotional muscle—seeking out a parenting group or meeting with a parent coach can provide crucial support. It doesn't matter which method or combination of methods increases emotional muscle and competence in mothers or fathers. What matters is feeling good about the work of accomplishing each step in getting to know your baby better.

Frances was a high-powered business manager, who was a single mom. She took pride in her self-sufficiency. When she found herself becoming enraged with her four-month-old son, who was not yet sleeping through the night, and irritated at work, she felt overwhelmed with failure. A friend suggested she join the Under Ones class at Allen Creek. Frances was distrustful but desperate, so she gave it a try. She was surprised and then deeply moved to find out that she was not alone in her predicament, that her anger and irritability were not signs of her unfitness to be a mother or an executive. She said in the group that she had always found it difficult to ask for help, but she was now listening to the other parents sharing their dilemmas and discovering that it seemed more like a strength than a weakness for them to do so. She also saw how the other parents were using their spouses for support. Frances then felt able to work on getting help from the group with her nighttime issue with Georgie. And she called her mother, who lived nearby, and began including her on a regular basis in Georgie's care. Frances and her mother began talking on the phone every day. Georgie's grandmother also visited in school and got to know Georgie's classmates and their parents. Frances and her mother together created a network of supportive relationships.

LIVING THROUGH YOUR BABY'S MILD DISTRESS

You and your baby are learning to depend on each other by sharing the whole range of feelings.

Parents also have to develop the emotional muscle to bear their baby's mild distress and recognize that this will not harm her. Attunement does not mean completely anticipating your baby's every need, thinking that you know what she wants before she signals. Normal, healthy babies and parents are actually tuned in to each other about 30 percent of the time.[8] What matters is parent and baby partnering to get back in sync, to repair moments of mismatch. In fact, babies learn a crucial lesson by making a signal of need that is then responded to; they feel their signals are effective and begin to trust that they are in charge of getting help when it's needed. This is a crucial building block for a feeling of agency, the sense of being in charge of oneself. We see this as the basis for developing a competent system of self-regulation.[9]

Newborn Stevie and his mother Marie came to the office to see one of us for a consultation. She had lost her mother during her pregnancy and was feeling overwhelmed about parenting. In the office, Stevie signalled his various needs for feeding, soothing, stimulation, and sleep. Stevie's mother, however, interpreted every emotional signal he made as a need for a diaper change. She changed him five times in our one-and-a-half-hour meeting. I thought that Marie was dealing with her own worry and helplessness by attributing to Stevie a very limited range of needs, mainly relief of discomfort at wetness. This was something Marie was sure she knew how to fix. She also did not seem to register that Stevie's signals were actually varied.

Over a few more meetings, by sitting next to Marie on the floor, facing Stevie, I could gently describe his facial expressions, body movements, and activity levels. I also modeled for Marie how to bear the uncertainty by enjoying the discovery process. "Oh, Stevie, you're opening your eyes wide and waving your hands and feet at us. You sure look involved in something. I wonder what you're telling us. Any ideas, Marie?" Marie wasn't sure. I said, "I'm not sure either, but pretty soon he'll probably let us know." Marie relaxed and then she pointed out that Stevie was pursing his lips and making sucking noises. She tentatively suggested he might be hungry. "Wow, he let you know what he wanted eventually. You just had to bear waiting for him to get there." Gradually, with persistence and effort, Marie learned to read her baby more accurately. She began to exclaim as she noticed Stevie's wishes emerging and changing. After some time, Marie was able to say, "Oh, Stevie, you're trying to tell me something. What is it, little guy? Let's figure it out." She then felt strong enough to try different responses until she found the one that met his needs.

KEEPING JOY AND LOVE IN THE PICTURE

*Make the effort to recall good times and
share them to maintain love.*

People talk about the joys of having children, but this is often a distorted idealization of the actual experience. Many children are unwanted, mistreated, physically or psychologically abused. Even under the best of circumstances, joy and love can easily be submerged by physical or emotional discomfort. Parents of new babies undergo sleepless nights, helplessness, worry, and uncertainty. It takes effort to access and hold on to good feelings. This effort takes practice and repetition. Holding on to good feelings about your baby stretches new parents when they have fewer reserves. Negative feelings can be very powerful; anger, irritation, helplessness, or regret can swamp the moments of joy during the day.

By the evening, after a long day of child care or work, a parent may find it hard to remember the good feelings. A memory fires the same area in the brain as the actual original experience, so telling someone else about the good times will revive and strengthen the pleasure in both the speaker and the listener.[10] It is therefore very important, whether it is a caregiver greeting a parent or the caretaking parent greeting the partner, that the good feelings of the day be shared first. Then both will strengthen their love for the baby. In the context of this shared love and pleasure, you can then share the difficulties.

This is where the availability of another loving, supportive adult is crucial to offer perspective, ideas, even humor. It's easier to see the funny side of a ten-pound person making an adult feel helpless when the exasperation is shared. It is also deeply important to have our enormous and irrational love for the baby validated and accepted by another. Whether it's a spouse, a grandparent, a neighbor, or the checkout clerk at the grocery store saying how darling she is, seeing your baby through someone else's eyes can restore you to a loving place.

There are times when a parent's best effort isn't enough and there are no people in the immediate circle to offer constructive support. A blaming or preoccupied spouse, a critical grandparent, a judgmental nurse—these can all be terribly undermining to a new parent's confidence and interfere with the development of the muscles needed to recall good times. That is when a parent group or professional help can be very useful.

RECOGNIZING WHEN TO SEEK EXTRA HELP

Be strong and brave enough to set aside shame or guilt when things aren't going as well as you expected with your baby.

The usual experience for new parents is a process of gradually learning to sort out the baby's own pattern of soothing, stimulation need, feeding, sleeping, and so forth. But some babies take longer than others for these patterns to emerge into a predictable organization. These are sometimes the babies who cry for no apparent reason or are hard to comfort. It takes emotional muscle on the part of parents to face their baby's distress and their own not knowing what to do. Sometimes, all parents can do is hold on to hope and confidence that things will improve and the baby will eventually settle down. In this predicament, parents need support to maintain optimism, and they need the strength to ask for it.

Other babies really don't seem to respond to ordinary interventions. This warrants investigation, to find out if there is an underlying cause for the baby's unusual distress or difficulty. Advice and support are needed to be able to stay with the knowledge that these factors may be internal to the baby and not necessarily the parents' fault. Parents have the challenging task of not reacting to their own helplessness by blaming themselves or the baby.

Marisa's mother, Diana, struggled to feed her; when Marisa was hungry, she screamed; when she was full, she screamed. Her mother felt she couldn't do anything right to help Marisa feel content and happy. She was being blamed by her in-laws and her husband for her feeding technique, her burping, her milk, and anything else that might make her responsible for the trouble. She too worried what she was doing wrong as she couldn't bear thinking that something was seriously wrong with Marisa. We met her at a playgroup in a neighborhood community center, where Diana came to obtain her food stamps. As we spent time with the mom and baby, it was clear that Diana was a competent, loving, and attuned mother. She was doing all she could and still Marisa could not settle and be comforted. We worked to support Diana in facing what she knew in her heart—her baby was struggling and she needed more help to find out why.

With our encouragement, Diana consulted a hospital specialist as her pediatrician had not responded helpfully to her concerns. Marisa was found to have a condition that made it difficult for her to get the full nutrition from her milk. She needed special supplements, and Diana had to adjust her diet as well. Diana's strength in using our support to seek specialized help gave her confidence to take good care of her baby as Marisa began to flourish.

OPENING YOURSELF TO THE REALITY OF BABIES' EMOTIONS

It takes strength for parents to acknowledge the full range and intensity of babies' feelings.

There is a lot babies can't do; they need adults to take care of them and meet the needs they signal. But there is also so much they can do. The full range of emotions is available to babies from birth. It is part of our evolutionary heritage and forms what neuroscientists call the core self.[11] While babies automatically have access to a wide range of positive and negative feelings, parents often have to overcome barriers to their own access to feelings. As a grown-up, there may be many feelings that have been blocked off, avoided, denied, or otherwise pushed aside. This can have roots in family history, cultural norms, and personality structure. Many parents therefore find it difficult at first to understand how varied and rich their baby's emotional life is. The intensity of infant emotions can also be hard to bear since babies feel their feelings with their whole bodies, and haven't yet developed any filters to modulate and master their own experience.

Julie brought her four-month-old to Under Ones class at Allen Creek and shared her dismay over how upset Sandy got if she didn't pick her up right away. "It sounds like she's in pain! Am I hurting her somehow?" The teacher suggested that perhaps Sandy was mad because she wanted her mom the minute she felt the need, and frustration can make anyone mad. "Can such little babies even get mad?" Julie asked.

The parents and teachers talked about all the feelings they saw the babies experiencing, both in class and at home. Everyone shared how hard it is to recognize anger in babies because parents may feel that they have to make sure their babies never get mad at them, or else they feel like bad parents.

Julie then said that she always felt like a bad girl when she got mad at her parents, and she was determined that her Sandy should never go through that. The other parents and teachers reassured her that anger was a useful signal of something troublesome and was bound to come into interactions between parents and children. The teachers compared the importance of pain as a physical signal with anger as a psychological signal; if we didn't feel pain, we wouldn't stay away from the hot stove, and if we didn't feel anger, we would never learn what we liked and didn't like. Everyone agreed that we all need to know when something doesn't feel good. The other moms and dads pointed out how lucky Julie was that her baby could signal frustration so clearly because then Julie could fix it.

The family consultant noted that there was a general point to learn from Julie's example. When babies have intense feelings, parents can feel helpless, uncertain how to understand it and not knowing what to do. Helplessness is hard for anyone to tolerate. Parents can deal with this by lashing back at the baby, getting angry with their voices or actions, shouting at or shaking a baby. This may make parents feel momentarily less helpless but can really hurt the baby and seriously undermine the parent-child relationship. The baby needs parents to absorb her feeling and transform it by reading it as a signal of needing something.

Another mom said that made sense and helped her understand why she had felt a spurt of anger at her baby kicking while she changed his diaper the day before. She had felt helpless and then guilty about being so angry and realized that she could have seen his kicking as his frustration at having to lie down for so long. Then she could have found a different solution, maybe singing to him or making faces.

These parents were developing the emotional muscle to acknowledge honestly what their babies were feeling, how they felt in response, and working to exercise other options. Parents can develop the emotional muscle to respond to helplessness with problem-solving rather than rage, blame, or withdrawal.

BEARING YOUR OWN INTENSE FEELINGS

It takes courage and strength for parents to be open to the whole range of their own feelings, especially fears and worries, and work to transform them into signals.

As with all feelings, anxiety can become overwhelming. The task, which requires emotional muscle, is to manage feelings and keep them at a useful signal level rather than an overwhelming state. This is not easy in relation to anxiety as any anxiety from the baby sets off mirror neurons in the mother's brain so that she feels the feeling too. This is an important survival mechanism, but it can swamp the parent, which will increase the baby's anxiety in turn, unless the parent can call upon other strengths. Parents can use their adult knowledge that this is a temporary moment; they can get another's perspective; and they can work to differentiate their own feelings from the child's. In this way, they are developing a stronger emotional muscle for tolerating their own and others' feelings and learning how to help their baby feel secure.

In all our work at Allen Creek—in day care consultations, with pregnancy and parent-infant groups, in private work with parents, with biological or adopted babies—we have found consistently that parents, especially mothers, struggle with anxiety that is sometimes very intense. They worry that their babies will die, be smothered, fall, be hurt by them, be scared, feel insecure, and so forth. Most of the time, parents simultaneously remark, with rueful laughter, that they "know it's crazy, but. . ."

When the mothers all talked in baby group one day about how often they got up in the night to check that their babies were still breathing, they were very relieved to hear that they weren't the only ones to do this. We added how useful and adaptive maternal anxiety could be since it motivated them to be alert to real dangers for their children and kept them focused on their babies' state.

Anxiety that is too intense can become overwhelming and interfere with pleasure, attachment, and the development of emotional muscle. Acknowledging, sharing, and understanding the value of your feelings creates an early strand of emotional muscle. We help teachers, doctors, nurses, infant workers, and others work with parents to strengthen their capacity to differentiate between the baby's reactions and their own.

As the first year progresses and the babies grow, there is generally a solidifying of attachment and a relative lessening of all-encompassing, potentially overwhelming anxiety around death, loss, or annihilation. It seems that secure attachment cannot be consolidated until experience helps parents move beyond the potentially traumatizing fear that their babies will die. Some parents do this quite quickly, reassured by watching their babies actually grow and flourish; most respond to support and encouragement from family consultants, physicians, teachers, and other parents; a few take longer and need extra help to make this progressive developmental move. All are developing emotional muscle by first opening themselves to their feelings and then allowing real experience to change them.

Mary and her mother Olive missed a mothers' group because Mary got her first cold. When they returned, her mother talked about how scared she had been the first time Mary sounded so stuffed-up in the night. Was she going to be able to breathe? When Mary woke up crying and coughing, Olive felt a little panicky for a minute. Then she reminded herself of what she knew to do about congested noses, wiped Mary's face with a warm cloth, and rocked her back to sleep. Olive said she realized then that she just had to deal with her own worries, and since Mary had gone back to sleep just fine, she guessed that she was a lot more worried than her Mary was! But Olive slept lightly that night, listening in case Mary needed her. When she called the doctor's office, the nurse confirmed that she was doing everything she could, and indeed, Mary was better in time to come to group the next week.

Olive had worked through an important sequence in building her emotional muscles. First, she pushed herself to bear her anxiety, not reacting to the helplessness of such a big feeling by denying it or succumbing totally to it. She differentiated her own feeling from Mary's, and then she kept her worry as a signal to help herself stay alert for her baby's needs.

Olive took her efforts a step further, wondering to herself why she had been quite so worried. She told her friends that she had remembered that her own mother was always terribly upset over even minor illnesses. Olive thought that she had probably learned that attitude from her mother; she determined to develop a sturdier, more realistic response to be prepared for all the times Mary was likely to get sick.

DIFFERENTIATING SEPARATENESS AND SEPARATION

*Growth is about transformation, not physical
separation.*

A lifelong task for parents that begins in infancy is to grow *with* your child, not *away* from your child. In other words, the goal of parent-child relationships is not to leave each other, but to transform the relationship to be close at each new level. Many theories of child development, bolstered by cultural norms, equate physical separation with growing up.[12] Parents can feel tempted or pressured to measure their child's successful development by how easily she separates. This often arises at day care or preschools where staff may say things like, "She did so well, she didn't miss you" or encourage parents to sneak out or drop their children at the front door to avoid tears. If a child is crying, staff often pushes parents to leave anyway, assuring them that the child will be "fine once you're gone."

Fear of separation is the first and most powerful anxiety. It is a survival mechanism, built into the brains of all mammals whose young need extended care after birth. Parents and babies both feel it. Babies feel it as equivalent to total loss, which literally means death to an infant. Parents can use their knowledge that brief physical separations are just that, and everyone will survive. This helps parents distinguish psychological and physical separation.

Physical separation is a goal sooner or later in childhood, but that is not the real issue. The important thing is recognizing and respecting the fundamental separateness of babies from the beginning. Then parents can work to create the kind of solid, respectful emotional connection that can be maintained but transformed throughout life.

In consulting work at day care centers, much of the effort with staff is to help them remember that their primary task is to keep the parent-child relationship vivid and present in the child's mind, and not compete by thinking that they are replacement parents. Equally, parents who use day care for their babies should keep the relationship alive in their own minds. You are apart physically, but not emotionally. It takes effort and muscle to contain the strong mixed feelings that separation evokes and to have the confidence that you are always the most important person to your child.

A day care director in a consultation meeting brought up a problem she was having with a new mother at the center. The mother insisted on staying with her baby for the first few days, and the director and caregivers were insulted, feeling that the mother didn't trust them. The caregiver felt that the mother was interfering with the child forming a bond to the caregiver and might be causing a separation problem.

The consultant reframed the discussion in terms of everyone's shared goal of supporting the baby's development. The goal was not separation but secure separateness in which mother and baby could keep each other in mind. How could the staff foster that? This led eventually to some major changes in the center, with caregivers making efforts to talk about home and parents, show babies pictures of their parents, sing home songs—in short, to keep the parent-child relationship alive in each baby's mind throughout the day. Parents were encouraged to call to check in and hear about their baby's day. Parents from this center expressed their appreciation and reported changes in their own feelings of connectedness to their babies.[13]

No matter how much your child changes, whether your child is at home or in day care from early on, the primary parent-child relationships are central and must be maintained. This takes enormous effort and strength on the part of parents and caretakers. When parents can do the hard work of retaining their knowledge that the child is a separate person from the beginning, as well as staying connected through their love, they won't react to each change in the child as a separation and loss.

Leila was mystified and felt pushed away when six-month-old Tarik had a growth spurt and simultaneously developed several new skills. He no longer accepted being swaddled for sleep, and she found herself worrying that he would somehow get hurt in his crib. He loved to roll over and over across the floor, and she said that she and her husband had been joking about how he would be going off to college before they knew it, when she had burst into tears. In the class discussion, the other parents reminded her that he had always been a separate person, who had enjoyed the swaddling she offered; now he was telling her that he wants something else. But he still needs her even if she doesn't yet know exactly what he wants. "We're always trying to catch up with our babies."

Anique shared her discouragement with the Under Ones group when she described her feeling that Francois, eleven months old, didn't seem to need her for much anymore. He was feeding himself finger food, had stopped nursing, and was getting himself to sleep at evening and nap times. She wondered why she was staying home with him. The parents who were there with their second children talked about remembering feeling exactly that way when their older children had made the clear move from the total dependency of infancy toward the increasing autonomy of toddlerhood. One mother said, "I keep saying to my kid and to myself 'I will always be your mom. We'll be together in new ways.'"

CREATING A POSITIVE CYCLE FOR STRENGTHENING EMOTIONAL MUSCLE

Competence, self-awareness, and emotional muscle are mutually enhancing.

New parents struggle with worries that they don't know what to do for their babies, that they might do something wrong, that they might hurt their babies or won't know what they need. This can become a vicious circle of helplessness. The alternative is a positive cycle of confidence, competence, and mastery. When a new parent feels more securely on top of what is going on, he or she feels competent and will actually be better able to meet the baby's needs. The goal is a combination of competence and confidence that you can learn to do what your baby needs. A parent called this thoughtful parenting, where you think about your goals and reflect on your reactions rather than just reacting. Then you experience the self-reinforcing satisfaction of mastery.

Sally's mother, Eleanor, talked about how she had spent a couple of days earlier in the week feeling really irritated and worried about Sally. She felt like she couldn't do anything right for her baby; none of the old methods seemed to work to get her to sleep. Eleanor and her husband had sat down to talk it through. As they went over what had been happening recently and brainstormed about the changes, they realized together that Sally was spending a lot more time awake now that she was nearly six months old. Eleanor was used to feeding Sally when she first woke up, but now that she was busily playing between feeds, Sally might be too hungry to go easily to sleep the next time. Eleanor tried switching to feeding Sally at the end of a play period, and Sally had begun to settle easily again.

Eleanor shared her insight that her own feeling of confusion and annoyance had actually signaled a change in Sally. She said it felt so good to talk it through with her husband. Eleanor felt relieved and proud that they had figured out what Sally needed, and Eleanor felt better able to anticipate bearing her own negative feelings the next time since they would probably recur when Sally made another developmental step.

Eleanor had strengthened her emotional muscles, using component skills at each step along the way. First she had tolerated her own uncertainty, then used her feelings as a signal that she had a problem to solve. She asked for help and used her mind together with her husband to figure out the situation and generate solutions to try. When things changed, she reflected on why and how and appreciated her own competence in making a difference. That pleasure was a self-reinforcing experience that keeps the positive cycle going.

THE EMOTIONAL MUSCLES USED BY PARENTS OF BABIES ARE

BEARING UNCERTAINTY AND FACING THE UNKNOWN

MAKING AN ALLIANCE WITH YOUR BABY

CREATING SUPPORTIVE PARTNERSHIPS

LIVING THROUGH YOUR BABY'S MILD DISTRESS

KEEPING JOY AND LOVE IN THE PICTURE

RECOGNIZING WHEN TO SEEK EXTRA HELP

OPENING YOURSELF TO THE REALITY OF BABIES' EMOTIONS

BEARING YOUR OWN INTENSE FEELINGS

DIFFERENTIATING SEPARATENESS AND SEPARATION

CREATING A POSITIVE CYCLE FOR STRENGTHENING EMOTIONAL MUSCLE

What do babies need to develop emotional muscle?

Security and safety from being overwhelmed are fundamental for all babies to survive physically and emotionally. Babies need predictability, consistency, attunement, and affection to feel secure. Infants are born with the capacity to recognize the attunement of their caregivers. Surprises and irregularity make babies feel helpless. A helpless baby has to spend too much energy just holding herself together; she won't have resources available to get to know her own signals, her important people, and the world around her. But even the best-attuned parents are likely to be out of sync with their babies a lot of the time and have to spend energy and time restoring attunement. It takes very hard work and emotional muscle on the part of parents to create the conditions in which their babies can thrive.

Even an enjoyable and nonstressful experience demonstrates how much work everyone puts in. We can see the relationship between parents' emotional muscle and the baby's emerging strengths in the story of Thea and her sippy cup.

Thea's mom described the night before when six-month-old Thea was sitting in her high chair, a sippy cup in one hand and a spoon in the other. She was trying to get the cup to her mouth, but the spoon was in the way. Her mommy and daddy watched her efforts as she twisted the cup, twisted her head, twirled the spoon, banged the cup with the spoon, and so on. After several minutes, Thea managed to grab the cup's second handle with the hand holding the spoon. She brought it to her mouth and sighed and gurgled. Her mom congratulated her dad on being able to let Thea work it out, persisting in trying to solve the problem.

To us, Thea's parents were using emotional muscle, resisting stepping in prematurely to fix the situation. They were working with the knowledge that babies can do much more than they are given credit for and wanted to help Thea do as much as she could for herself. They could see that Thea was busy, that the frustration was not overwhelming her, and therefore the work was good for her. Thea was learning persistence, trying different solutions and tolerating frustration. Then she had the intense satisfaction of mastering the challenge.

Physical muscles are inborn and grow at their own rate as long as nutrition, space, and opportunity for activity are provided. Infants' social, psychological, intellectual, and emotional capacities will also unfold when parents and caretakers follow the baby's active lead, working to attune themselves to her feelings, needs, intentions, exploration, and attachment. Emotional muscles are part of this complex development and can be fostered by parents building on and reinforcing the working of the baby's growing personality at each stage. This is a lifelong process, but it is best started in infancy.

What babies learn

ANTICIPATION, DEPENDABILITY, AND FLEXIBILITY
TRUST, CONSTANCY, AND ADAPTABILITY
UNDERSTANDING CONSEQUENCES AND CONTROLLING IMPULSES
INITIATIVE, RESPONSIBILITY, AND FOCUS
COMPETENCE

How parents help babies build emotional muscle

Babies are very busy. They are constantly figuring out what is happening, making connections, putting together cause and effect. The more we support the baby's learning about her experience, the more competent she will feel and the stronger she will be emotionally. "Infants learn more from their own actions than from observing others."[14] Each of the points that follow speaks to different ways that parents can set the stage for babies to learn from their own experience, trying new actions, putting things and ideas together in new ways, discovering the world inside and out to build their own emotional muscles.

ANTICIPATION, DEPENDABILITY, AND FLEXIBILITY

These muscles can be developed from the beginning to
help your baby feel secure.

Parents can promote this growth by

- **ESTABLISHING ROUTINES**
  You can initiate some routines even before your baby has settled into a predictable pattern. For instance, you can change her diaper at the same point in the feeding/sleeping cycle and sing the same song while doing it. This builds on babies' inborn capacity to make connections. As routines become dependable, your baby may relax. Very soon, a baby crying for a feed will stop as soon as she hears her parent's footsteps coming. She is anticipating that the milk is coming soon and is able to bear her hunger and frustration for a few minutes more.

- **ANTICIPATING CHANGES OUT LOUD**
  Talking about upcoming changes helps babies begin to predict what will happen next. Transitions are hard for everyone, especially babies—some advance notice may reduce distress and crying by setting up a familiar connection.
  A young mother said that she had thought talking to her newborn was just "too silly." But four-month-old Sammy screamed every time she put him in the car seat and tried to buckle him in. She then tried telling him beforehand that they were going in the car and that he

would be putting his arms through the straps, getting all buckled in nice and cozy to be safe. He stopped screaming and arching, instead looking around with interest. Sammy's mother experimented with anticipating other transitions, for instance, making sure to say "1-2-3 up!" before picking him up. Sammy's day and his interactions with his mother became much smoother in general. They both felt more capable. Anticipation is an emotional muscle that babies can develop.

- **SIGNALING AND STRUCTURING TRANSITIONS**
Signal and structure transitions with music or song so that the baby knows what is happening and knows that it will end.
Diaper changes seem relatively easy with newborns, but they become squirmy and difficult as the baby grows and develops more physical activity as well as interest in looking around and reaching for things. Singing a particular song or playing a particular game during each change will help hold the baby's interest and increase her tolerance for having something done to her. A pleasurable interaction strengthens the baby's capacity to wait.

- **USING WORDS TO ANTICIPATE PLEASURE AFTER A NECESSARY DELAY**
"The milk will taste so good as soon as it's warm enough."
"When we go outside, we'll see all the cars going by."

- **EMPHASIZING THE PLEASURE BY NAMING IT AGAIN**
"That milk sure tastes good, doesn't it?"
"We're having fun looking at all the cars."

TRUST, CONSTANCY, AND ADAPTABILITY

Changes are part of life, but they can also be overwhelming for parents and children. Babies adapt better to changes that are gradual—they need manageable amounts at a time so that they don't start to feel completely helpless.

Parents can promote this growth by the following:

- **MAKING CHANGES GRADUAL**
Many parents have their babies sleep next to them or close by right after birth. When they decide it is time for the baby to sleep on her

own in her crib, it makes the task manageable for the baby if it starts with only one nap a day. When the baby has mastered that change, another time can be added until all the naps and the nighttime sleep are in the crib. Manageable change leads to mastery.

One of the biggest changes that faces babies and their parents is when parents plan to include alternative care for the baby, either in the home or at a day care. The feelings around the separation are intense, and we have talked about the parent side of it in relation to transforming the relationship with your baby as she grows. Here we want to stress that time apart is one among many changes that parents and babies can face together. The same principles hold for any changes—gradual and predictable are best.

The goal is for the baby to be able to master the changes from a position of strength. That means helping the baby to develop the emotional muscle that will sustain her through the separated time. Here the analogy with developing physical muscle is very clear—no one would start lifting two hundred pounds! You start gradually and work up to the needed level.

"I'm going to get a glass of water in the kitchen. I'll be right back."

"Nana is going to stay with you while I'm at the gym for an hour. I'll be back when it's time for bath."

"We are going out to have dinner in a restaurant after we put you to bed. If you wake up, Ginny, your babysitter, will be here. And then we will come back and give you a kiss while you're sleeping, before we go to bed."

"Today we are going to visit your day care. This time I will stay with you while we look at the rooms and talk to the people."

"When you are at day care today, I will be thinking of you, and Mary (your caregiver) will show you my picture to help you think of me."

As we noted earlier, many day cares recommend that you leave your baby and walk out. They say that the baby will cry for a few minutes and then be fine. That is probably true. Babies can accommodate to a wide range of situations. But if your goal is not to have your baby just cope but rather to master her experiences and grow from them, then each event and change in her life is another opportunity to strengthen her emotional muscles for further development.

- **REINFORCING POSITIVE MEMORIES**

One way to strengthen your baby's capacity to keep you in mind and thereby be comforted internally during separations is to reinforce her memories of your happy times together. Talking about them and telling the story of the nice time at the playground or the yummy yogurt at breakfast creates and recreates a strong mental image. Research confirms the specificity, accuracy, and persistence of babies' memories.[15]

Karl talked at a parent evening at a large day care about what a wrench it had been for him and his wife when they first left their son. "And if it was hard for us, what about him? He's just a little guy. The director suggested that we bring his favorite blanket from his crib and also asked us for a picture of the family. We were kind of surprised, but she explained how they would use it to help him when he missed us."

A mom described what happened when grandparents recently arrived for a visit. Her ten-month-old, Jake, had looked really wary since he hadn't seen them for four months. Her husband had immediately taken him into his room and showed him the picture of his grandparents, the one they often said good night to. It showed them all together by the lake the summer before. Jake then beamed and warmed up to them soon. Another parent talked about using videoconferencing on the computer to stay in touch with relatives. "It's great," she said. "They only stay on about five minutes and sing a song or read a story, but she really looks forward to it and seems to recognize them. When we visited them, there was no hesitation."

UNDERSTANDING CONSEQUENCES AND CONTROLLING IMPULSES

It expands babies' knowledge when parents notice and talk about cause and effect. When you help your baby realize she has actually made something happen, you are laying a foundation for important emotional muscles. She will need to learn how to differentiate real and pretend, wishes and actions, ideas and behavior. Clearly limiting undesirable actions is the first step in her learning how to have the muscle to control her own impulses.

Parents can promote this growth by the following:

- **NOTICING AND TALKING ABOUT CAUSE AND EFFECT**
  "Look, you kicked your foot and the toy bounced up and down."
  "Wow, you made a big sound on the drum when you tapped your hands on the top."

If the baby bites her mother's breast, or any other part of a parent's body, you can firmly and loudly say "No, it hurts me when you do that," then immediately take the baby off the breast for a minute before resuming feeding or interrupt the game.

Research has demonstrated that babies make connections from the very beginning. They especially register emotions and then connect them with tones of voice. If you create conditions for a three-month-old to be able to reach for and successfully grasp an object, she then can understand that someone else reaching wants something too and will enjoy getting it. The point of citing this research is to demonstrate how much is going on inside babies' minds very early. [16] Babies have a very sophisticated understanding that other people have desires, intentions, and goals as determined by their actions. The emotional muscles that can be developed on this foundation will be important throughout life; parents have to work to counter the prevailing careless assumption that babies don't know what is going on.

INITIATIVE, RESPONSIBILITY, AND FOCUS

Pleasure from doing things motivates babies to practice their skills.

Parents can promote this growth by

- **PLAYING WITH YOUR BABY**
Play is an important arena for parents and children to connect pleasure with skills and for babies to develop a sense of agency. Play is a built-in motivation for all mammals and is seen from birth in human infants. At one week, babies engage in reciprocal play, making sounds, facial expressions, and movements back and forth with adults.[17] Researchers have described the importance of rough-and-tumble play for neurological development, especially capacities associated with attention and impulse control.[18] When we are talking about infants, we prefer to think of gentle-and-tumble play. These are the games, songs, finger plays, tummy times, bouncing knees, dancing, and so forth that bring forth smiles, gurgles, and belly laughs. The pleasure of parents and babies at these moments is mutually reinforcing, contributing to a strong positive relationship. The baby or the parent may initiate the

play; even very young infants may start a game that they have enjoyed before with a parent. It is the parent's job, however, to learn the baby's signals and know how to keep the excitement and pleasure manageable, knowing when to stop before the game becomes too much.

In response to a column about the importance of regular play, a mom called Nell wrote in with the following story. She described how, every time she changed Kyle's diaper, Nell played a game with him, she raised his arms over his head, crowing and exclaiming, "How big is Kyle? Soooo big!" One day, when Kyle was three and a half months old, Nell was surprised when Kyle raised his arms above his head as soon as she had laid him on the changing table that morning. When she said the words, he grinned at her and repeated his action several times. When she had finished changing his diaper, she told Kyle they would play one more time and then go downstairs and show Daddy what he could do.

The emotional muscle Kyle was developing was in his registering the pleasure, remembering it, initiating it, and reproducing the good feelings with his mother. Through play, pleasure becomes something the child can create rather than a chance accompaniment to something that comes from the outside world. It is sometimes hard for parents to follow the child's lead, especially when a game is repetitive, but he will be stronger from the experience of genuinely generating pleasure for both people.

COMPETENCE

*The feeling of competence is the pleasure that fuels
realistic functioning throughout life.*

Parents can promote this growth by

- **PROVIDING AND VALIDATING EXPERIENCES OF SUCCESS**
  Mastery of developmental tasks is another source of pleasure as competence is deeply satisfying and feels good to both parents and children. Early experience of developing competence creates a strand of emotional muscle that will stay important throughout life. Babies need to accumulate pleasurable memories and to have a pleasure/unpleasure balance that is weighted to the positive side. The more connections that parents can provide between mastering the tasks of daily life and good feelings, the happier and stronger your baby will

be. This prepares her to enter the next phase of development well equipped with emotional muscle to meet new challenges. Just as the body uses calories to build and sustain physical strength, pleasure is the fuel for emotional muscle.

Jeannette laughed in baby group when she said no one believed her that her three-week-old baby Pauline was smiling at her. She demonstrated that when she smiled, Pauline did indeed respond with a big grin and waved her hands. "See, I don't care if my mother says it's gas." And turning to Pauline, "Aren't you a big girl, what fun we are having!" The rest of the group of mothers, fathers, and teachers all looked on with pleasure as Jeanette and Pauline beamed at each other. A few weeks later, Pauline was initiating the exchange of smiles, gurgling with pleasure when her smile evoked her mother's response.

Jeannette was reinforcing Pauline's pleasurable experience of effective interaction with another person. This exchange between them is the root of competence and motivates the development of emotional muscle.[19] A cycle of positive feelings is being created, where success leads to feelings of effectiveness and competence, which lead, in turn, to pleasure, which strengthens the motivation for mastery.

HOW PARENTS HELP BABIES BUILD THE EMOTIONAL MUSCLES OF

ANTICIPATION, DEPENDABILITY, AND FLEXIBILITY
Parents help by
• ESTABLISHING ROUTINES • ANTICIPATING CHANGES OUT LOUD • SIGNALING AND STRUCTURING TRANSITIONS • USING WORDS TO ANTICIPATE PLEASURE AFTER NECESSARY DELAY • EMPHASIZING PLEASURE BY NAMING IT AGAIN

TRUST AND ADAPTABILITY
Parents help by
• MAKING CHANGES GRADUAL • REINFORCING POSITIVE MEMORIES

UNDERSTANDING CONSEQUENCES AND CONTROLLING IMPULSES
Parents help by
•   **NOTICING AND TALKING ABOUT CAUSE AND EFFECT**

INITIATIVE, RESPONSIBILITY, AND FOCUS
Parents help by
•   **PLAYING WITH YOUR BABY**

COMPETENCE
Parents help by
•   **PROVIDING AND VALIDATING EXPERIENCES OF SUCCESS**

ONE-YEAR-OLDS AND THEIR PARENTS
BUILDING EMOTIONAL MUSCLES

The infant of a short time ago has become a charming, funny, exasperating, and complex person. Many new capacities flower as young toddlers look together with Mom or Dad at something outside them both and learn about it. Jumping off from the nine-month revolution[20] in brain functions, toddlers learn at an incredible rate. By two years of age, many of the essential building blocks for social and emotional understanding are already in place. Parents have a big shift to make, trying to keep up with their toddler's swift rate of change and develop the new emotional muscles needed to address the challenges of this phase. Toddlers increase their independent activity. They have achieved new physical, intellectual, and emotional skills. This comes side by side with a strong need for help to stay safe, to manage their intense feelings, to channel their energy, to learn how to be in charge of themselves.

Whether they are good crawlers who can't talk yet or toddlers with some words, the one-year-olds now need their caregivers in very different ways from when they were babies. They make their needs, wishes, and choices quite clear, and they respond with noisy protest if the grown-up doesn't understand or agree. It is hard for parents to know how to support toddlers' ambition and how to deal simultaneously with the many times they have to say no. Despite toddlers' new skills for running, climbing, carrying, playing alone for a time, and so forth, the children still need a great deal of physical protection and watchfulness, especially now that they are so mobile.

Sixteen-month-old Georgette and her mother dropped into school to pick up some papers. While her mother took thirty seconds to say hello to the teacher, Georgette made a beeline for some artwork drying on a rack. Her mother ran after her and swooped her up just before Georgette touched the wet paint. "Meeeee," shouted Georgette, and

"Nooo," laughed her mother. How could they negotiate the wishes going in opposite directions?

Twenty-month-old Harry was beginning to move away from his mother at his regular playgroup, sometimes venturing to the other side of the room. His mom tried to remain attentive, but not follow instantly, giving him time to explore activities on his own. She talked with other parents about her surprise that it took some effort to see what Harry would do on his own, but she was enjoying his greater independence. One day, however, Harry quickly climbed to the rounded top of the soft cushion tunnel, which was not a stable place to stand on his own. As he teetered there, looking unsure whether to smile or cry, his mom immediately came close, took his hand, and said, "You climbed up to the top, way up high. Now I'll hold your hand to be steady, and then you'll come down the other side." Harry beamed with pride and used his mother's supporting hand to jump down safely.

What parents learn

TOLERATING SADNESS

*Tolerate sadness about change by enjoying
what the changes mean.*

At Allen Creek, we have a junior toddler class for children between one and two years old who attend with a parent. The goal is to strengthen the parent-child relationship by helping parents work together with their children. All the parents in the junior toddler group express pangs of sadness and loss, pressing a hand to their hearts as they talk about their children moving away from them, not needing constant physical contact anymore. Family consultants remind the parents of how powerful separation experiences are for all of us. The parents often say they feel that they have lost their value and importance to their child.

At the beginning of the school year, parents of the newly mobile one-year-olds sometimes feel at a loss about what to do with their children in class. They are struggling to regain a comfortable level of confidence and sense of competence with their toddlers. Playing together at home or at school, at the playground or a group provides a context for parents to find new ways to be close to their children on the new level and find pleasure and pride in their children's growth.

With a mixture of sadness and impatience, Ute's mother said in parent group, "Now that she is weaned, I feel useless. Anyone can change diapers and pick up toys over and over. I've gone from being the center of the universe to being her maid. This doesn't feel good." Another mother said, "When he was a baby, I knew what he needed. We were so close, and it felt so good to meet his needs and see him smile and relax and snuggle in. I really miss that."

As the discussion continued, the parents and the family consultants began to look at the problem from a longer perspective. They talked about the many different developmental transitions ahead and how the experience of change is almost always mixed. It's hard to say good-bye to the familiar and greet the new while it's also exciting to see what's coming next and shape the future. The move from infancy to toddlerhood is the first of many ongoing chances for parents to practice the adjustment.

A parent with an older child pointed out that the wonderful parts of babyhood persist throughout life—parents and children continue to love each other, show affection, feel helpful and close. No one ever has to say good-bye to those things. "And we don't have to feel sad leaving behind broken sleep and constantly carrying the baby. I thought it was all over when my older daughter turned one, but so much has happened since then that I can't tell you how satisfying it is to watch her keep growing." The family consultant underscored this point, noting that the enormous growth of the next stage of life will bring its own joys and satisfying achievements. Sadness only comes with love. In order to maintain love, parents need the muscle to tolerate sadness. It's easier to bear sadness when you remember that the love continues and grows.

The parents in the group at Allen Creek teach us that everyone has mixed feelings at times of developmental transition. The support of family, partners, or a group can help you develop the strength to tolerate the inevitable sadness. But even just knowing that this is your first of many such times helps to motivate parents to stretch their emotional muscles and build their capacity to master change.

TRANSFORMING THE RELATIONSHIP

Enjoy working at the new ways you are
important to your child.

Ute's mother and the other parents were struggling with the feeling that they were no longer important to their children. She was uncertain how she could be useful in Ute's increasingly independent world. A risk for parents at this point in their children's development is to think of babyhood as blissful, as an ideal time, a garden of Eden. Or they may go to the opposite extreme and think that their child is so big that she can do much more than she is actually ready for.

James's mother talked to her family consultant about what a hard time she was having with her seventeen-month-old boy. She felt badly that she wanted her baby back. "He used to be so sweet, and now he doesn't mind me and he says no all the time. What happened to that baby who ate well, let me put him down to sleep, and played happily in his playpen? I could do everything for him." As they talked about how helpless James made her feel currently, she exclaimed, "Oh no, it sounds like I am having a hard time not having total control!" The family consultant reminded her that she had talked, when James was a baby, about the hard work involved in helping him settle into a routine. She had never been in total control but had worked with baby James to find a good pattern. Now that he was older and had ideas of his own, she could think about working together with him in the same way, mastering the new challenges together.

When James's mother brought up this conversation in the group with other parents, someone remarked, "Neither of you is the boss." Everyone reflected on what a hard idea that was since parents have to keep children safe, setting limits and deciding what's important. Toddlers, however, also have strong developing capacities, and parents are challenged to work out what they can actually manage. Then they won't pitch demands too high and create frustration and failure.

Tania's dad talked about his annoyance when Tania cries in the morning when he is going off to work. "She seems like such a baby then when the rest of the time she wants to do everything herself." The family consultant remarked that Tania was showing her dad how important he is to her and how much she misses him during the day. If he could appreciate Tania's new capacity to think about him when he was gone, he could tolerate her sadness, talk about it, and acknowledge how important they are to each other. Tania's sadness is a sign of strength and achievement, not a clingy weakness. Change does not lead to separation but is one of many opportunities to transform the relationship.

These parents show us how the idea of emotional muscle provides all parents with more opportunities to promote pleasure and growth. By talking with Tania about how they would both miss each other, think of each other during the day, and be so happy when they saw each other at suppertime, Tania's dad strengthened his own capacity to bear a hard feeling, reinforced his connection with his little girl, and gave her tools to master her feelings.

WORKING TO STAY IN TUNE WITH YOUR TODDLER

Take time to listen to your toddler's words,
gestures, feelings.

Infancy demands a lot both physically and psychologically from parents. Parents are pulled into the baby's own needs and rhythms. Toddlerhood is different. Instead of signaling a limited range of immediate needs, as babies do, toddlers are trying to convey very complex ideas, desires, and wishes. They use their gestures, bodies, feelings, and play to communicate what they want. Parents have a different response to a child's needs and a child's wants. No parent would consider refusing to feed a hungry baby. But a toddler who wants yet another book before bed poses a dilemma. It can be a difficult adjustment for parents to shift gears and resolve conflicts between their own resurfacing adult needs and those of the child. Working on strengthening the emotional muscles needed for this adjustment leads to the possibility of finding pleasure in these changes. A first step is to learn how to read your child's new signals.

Timothy's father, Jeff, described how exasperated he was when he couldn't get nineteen-month-old Timothy to stick with his nighttime routine. At the end of the day, Jeff was tired and wanted to get on with his evening with his wife. He felt thwarted every step of the way, with Timmy resisting and fussing, always pulling in the opposite direction from where his dad wanted to go. Then Jeff said that he had a flash of inspiration.

He realized that Timmy's behavior wasn't random, it must mean something. Jeff stopped arguing and asked Timmy what he was trying to do. Timmy beamed and grasped his dad's hand, taking him over to the bookshelf. Timmy took a special book and handed it to his dad. Jeff then understood that Timmy wanted that particular book for story time even though he couldn't say it in words. Jeff said, "Oh, I get it. We'll read this book as soon as you have brushed your teeth and got jammies on." Then Timmy happily went upstairs to brush teeth.

Jeff had drawn on his own strengths and experience to realize that something more than mindless defiance was going on. By listening to his little boy's gestures and discovering their meaning, Jeff moved further into the new level of relationship with Timmy. To stay in tune with a toddler, you have to remember that their behavior has meaning.

Play increasingly becomes your toddler's way of learning, mastering, working things out, expressing feelings. Toddlers start pretend play early in the second year. The first stage in pretend play is imitation, where they talk on toy phones, offer tea, and put their dollies to bed.

Danny, sixteen months old, began frequently picking out a toy cell phone from the basket in his playgroup and walked around, holding it to his ear. After the teacher noted that his mother was just watching Danny do this, she chose a phone for herself and modeled joining into Danny's game. The teacher said, "Hello, Danny, how are you today? Are you going to the store?" After a few times, when his mother saw how enthusiastically Danny responded to his teacher's involvement in the game, his mother joined in too. She picked up a phone and began to talk about what they might want to buy at the store.

Danny's mother told the teacher how surprised she had been that Danny could pretend at such a young age. The teacher brought similar examples and talked about how important parents' enjoyment and participation can be for their children's intellectual and emotional growth. If parents aren't alert to notice the beginnings of imitation and don't respond, their child may stop trying. This teacher had been trained to include the idea of emotional muscle in her classroom interactions.

Pretend play, even at the level of direct imitation, is the beginning of an important pathway that continues throughout development. Toddlers beginning this kind of play are learning the difference between pretend and real; they are discovering ways to make sense of their experience; they are learning channels for dealing with feelings; and they are practicing doing more grown-up things. Parental pleasure in play is important in making it fun and worthwhile for children to pretend and imagine. It takes emotional muscle for parents to stick with the complex new demands and not get bored or angry or dismiss their child's new ways of communicating as nonsense.

Thea's dad described a new development in her play. Thea, twenty months old, had been imitating her parents for some time when he noticed her one day looking around the living room, behind the couch, under a pillow, and in the bookcase, saying what sounded like "Cheese?" Thea's parents could not figure out what she was doing, and Thea got more frustrated and frantic. They were also getting irritated and wanted her to stop. They said, "Thea, we know you are trying to tell us something and we are sorry that we can't understand, but we will try again in the morning."

The next day, when they went to the babysitter's, Thea ran straight to the table and grabbed a book, insisting that her mom read it before leaving. It turned out to be a story in which a mouse searches for cheese all over the house. Thea had been pretending to be the mouse! That evening, her parents played mouse with her, and they all enjoyed going all over the house saying "Cheese."

Thea's dad told this story with rueful astonishment; he said, "She's into literature and we weren't keeping up! Thank goodness we stuck with it, and Thea showed us what was important to her."

Thea was indeed entering simultaneously, through this way of playing, into two important pathways of development. She was embarking on a long journey of the imagination, starting her understanding of language, literature, metaphor, narrative, sequence, and more. She was also exploring the differences between real and pretend that will occupy her well into adolescence and beyond as she engages increasingly with the real world and learns to differentiate what is in her mind from what is outside. She may also have been doing what she could to make a connection between activities at her babysitter's and at home, using her new imaginative skills in an effort to master separation.

Thea's dad was strengthening his emotional muscle of flexibility, stretching himself to trust that Thea's behavior was meaningful and sticking with her long enough to figure out her new capacities for making meaning and communicating.

CREDITING THE POWER OF LANGUAGE

Continue and expand the effort to put everything into words.

Children have a very long period of active receptive language from at least six months old until close to two years of age before they can express themselves in words.[21] What this means is that they are taking in and understanding what you say and how you say it. Although it's hard for parents of infants to believe that such little ones understand their communications, parents must make this step with their young toddlers and develop trust in their children's capacities. This next step builds on the preference your baby showed for your face, voice, and speech. Newborns engage in proto-conversation; toddlers actually participate in real conversations, taking in both simple and complex meanings. They may not respond in words, but their actions and the changes that come after explanations and discussions show that they have fully understood.

Sachiko's mother, Ayano, arrived at her school one morning in tears. She had never driven in snow before, and her car had skidded on a turn. She was terrified, and Sachiko, sixteen months old, was screaming. The car was all right, but they were both distraught. They calmed down and came to class, and Sachiko seemed to enjoy herself as usual although her mother, Ayano, was subdued. At the end of the morning, however, Sachiko screamed and arched her back when her mother tried to put her in her car seat. One of the teachers had walked them to the car, intent on reassuring Ayano before she got behind the wheel again. When Sachiko seemed so distressed, the teacher suggested that her mom sit in the backseat next to her for a while and talk about what had happened. Ayano did that, telling the story a few times while Sachiko gradually settled. She accepted being buckled in and they left for home.

The teacher telephoned them that evening to check in and heard that Ayano had tried to take Sachiko to the store in the afternoon. The same screaming and arching had happened, and Ayano was very worried about getting to school the next time. The teacher suggested that Ayano go to the car a few times beforehand and just get in with Sachiko on her lap, playing and talking about going places in the car. Ayano could tell her that mommy had been very, very scared and that made Sachiko scared. Now, however, Mommy was going to drive very slowly and carefully, and they wouldn't be scared.

The next week, Ayano said that Sachiko had finally relaxed only when she explained the feelings part, when she talked about her own fear and how scary that must have been for Sachiko.

It takes emotional muscle to have confidence that your child, who is not talking yet, can respond to your words and tone. It also demands persistence for parents to spend the many months of talking, explaining, naming, differentiating, and connecting that go by before the toddler begins her acceleration of expressive speech and communication.

Janet's mother told a story of walking through the supermarket and seeing two adults, each with a toddler in the shopping cart, talking together over the children's heads about a terrible car accident. She said that the children's eyes were round as saucers, but their parents seemed unaware that the kids were listening. Her parent group discussed how young toddlers might not understand all the content, for instance, of a discussion about a war, but they would take in that something bad was happening along with the tone of anxiety or anger.

Gloria, who slept with her parents from birth through well into the second year, was both clinging and angry with her mother, Natalie. She scratched and pinched her mother while nursing frequently day and night. Natalie and Gloria had been unable to establish a harmonious, mutually regulated feeding and sleeping pattern. Gloria's main communication with her mother appeared to be defiant head shaking, signifying an emphatic "No!" whenever she was frustrated in any way. Natalie had questioned the idea of putting anything into words to a baby; she felt silly talking to someone who couldn't answer.

In consultation with Natalie, I endorsed the idea of her talking to Gloria, suggesting that she try for a while to set limits in words and explain things even if it felt artificial. That way, she could see if it would help to expand the repertoire of interaction between them. I supported Natalie over some weeks as she continued to try.

Natalie's efforts paid off; she returned, glowing with the news that Gloria had begun nodding her head "Yes!" Greatly expanded communication rapidly followed, and Natalie was proud to report how Gloria could find her shoes when asked and so forth. Gloria soon began sleeping longer through the night and began to touch her mother more gently. Natalie felt stronger in using words to work together with her little girl to manage challenging moments and enrich happy times with words that made sense of those experiences.

Parents' patience and persistence have big impact on toddlers' language development. Responding promptly with a smile, a touch, or words to your child's babbling and vocalization, even before there are recognizable words, accelerates the rate of language acquisition. Part of the emotional muscle parents can work on during this year is taking the trouble to stay responsive as it will pay off in the shared capacity to use words to solve problems.

MAINTAINING RESPONSIBILITY FOR YOUR TODDLER'S SAFETY

Decide what's truly important to you for the health and safety of your child.

Old worries about your child's safety recur now that she can move around, hide, and climb. On the one hand, these are realistic since toddlers are truly active and curious, able to move quickly out of sight, where they can do something destructive or dangerous. On the other hand, parents carry many worries of their own that may or may not apply to their own children. If these worries are irrational and intense, they can lead to overprotectiveness, which limits your toddler's growth or creates constant battles. Extreme worries can also lead parents to withdraw, leaving a toddler unprotected from the real hazards of home and the outside world.

There are many things that parents can work out together for keeping their children safe. An important distinction to make is between what are real dangers and what are irrational fears.

Victor's mother, Rose, brought to a parent group her fear that he would electrocute himself as he was so interested in the lamp cords and plug sockets. She worried that he might drown in the dog bowl as he toddled into the pantry out of her sight. She complained that this was much harder than when he was happy to sit in the playpen with his toys or even than when he wanted to be carried everywhere. He had never gone out of her sight before. Another parent said, "I really don't think he'll drown in the dog bowl, but what have you done about the light socket?" Rose said she had been too anxious and frazzled to tell the difference and hadn't done anything.

Other parents chimed in, talking about how curious the children had become—"Nothing is safe anymore. They're into everything!" Another mother said that she finds herself saying no all the time. She hated how that feels and worried that her baby would stop loving her or, even worse, stop feeling loved.

The family consultant used Rose's worry about Victor to talk about parents using their anxiety as a signal (as they learned while their children were babies) and childproofing their homes to the extent practical. This gives parents the confidence to say no when it is actually necessary while reducing the number of times you have to frustrate your toddler.

All the parents generated ideas about what they should actually do to childproof the house, like putting plug covers on the open sockets and gates on the stairs, locking the outside doors, and so forth. But they realized that no amount of childproofing can eliminate all dangers. There will have to be some things that are really forbidden. As they talked, they realized that they were working out how to teach their children to keep themselves safe. For the lesson to be absorbed, the guidelines have to be consistent and parents have to stick with them. It is important to say no not only to keep your child safe, but also because of what comes along with it, that is, the building blocks of independent safety and good judgment.

Jenalle's mother had noticed in the playground that Jenalle was looking back at her periodically. "It feels like she's checking in, but I'm not sure about what." Jenalle's mother said she was doing it whenever she got near the playground gate and when she approached the climbing structure with the big slide. "Good for Jenalle," said another parent. "She's making sure you say it's okay!" The family consultant agreed, remarking that Jenalle already seemed to feel secure that her mother was a reliable guide to what she could safely and enjoyably do. Mom's face was giving Jenalle a useful signal about whether to go ahead or not. Jenalle's mom laughed and noted that she frowns when her daughter approaches the gate, and was nodding and smiling when Jenalle wanted to try the shallow steps up to the bigger slide.

Charlie's parents described how they had built on this idea to decide how to handle going to the playground. Charlie's mom had realized that she was really scared by the big slide, and Charlie always wanted to try it. She was sure her face and body conveyed her worry loud and clear.

His dad thought Charlie could manage it and wanted to help him learn how to do it safely. So they decided that Charlie's dad would be the one to take him to that playground, and his mom would go with Charlie to a different one until Charlie could be dependable on the big slide.

What we can learn from the parents in this group is how necessary parental watchfulness and judgment are for keeping toddlers safe. Most toddlers look to their parents for guidance. So parents have to work to figure out the difference between real dangers and imaginary ones. It takes some moral courage for parents to examine their own fears. Victor was not going to drown in the dog bowl, and Charlie's mother realized that her worry would limit his growth. If you convey indiscriminate worry, your child will soon discount your prohibitions or, like you, become frightened of everything. Neither outcome leads to emotional muscle in your child or the continued growth of trust between you.

There are probably hundreds of moments every day when parents give guidelines with their faces, voices, and sometimes physical interventions to their toddlers about what is and isn't safe. Parents have to work to be a reliable resource for this critical information—their little ones are taking it in and making it part of their capacity to keep themselves safe. Consistent reactions help the children make sense of the outside world.

SETTING REALISTIC AND APPROPRIATE LIMITS

Trust that your child will still love you.

Realistic, clear, and consistent limits are an expression of love even when they momentarily frustrate and anger your child. Keeping your child safe is central to your love and care. Parents' major worry at this age (one to two) seems to be that their children will stop loving them if they enforce rules. When limits are not too harsh, too lenient, or too inconsistent, children appreciate them and feel more secure. The emotional muscle to set limits for your child is crucial throughout her life and will make future times easier if practiced from the beginning and transformed as your child grows (think adolescence!).

Rose, who had earlier articulated her fear that her newly mobile toddler, Victor, might drown in the dog's water bowl, described his momentary defiance over her appropriate limit setting a few months later with an astonished observation that "his anger was temporary. Even though we say no, they still love us!"

Enjoy your responsibility to interpret reality
to your child.

Sometimes saying no and setting limits is part of teaching her about what is possible and what isn't, what's real and what isn't. This is critical information for your child. Knowing that she will grow from having a better understanding of the difference between what is real and what is a wish or an idea helps parents tolerate the sometimes painful task of prohibiting and limiting.

Eighteen-month-old Yolanda was a bundle of energy, climbing, running, and tumbling all day. At the playground near her house, she climbed to the top of the big kids' slide faster than her mom, Ursula, could catch her. Her mom scrambled after her and held her in her arms. She told Yolanda that she could see she was getting to be a very good climber but that this slide was still too big for Yolanda to do alone. Ursula said they could do it together, and someday, Yolanda would be able to do it all by herself. Right now she could use the toddler slide all by herself, which Ursula knew felt very good to Yolanda.

In enforcing the limits and explaining the important distinctions, parents' consistency gets the message across. It isn't easy for grown-ups to stick to the rules all the time, but the resulting strength for both parents and child is worth it. It takes muscle to shoulder the responsibility to make sense of the real world to your child. Parents represent reality. You are the ones who introduce your child to the larger world, make sense of it, and make it accessible and manageable.

FINDING THE POSITIVE IN YOUR TODDLER'S ACTIVITY

Respect his growing need to be in charge of himself, to
explore, and have an effect on the world.

Thinking about each challenge from his point of view helps you to understand why it's important to him and to find your toddler's positive urge and pleasure in his new range of activities.

Thirteen-month-old Jenny was a very active explorer, pulling herself up to open all the lower kitchen cupboards. Her mom, Carol, told how she had pulled a stack of platters out, and one of them had cracked when it hit the floor. Jenny was frightened and Carol was angry. "Look what you did! That's what happens when you get into the places you shouldn't!" Carol was telling this story to the parent group as an example of setting limits, but she also shared that she felt badly about how angry she sounded and how frightened Jenny seemed afterward. She asked the group what they thought.

The other parents first expressed their support and shared their own recent similar experiences. Some of the behavior was simply messy, but some was destructive. This led to questions about what Jenny was actually trying to do. The plate had cracked, but was that her intention? The parents and the family consultant tried to imagine together, putting themselves in Jenny's place.

With that perspective, all agreed that Jenny was exploring her newly expanded world now that she could reach the knobs and do so much more independently. What was behind those cupboard doors? How do they work? How can I play with these pretty flat things?

The group concluded that toddlers need adults to recognize their new needs and interests and, where possible, make changes that will make curiosity and exploration safe, positive, and fun. They talked about how they would go home and look at their houses with new eyes, probably rearranging a lot of things. Marge, a mother with an older child, described how she had recently taken all the breakables out of the lower cupboards in her kitchen, replacing them with plasticware and light pots. Her toddler spent long periods playing happily with her in the kitchen, opening and shutting the doors, taking out the contents, banging on pans with a wooden spoon, rearranging them, and putting them away with her when she sang the cleanup song from school. What Marge most enjoyed was the shift from constant vigilance and annoyance to how pleasant it felt to be doing things in the kitchen together.

These parents were working on important new strands in their emotional muscles. They realized that, instead of just getting into a fight, they could use their annoyance as a signal that something needed to be changed with their toddler. Then they could put themselves in their toddlers' shoes, using empathy to point them to problem solving.

ACCEPTING YOUR ROLE AS A MODEL

Decide what character goals you want to offer your child—model that behavior.

In the discussion after a community lecture about thoughtful parenting, John, the father of twenty-two-month-old Jeremy, described how shocked he was to hear Jeremy swearing from his car seat as they were stopped at a red light on the way to school. It was a sharp reminder to him of how he often got angry in the car, one of the few places he allowed himself to express his chronic irritability. He hadn't realized that his little boy would be learning so much from him so quickly. John said he wasn't sure how easy it would be for him to change his habits. He said the kids were able to change more quickly than he could. One of the mothers in the audience said that she also felt very challenged by this new responsibility. She had heard a whining tone in her little girl's voice that echoed her tendency to complain and feel sorry for herself.

The lecturer not only pointed out that parenting can be very humbling in this way, but also was presenting them with an amazing opportunity to change lifelong maladaptive habits. It is sometimes easier to do something for the sake of one's child than for oneself alone.

The audience was thinking about the emotional muscle needed to look honestly at themselves, change if necessary, and set an example of the kind of person they want their child to become. Most people don't realize how much little children understand before they can talk—not just words but also the intentions of others.[22]

The lecturer proceeded to illustrate this point. He told about a mom who described unloading the car after arriving home from the store. The toddler was "helping" as usual, taking things out of the bags and putting them on the floor. Mom reached toward the table to set down her keys, and they fell short. The twenty-three-month-old picked them up and put them on the table, reading her mother's intention rather than imitating what actually happened.

After describing this incident with the keys, he told a story about a little girl called Ellyn. Ellyn's dad had said, "We had some visitors over and I had papers spread out in the den. One of the visitors started in that direction, and I really didn't want them to go in and see the mess. Ellyn's not quite two, but she went over and shut the door to the den. I swear she knew what I wanted even though I hadn't said anything."

These toddlers were demonstrating the sophisticated social skills they had already developed to see and act on feelings and wishes below the surface in other people. These skills are crucial to their development, but it is sometimes surprising for parents to feel that even their tiny children can see through them. It takes fortitude for parents to expose themselves to scrutiny like this and realize that honesty about their intentions and emotions will be good for their children. Parents are challenged by the reality of their children's perceptive capacities and can use this opportunity to model desired behavior and attitudes.

HOLDING ON TO THE LONG-TERM STRATEGIC GOALS OF MASTERY AND AUTONOMY

This will be a central theme throughout. The first step started at birth with your recognition that your baby is a separate person. By one year, you can define the goals for her development. At each age, you will add new parental emotional muscles to help your child work toward mastery.

Rise above control battles to remember
what you want for your child.

Intense toddler feelings and their constant activity can pull grown-ups into the moment-to-moment details and make it hard to keep the bigger picture in view. The overarching goal is mastery and autonomy for the child. Each struggle is an opportunity to work toward those goals. Rather than experiencing the relationship as a battle over who's in charge, it is important to remember that parents and toddlers are actually working toward the same aims—they both want the child to be able to be in charge of herself in a competent way one day. The challenge for parents is to build emotional muscle by turning daily power struggles into collaborative steps on the path to growth. To do this, you have to respect her autonomy and support age-appropriate mastery.

Janet's mother, Irene, was worried that Janet's appetite had diminished—was she getting enough nourishment? Irene had begun following Janet around the house with snacks on little plates, trying to convince Janet to eat more.

When the group discussed this situation, it became clear that there were several things going on at once. One was that toddlers' rate of growth is not as steep as for babies, and therefore Janet probably didn't need as much food as before. The teachers had reminded Irene to check this with her pediatrician. For most children, parents who don't make an issue over food intake will find that the child's own appetite is self-regulating.[23]

Second was that Irene was struggling with the change from being completely in charge of Janet's intake, with bottles and baby food, to Janet making her own choices from the finger food available at mealtimes. Irene had to first remember that she was still and would always be very important to Janet, and that her ultimate goal was to have Janet be in charge of her own feeding. Rather than making meals into a struggle over who was the boss, Janet's new level of appetite and skills provided an opportunity for mother and daughter to work together in a new way.

Another factor was that Janet's expanding world was so attractive to her that she didn't want to interrupt play and settle into her high chair. The group suggested that Irene make sure to give Janet some preparation for when playtime would be over and they would get ready for a meal together. Sitting down and enjoying social time with Mom would be an incentive.

Food and meals are a common area of friction with toddlers; there are many books and sources of advice about nutrition and feeding. What is important here is the way Irene could use the arena of feeding, like any other throughout the day, as an opportunity to develop her own emotional muscle of handling the situation in a way that moves them toward important goals of mastery and autonomy. Parents of young toddlers are pushed to find a new level of comfort in sharing control with their children, allocating responsibility in new proportions. Each part of the day's routine is an opportunity for practice.

Trust your child's growing capacities.

When scientists talk about self-regulation,[24] they mean competent mastery of needs, feelings, and impulses. Mastery builds on emotional muscles, which, in turn, lead to greater mastery. Parents can be taken by surprise when toddlers insist on doing everything for themselves. "Me do it" can feel like a tidal wave, taking over the whole day and night, leaving little room for gradual transition into the new phase. "Me do it" is a healthy wish for mastery to be in charge of themselves. It is as if they have got up on their feet and are ready to charge out into the world. Toddlers don't realize how little they can actually yet do, but it is hard for parents to realize how much they can. These issues show up most in the basic arenas of feeding, sleeping, and activity.

Janet's mother Irene reported back to the group some weeks after the first discussions that, to her surprise, mealtimes had stopped being a battle. Irene still struggled inside when Janet said, "All done," after four bites of peas, leaving her chicken and berries untouched, but she was hanging in there, helping herself by taking notes on what Janet ate. When she looked them over at the end of the week, she realized that Janet was eating a pretty balanced variety of foods, just not all on the same day. "Whew, it's such a relief to know she's eating right and maybe even a greater relief not to be fighting and anxious all the time. We're having more fun."

Olaf's dad, Stig, talked about how hard it was to "get him to sleep." After various suggestions from parents about bedtime routines and ways to talk about it with Olaf, one of the family consultants noted, "You said 'get him to sleep.' That sounds like it relates to one of the biggest issues we deal with in toddlerhood—who owns my body?" The group discussed the difference between parents' deciding on bedtime and the child deciding when to go to sleep. The family consultant underscored that we all want the child to develop a sense of ownership of his own body. This is basic to developing toilet mastery, to his ability to keep himself safe, and to protecting his physical and emotional privacy as he grows. Adults are still in charge of caring for children's bodies, creating good conditions for healthy timetables of sleeping and waking, but no one can "make" someone else go to sleep. Here was another instance of the challenge in beginning to share responsibility with the toddler.

A few weeks later, Stig described the work he was doing every night to keep himself from going back in Olaf's room and scolding when he heard Olaf singing and talking to himself, sometimes for up to an hour. Stig realized that his annoyance came partly from worry that Olaf wouldn't get enough sleep and be cranky the next day and confessed that another part of it was irritation at not being in charge. A member of the group suggested that Stig keep track of Olaf's cranky days and see whether they might be about something else, in case the crankiness was a separate issue from how much sleep he got.

One of the mothers described how she had made a point of listening on the baby monitor to what her son was actually saying in this time before sleep; she was amazed at how he was going over the whole day, recounting details and repeating phrases he had heard. "It was really fascinating to hear what his take on the day was, what stood out in his mind. I learned a lot from listening to him."

Another month later, Stig said that he wanted to report back on Olaf's sleep situation. "Actually, I think I am talking about my own changes more than Olaf's since I have had to work out how to let him be in charge of his own body and how to pay closer attention to what things may mean to him." He described tracking the cranky days, asking his wife and the babysitter to notice more specifically what was going on.

Olaf's parents had worked hard to develop a care plan that maximized each of their time with him. They shared his care with a babysitter on a regular, but complicated, weekly schedule. It turned out that Olaf's cranky days were almost always those days when his mom left early for her shift before he awoke. Stig and his wife were upset when they figured this out but swiftly found creative solutions, making use of Olaf's new capacities for memory and connection. They reminded him the night before that his mom would already be gone to work when he awoke and then showed him the little framed picture of her that she would leave next to his bed for him to see right away in the morning. Stig made sure on those days to talk about Mommy at breakfast and how she too had eaten yogurt and banana before she left for work.

With the help and support of the parent group and their family consultants, Stig and his wife were able to surmount their own frustration and increase their trust in Olaf's capacity to be in charge of his own body, particularly of sleep, and offer him new tools for mastering his feelings on days he was missing his mom.

Lindy's moms announced ruefully that they had a funny story to tell after returning from a family reunion over a holiday weekend. Lindy, twenty months, was an active, curious child, happy to explore new places and usually interested in new people. The family reunion included familiar and new relatives and children of all ages, including some other toddlers. Lindy joined enthusiastically in running around the lawn with the other kids the first afternoon but puzzled her parents when she refused the next morning, sitting herself down under a tree at some distance instead. Her mom offered to come with her to join the others, but Lindy said no. Her parents didn't fight with her about this and just sat down too and sang a few songs. But another relative came and coaxed with more emphasis. Lindy's mom said she felt annoyed that this aunt was so pushy.

Other parents chimed in with stories of how hard it can be with family members or friends who don't allow their toddlers as much latitude to decide for themselves, especially about food, and also about joining in. Lindy's mom then described Lindy's loud and enthusiastic participation at the next meal, where several children and parents shared a table with conversation and passing of food. Her conclusion was that Lindy was taking good care of regulating her own stimulation, joining in when she felt good about a high level of activity, interaction, and noise and chilling out when that felt like what she needed. Lindy's mom said it was a bit rough to defend Lindy against the relatives' asking "What's wrong?" but that she was proud of her daughter for knowing what she needed.

Lindy's parents were exercising their capacity to trust Lindy's capacities and defending that parental position even when pressured by loved ones. They kept in mind that they and Lindy were working together to move forward toward mastery and autonomy for Lindy.

ENJOYING THE STEPS ALONG THE WAY

Cultivate patience and pleasure instead of disappointment.

Parents have many wishes for their children. Keeping your eye on the overarching goals of mastery and autonomy helps you rise above daily power struggles. This helps you to keep perspective, but it can also make it hard to enjoy the steps along the way. Toddlers can't see the whole picture, but they can register the disappointment and impatience of grown-ups if they fail. They need grown-ups to offer them experiences of success graded to their capacities, and they also need us to feel genuine pleasure at their mastery of each tiny step.

Donny's father, Jake, had bought a new toy, which required a somewhat complicated maneuver to work. He complained to his wife that he had shown Donny four times, but the boy still wasn't getting it. Jake was disappointed as he had been excited to find a toy he had loved as a child and had looked forward to playing this with his son. His wife reminded him that he was three when he enjoyed that toy, not one like Donny. Together they figured out that Donny and Jake could simply enjoy pushing the toy around the floor for now. When Donny was older, Jake could show him how to manipulate the various levers.

With his wife's help, Jake was strengthening his capacity for patience and finding the right level for shared pleasure with Donny. Rather than a painful interaction with Jake disappointed and Donny feeling badly about himself, father and son had a fun time together.

Sophie, mom of wenty-one-month-old Thea , described how angry Thea was one day at lunch. Sophie had put Thea's milk in a white cup and her juice in a yellow cup. Thea banged the table, kept saying something in increasingly loud tones, and was unwilling to proceed with her meal. Sophie could not figure out what the trouble was or what Thea wanted. Instead of giving up, or assuming she knew what was the matter and imposing a solution, or getting annoyed, Sophie stuck with explaining to Thea that she was trying to understand but that Thea should help her get it by telling her until they could figure it out together. At that point in time, Thea knew some color names and had words for *milk* and *juice*. Thea tried her different versions of the relevant words and soon was able to put the words together.

Thea and Sophie both beamed when Sophie said, "Oh, now you have helped me understand. You want the milk in the yellow cup and the juice in the white cup. I think we can handle that." Sophie felt it was worth rinsing the cups and changing the drinks to reinforce Thea's big effort to communicate.

Sophie was exercising patience and selecting communication as the most important current step in Thea's development. She challenged Thea to do something she could succeed at with work, and then they could enjoy the success together.

THE EMOTIONAL MUSCLES USED BY PARENTS OF ONE-YEAR-OLDS ARE

TOLERATING SADNESS

TRANSFORMING THE RELATIONSHIP

WORKING TO STAY IN TUNE WITH YOUR TODDLER

CREDITING THE POWER OF LANGUAGE

MAINTAINING RESPONSIBILITY FOR YOUR TODDLER'S SAFETY

SETTING REALISTIC AND APPROPRIATE LIMITS

FINDING THE POSITIVE IN YOUR TODDLER'S ACTIVITY

ACCEPTING YOUR ROLE AS A MODEL

HOLDING ON TO LONG-TERM STRATEGIC GOALS OF MASTERY AND AUTONOMY

ENJOYING THE STEPS ALONG THE WAY

What do one-year-olds need to develop emotional muscle?

Toddlers are facing new challenges from more complex emotions and worries. They are dealing not only with many new experiences from outside, but also need the help of grown-ups to deal with potentially overwhelming feelings from inside.

Toddlerhood is a critical time for children to begin forming emotional habits. We are purposely calling these habits as everyone uses the ideas of good and bad habits as part of how they judge themselves and others. Strong emotional muscles that lead to forming positive emotional habits create mutual enjoyment in interactions between children and others. How children learn to deal with their strong feelings and whether they see themselves as agents or victims in the world depends largely on patterns established in their relationships during toddlerhood.

Young toddlers need to learn what they are in charge of, what parents are in charge of, and what no one is in charge of.[25] This is a long process, and there is a lot of potential for control battles as parents and children sort out these categories and adapt to the changes that come with growth. For optimal development, young toddlers need parents who have already developed some emotional muscle and are willing to take on the challenges of transforming the parent-child relationship and generating new strengths.

What one-year-olds learn

> *SELF-CONTROL, SELF-AWARENESS, SELF-REGULATION*
> *TOLERATE MIXED FEELINGS*
> *RESPOND POSITIVELY TO CHALLENGES*
> *MAKING MEANING OF EXPERIENCE*
> *AGENCY AND RESPONSIBILITY FOR ONESELF*
> *EMPATHY*

How parents help one-year-olds build emotional muscles

SELF-CONTROL, SELF-AWARENESS, SELF-REGULATION

Managing negative feelings is a major challenge throughout life. People need strong emotional muscles to master that task. The necessary emotional muscles start developing in babyhood and continue with new components added each year.

Just as you teach your child the names of everything in the outside world, it is equally important to equip her with tools to think about her inner experience.

Parents can promote this growth by

- **NAMING FEELINGS, THOUGHTS, AND DREAMS**
Parents in an Allen Creek junior toddler group became very skilled at reading their children's emotional signals and labeling the feelings appropriately. They could recognize and name happiness, frustration, excitement, sadness, hurt, and disappointment. But they found it very difficult to name anger. Parents felt uncomfortable about attributing

such a mean, negative, destructive feeling to their little children. They also worried that it would stir up their own anger if they got too close to the children's strong anger.

Jenny shrieked with excitement and pleasure at the playground swings. It was very hard for her to leave when her dad said it was time to go home. Often the situation turned into a battle. Jenny's dad said he hated the feeling of picking her up and carrying her home kicking and screaming, but he didn't know what else to do. It also made him mad that she wouldn't leave when he had already spent so much time playing there with her. "Why isn't she grateful? Or at least, why isn't it ever enough?"

The other parents in the group sympathized; everyone had experienced similar scenes. The family consultant suggested that they think about why Jenny didn't want to leave. All agreed that she was not actually being naughty or ungrateful. Rather, she was having such a good time that she didn't want it to stop. Jenny's dad said, "Oh, she's having too much fun. That puts kind of a different spin on it. She's angry because I'm stopping her fun." The family consultant suggested that he try putting Jenny's feeling into words. He could prepare her a few minutes ahead for going home time, and then talk about what fun she was having and how she wanted it more and more. He was glad she liked it so much, and he understood that it made her angry and felt hard to leave the park, but they could have all that fun again another day.

A few weeks later, Jenny's dad said that their outings were really different. "Jenny bounces over and takes my hand, and chatters all the way home. I still can't make out her words, but I think she's talking about going on the swings tomorrow."

Acknowledging Jenny's pleasure and validating her wish to have it continue helped her understand her anger and hold on to the good feeling, rather than focus on losing it. Then she could anticipate the future. The power of words builds the emotional muscles to stop, listen to oneself, identify the feeling and its cause, and then address the cause. The beginning capacity to delay because of imagining the future depends on being able to think about it. Words are essential tools for these emotional muscles.

- **NAMING AND OFFERING WORDS AND GESTURES AS SUBSTITUTES FOR ACTION**
  Support the change from feeling emotions in the whole body to experiencing them as internal mental signals. This is a task that

will occupy your child well into preschool, but the work begins for one-year-olds.

Mariana's mother, Zita, described her growing puzzlement over Mariana's continued tantrums. She always made her daughter sit on a certain step for three minutes when she had a tantrum, but it didn't seem to make any difference. Zita said, "She's about to be two and I don't feel I have the right tools to deal with this." All the parents in the toddler group wanted to know how to handle a meltdown, the times when their children became overwhelmed by their feelings. This usually referred to anger, but it could be sadness or any upset. The main strategy parents had was time-out, sending the children to another room until they could stop.

In discussion, the group came to the idea that, as upsetting as the meltdown was to the adults, Mariana and the other children were not intentionally being bad. The children were overwhelmed and helpless to handle their feelings alone; they needed a grown up to help them master the emotions, in a "time with." Zita could stay with Mariana and talk to her about her feeling getting "too big" for her to feel in charge. She could sit with the child and help Mariana use her own strong muscles to make the feeling just right to hold in one hand, then they could look at it together and figure out what to do.

The parents understood that the aim is to master the feeling and turn an overwhelming state into a useful signal. In this context the family consultant could introduce the idea of emotional muscles, analogous to the physical muscles the children were rapidly developing.

The emotional muscle the children were beginning to work on was the capacity to modulate and master their feelings. This is a long developmental path, but the initial effort and practice belongs in the second year of life, when their parents could help them begin to take responsibility for their feelings and share the effort to move beyond feelings to address whatever is needed.

- **ASSIGNING APPROPRIATE RESPONSIBILITY FOR FEELINGS FROM THE BEGINNING**

Many parents call themselves Mommy or Daddy, avoiding using pronouns like I or you. An unexpected consequence of this style of talking is that it distances the person from the feeling. But we grown-ups have to take responsibility for our feelings if we expect our children to develop the strength to bear whatever feelings they have. Owning feelings by saying, for instance, "I feel mad when you won't help put your pajamas on because I don't want to miss our reading time," sets an example and gives a child permission to own her feelings and express them in words when she is able to.

Nora's mother Gina talked about growing up in what she called a pretty cold household where no one was supposed to have any feelings. She was determined to bring Nora up differently and was quick to name and acknowledge all Nora's feelings. But whenever Gina described a problematic exchange between them, she quoted herself as saying, for instance, "Mommy gets mad when you won't get your jacket on." When we discussed taking ownership of feelings, Gina gasped, "Oh, my goodness, I thought I had gotten past it, but I'm doing a version of what my parents did. I'm pushing away the feelings."

A couple of months later, when she reported negotiating a bedtime dispute with Nora, Gina said, "I told her that I was tired of having an argument at night and that I wanted us to talk about it in the daytime. I said I would be so happy when we could have a cheerful bedtime." We noticed and praised Gina's use of I in her conversation with Nora. "Yeah, you're right," said Gina. "I've been owning my feelings in my words, and nothing bad has happened. My kid still loves me and I love her. It's easier to discuss things and solve problems. It's almost as if we had to commit fully to the effort before we could expect her to. Plus, I feel even better about being the kind of parent I want to be. I guess progress is possible between generations. It was pretty powerful, but I just had to break the habit of disowning my feelings."

Twenty-three-month-old Jeremy's mother told of going on an errand before a promised walk to a new park. The errand took too long, and Jeremy was very upset. Jeremy was crying, and she was irritated when she realized that she shouldn't blame Jeremy for being angry. "I felt really bad, actually guilty, since I had made him wait several times that day and the day before. I wouldn't do that to a friend, so it didn't feel good to do it to my kid." She apologized to him, explaining that she had spent too much time in the store. She told him she understood that he was disappointed and angry with her and promised to go for the walk the next morning.

Even though it was pouring with rain the next day, they went out and had a wonderful time splashing through the puddles together. Jeremy threw his arms around his mother's neck, getting them both even wetter, and shouted, "Thank you, Mama!" His mom laughed and said she felt the fun and the thanks were both related to her taking responsibility for what had happened. Jeremy had been able to let his negative feelings go when they weren't all mixed up with his mother's. "I never imagined apologizing to a one-year-old, but the whole thing really felt good."

By the middle of the second year, children can tell the difference between their own and others' feelings. The more adults are honest about their own feelings, the more toddlers will learn to deal with theirs. The emotional muscle Nora and Jeremy were being helped to develop was differentiating whose feelings are whose and taking responsibility for their own.

TOLERATE MIXED FEELINGS

*It is one of the major tasks of toddlerhood for parents
and children to cope with strong or mixed feelings.
Initially, children can only deal with one feeling at a time.*

Parents can promote this growth by

- **HOLDING ON TO LOVE EVEN IN THE MIDST OF ANGER**
  Young toddlers need their parents to be strong enough to contain mixed and conflicting emotions. This helps the children develop the same capacity.
  Sarah started a parent group meeting, saying, "I'm in shock! My dear little girl spent the beginning of this year just so smoothly. I admit I was congratulating myself that I wasn't going to have the hassles I read so much about. Alana just turned seventeen months, and it's like she pulled a switch. She stood there today on her little feet, clenched her fists and glared at me and then shouted 'No!' when all I said was 'Let's get our coats on.' First, I was astonished and then I began to get mad. I guess we're starting the terrible twos early. We finally got out of the house, but I really feel at a loss. Is this what I'm in for the next two years?"
  Other parents in the group talked about how startling this developmental change can be and wondered what happened right before Alana's defiant stand. Sarah explained that Alana was playing with her farm when it was time to go out. The family consultant said she thought that Alana was happy playing and then was angry to be interrupted; her

anger filled up all the space, leaving no room for the good feelings she was having just before, or her love for her mother and trust in her general good will. Since toddlers cannot at first manage more than one feeling at a time, the adults have to carry the full range temporarily and then hand them back when the toddler can receive them.

The family consultant suggested that next time, if giving Alana some notice that playtime will soon be over doesn't stop an angry outburst, Sarah might put Alana's anger into words. Then Sarah could remind her that they were having fun and will have fun again even though Alana is so angry right now. Another parent said his child seemed comforted when he told him that his angry feelings would soon go away; knowing he wouldn't have those big feelings forever seemed to make him less overwhelmed by them.

Parents are sometimes frightened and ashamed of their own anger and afraid that their child's anger means the child will hate them. It helps to remind yourself and your child that you still love him even though you are angry at what the child did. You can also say to him, "I know that you're angry at me for saying you can't have another book tonight, but I remember that you still love me even when you're angry, and I know you will remember it soon."

Young toddlers take a long time, usually well into the two-year-old year, to be able to hold mixed feelings. But when parents convey their secure knowledge and trust that the whole range of feelings is manageable for both child and parent, toddlers begin to take in the message and feel relieved of the worry that their strong feelings will render them helpless. They are gradually building the emotional muscle of tolerating and containing their feelings.

RESPOND POSITIVELY TO CHALLENGES

Challenges stretch capacities and promote growth in general; they actually help children develop emotional muscle.

Parents can promote this growth by

- **SETTING EXPECTATIONS AND MAKING DEMANDS THAT ARE GEARED TO YOUR CHILD'S DEVELOPMENTAL CAPACITIES**

Expectations that are pitched too high are discouraging; failing sets up a cycle of bad feeling that reinforces not trying. This can have profound effects on later involvement in learning. Expectations that are pitched too low make children anxious about their abilities; if the grown-ups don't think the child can do it, children take that in, think they are incapable and don't try.

This came up in toddler parent group discussion with family consultants as the kids began to have regular playdates and the parents were concerned that their children didn't want to share. Were they being selfish? Did they lack empathy? At what age should children be expected to share? Should they just not have playdates? It was a topic of great concern.

Parents reflected on their own childhoods and recalled that it was a fraught issue for many. They wondered why this emphasis on sharing? Many realized that it felt as if it reflected on the parents; if their child couldn't share, they must be spoiling her or bringing her up badly.

The issue was discussed in parent and staff groups at Allen Creek. We then realized that sharing was not an accurate way to think about the problem. After all, you can't really share a truck—you can't cut it in half like an orange. *The goal was to teach the children how to take turns.* Luckily, this is not completely new learning. Babies already know how to take turns from hundreds and thousands of experiences of playing games with parents and having conversations where each takes turns making a noise, then pauses to watch and listen to the other.

What the children needed was not to be forced to share but rather to have assurance of "a whole turn."[26] They needed to know that the parents/teachers would help them have the whole or full turn. When this was implemented, the parents noted that everyone relaxed at home and at school. Sharing no longer became an issue. When the teacher said, "Joe wants his whole turn with the truck. When he has had his whole turn, then you can have a whole turn." Joe often would soon happily hand over the truck.

Following through on the promise to protect each child's whole turn soon bore fruit in all the children playing more harmoniously at home and at school. Zach was angry and bewildered when his mother kept insisting that he give up a toy to another child to share and be nice. Soon he became a leader in enjoying and enforcing the idea of whole turns.

With the help of parents and teachers, all the children had strengthened their emotional muscles; they were strong enough to wait for a turn, to tolerate their frustration and disappointment if someone else had the desired toy first, and then to feel good about handing the toy over when they were done. The challenge was an appropriate stretch for their developmental abilities, and all the children responded with pride and social growth. The idea of a whole turn has proved useful in many different settings and situations.

- **OFFERING GRADED OPPORTUNITIES FOR EXPERIENCES OF SUCCESS AND PLEASURE FROM COMPETENCE**
Snack is a regular part of the day in all day cares and preschools. In many centers, however, the children aren't allowed to do anything for themselves. At Allen Creek, we experimented with doing it a different way. In the one-year-old class, children are expected to sit in a little chair at the table, with a parent beside them, and are given the opportunity to pour their own water from a small pitcher into their small cups. They feed themselves, at first with finger food and soon with spoons and forks. They ask for more if they want it, deciding if there is part of snack they don't want. When they are finished, they clear their places, putting the trash in the bin and the dishes in the sink, then wipe their place with a sponge, which they replace in the basket before going over to circle time. At the beginning of the year, few can perform all these tasks; many have no experience of drinking from a cup or pouring. Adults help with every step. But eventually, all the junior toddlers become very adept at most of these tasks.

Brandon's mom, LaTeesha, did not let him try to pour his water because she was afraid he would spill it and make a mess. The teachers reassured her that what he could learn was worth a few spills and suggested that LaTeesha put only a very tiny bit of water in the pitcher. Then she could help Brandon hold his cup steady on the table with one hand and the pitcher in the other. Together they could aim the water successfully. Brandon and his mom both beamed, then Brandon proudly asked for more water, and they repeated the sequence many times.

Helping toddlers accomplish the various tasks of daily life successfully takes many, many repetitions and a lot of patience. Parents have to call upon their own emotional muscle to persist in teaching, breaking the task down into steps that seem tiny to a grown-up and resist doing it for the child because it might be faster or easier, or rushing to the next step before the child is ready. Then the child will experience the wonderful pleasure of accomplishment that motivates and reinforces her developing and using emotional muscles of trying and persistence that are crucial for all later learning and work.

MAKING MEANING OF EXPERIENCE

Babies can understand physical cause and effect very early in life. Toddlers add the capacity to understand emotional cause and effect.

Parents can promote this growth by

- **EXPLAINING EMOTIONAL CAUSE AND EFFECT**

Walter, twenty-two months, suddenly started crying loudly in the one-year-old class, startling everyone in the room. His mother leaned over, asking him what was wrong, but Walter couldn't tell her. He just kept crying. Nearby parents and children looked mystified too, and the other children got worried faces. Their parents reassured them that Walter's mommy would help him and that they didn't have to worry about him. The other children turned back to their activities, but Walter didn't calm down.

His teacher came across the room, crouched down to be at eye level with him, and said, "Walter, I think something happened that made you scared and angry. We can figure out what it was and help you with those feelings." Walter began to sniffle and looked at her with some curiosity. The teacher looked around, including Walter's mother in her gaze. "Let's see, what were you doing right before you got upset?" she asked. Walter's mom picked up the cue and said that he had been playing with the fire engine that has the moveable ladder.

When his mom described his game, Walter raised his hand and showed his mom and teacher a pink spot on the back. "Oh," they both said, "you pinched your hand in the ladder." His teacher added, "That must have hurt and it surprised you too, especially since you love the fire engine and that has never happened before." Walter gave a big sigh and stopped whimpering. But he didn't return to the fire engine. The next time, his mom and his teacher both talked about how startled he had been when his beloved fire engine hurt him. Walter listened and watched while his teacher showed him how the ladder could safely be swiveled, but he didn't go back to his favorite toy until the third day.

When Walter's mom described this incident in parent group, everyone was struck with the idea that Walter had not been crying from continuing pain alone. Rather, he was crying because he was confused, surprised, and indignant that his beloved fire engine had hurt him. Once he felt understood and the sequence between his physical hurt and the multiple feelings was made, he calmed right down. Walter's mother said she had learned by watching the teacher how important it was to make the emotional connection explicit; she had been experimenting with this ever since and had seen Walter become more able to manage his feelings. "This is a powerful tool for us both!"

All parents can learn from this sensitive Allen Creek teacher and Walter's responsive mom what a helpful tool it is to take the time to figure out what the trouble is and explain it. That puts the child in charge of his feeling. As toddlers take in more and more about the world around them and have correspondingly complex internal experiences they work to make sense of it all. Organizing our experience is a powerful urge in everyone; the process of doing so promotes growth; the pleasure of understanding becomes a motivator and goal in itself. The emotional muscle of working to have a realistic understanding of inner and outer life is part of later learning and relationships. Walter's mother and teacher were equipping him in a very basic way to be strong enough to handle pain, challenge, and distress.

AGENCY AND RESPONSIBILITY FOR ONESELF

Children this age can begin to feel good about being a competent person who can effectively put wishes into action. This is central to a secure identity.

Parents can promote this growth by

- **OFFERING YOUR CHILD GENUINE CHOICES**
Keeping in mind the overarching goal of mastery and autonomy for children, parents have to assess what their child is capable of being in charge of and do a self-assessment of what you are really willing to let your child be in charge of. Then you must follow through and mean what you say.

Sylvia's mother, Louise, wanted to share a story in parent group. She talked about how she had made a decision early on to let Sylvia choose her own clothes, just as she wanted to let Sylvia choose what to eat. "I figured I had to really mean it and stick to it no matter what she chose. It has worked pretty well since her enjoyment has motivated her to learn. She can really just about completely dress and undress herself. I've tried to make sure that what is available in her drawer is reasonably suitable, but she is such a warm kid that I couldn't gauge the seasons well using my own sense of what would be the right weight clothes."

Other parents chimed in with their observations about Sylvia's various choices, reminiscing with humor about the day she came to school in snow pants and a tutu. Kyle's father agreed about the temperature debate. "I have given up fighting with him about a jacket. I just make sure we have it available, but it was really hard to let such a little guy be in charge of whether he wears a jacket or not."

Louise said that even though Sylvia often chose pretty unusual outfits, she had so far not really minded. What she wanted to recount, however, was what happened when Sylvia's grandmother had been visiting recently. She felt a conflict between her feelings of agreement with her mother about clothing choices and her parenting intention to let Sylvia be in charge of her clothes. The grandmother had protested when Sylvia wanted to wear her pajamas to the supermarket. Louise said she actually agreed with her mother that the pajamas weren't the best choice, but she also wanted to stick to her parenting philosophy of offering Sylvia choices whenever feasible.

The other parents sympathized with the dilemma and brainstormed about the issues involved. Even though clothing choice itself felt relatively superficial, the principle involved was serious, and the group understood the family consultant's remark that choosing between two positive values was going to be a challenge throughout their lives as parents. Thinking through the potential implications of different choices was a useful effort for the parents since they were going to be faced many times with how to reconcile these conflicts. Should Louise forbid Sylvia to wear her pajamas to the supermarket because her grandmother didn't approve and because she herself didn't find it appropriate? Or should she stick to her plan to give Sylvia freedom of choice about clothes despite her own discomfort with the choice? One mother raised the question, "When is she going to learn that pajamas are actually not the right wardrobe for the supermarket if you don't tell her now?"

Louise said that she had thought hard and ended up deciding not to intervene as she had realized that these clothes did not have any of the same meanings to Sylvia as they had to herself. Sylvia didn't really see much difference between her pajama bottoms and her cotton jersey pants. She remembered the principle of seeing her child as a different person from herself and felt the stretch to her own emotional muscles to maintain that view. She decided that Sylvia's growing autonomy was more important than her mother's position about what was socially acceptable. Louise felt that she could teach Sylvia later about social norms when her little girl had a greater appreciation of other people's reactions.

Louise had made a choice about what Sylvia could be in charge of and Sylvia clearly benefited from having such a wide area of autonomy. Sylvia was able to dress herself before she was two years old and took great pleasure in making choices. The emotional muscle Sylvia was developing was consolidating her sense of agency and using it to practice skills of self-care.

EMPATHY

Successful children and adults have the capacity to perceive, understand, predict, and respond to others' feelings. This is a learned skill.

Parents can promote this growth by

- **SETTING THE EXAMPLE, EXPLAINING AND ENCOURAGING**
  In Allen Creek's workshops for day care providers and preschool teachers, we routinely suggest that teachers deliberately do a running commentary of what they see others feeling and what they are feeling. This sets an example that parents soon follow. The children hear grown-ups saying things like, "I notice that Johnny is frowning. I wonder what might be upsetting him. I'm going to see what might help him feel better."

Allen Creek teachers use the example of Toko to illustrate the effects of this approach to nurturing empathy.

Toko, fifteen months old, loved his one-year-old class and the friends he saw there regularly with their parents. One day, he was busy with the garage at the far end of the room when he saw Janie hesitating at the classroom doorway and clinging to her mother's leg. Toko went to the shelf and picked up the doll Janie usually liked to play with. He walked over to the door and handed it to her. Janie then came happily into the room and hung up her coat.

Toko had learned to notice and feel concern for his friends' feelings because everyone around him exercised their emotional muscles of empathy and putting things into words, interpreting reality in a way he could understand. When he showed empathy and helped another person, parents and teachers appreciated him with words and expressions. It became a pleasure for him and the other children to be kind and caring to each other.

Sometimes, empathy can be accessed only after interfering feelings have been cleared up. A day care teacher brought the following story to a workshop.

It took the first couple of months of school for Sally and Amy to work out their possessive battles over the toy baby stroller. It was clear that the stroller was very precious to Sally, and she frequently asserted her right to play with it. One day, a younger child was going to join the class. The children had been prepared, but no one was sure how the older ones would react. Sally went straight for the stroller at the beginning of class, piled in several baby dolls, and took them for a walk around the classroom. Then she carefully took each one out, put them to bed in the cradle, and pushed the stroller over to Bettina, the new girl. Bettina beamed at Sally, and Sally smiled and patted her.

Sally took pleasure and satisfaction in enjoying her whole turn, recognizing when she had finished and allowing Bettina to have her turn. Sally was only just two years old, but she was able to think beyond herself, imagine Bettina's situation and feelings, and offer the younger child something precious to herself. The teachers had been able to support Sally's empathy and sense of agency, and Sally built on that support to help another child. Toko, Sally, and other young toddlers show their capacity to recognize the full range of feelings in others and regulate their own emotions to relate empathically to others.

HOW PARENTS HELP ONE-YEAR-OLDS BUILD THE EMOTIONAL MUSCLES OF

SELF-CONTROL, SELF-AWARENESS, AND SELF-REGULATION
Parents help by
• NAMING FEELINGS, THOUGHTS, AND DREAMS
• ASSIGNING APPROPRIATE RESPONSIBILITY FOR FEELINGS

TOLERATING MIXED FEELINGS
Parents help by
• HOLDING ON TO LOVE EVEN IN THE MIDST OF ANGER

RESPONDING POSITIVELY TO CHALLENGES
Parents help by
• SETTING EXPECTATIONS AND MAKING DEMANDS THAT ARE GEARED TO YOUR
• CHILD'S DEVELOPMENTAL CAPACITIES
• OFFERING GRADED OPPORTUNITIES FOR EXPERIENCES OF SUCCESS AND
• PLEASURE FROM COMPETENCE

MAKING MEANING OF EXPERIENCE
Parents help by
• EXPLAINING EMOTIONAL CAUSE AND EFFECT

AGENCY AND RESPONSIBILITY FOR ONESELF
Parents help by
• OFFERING YOUR CHILD GENUINE CHOICES

EMPATHY
Parents help by
• SETTING THE EXAMPLE, EXPLAINING, AND ENCOURAGING

TWO-YEAR-OLDS AND THEIR PARENTS
BUILDING EMOTIONAL MUSCLES

Older toddlers between two and three have made an astonishing leap forward in development. Their bodies are capable and coordinated, with growing physical skills consolidating rapidly. Their minds are active and complex. Their relationships are nuanced and their internal life has its own stamp while their feelings are varied and changeable. Most vividly, their rapidly emerging expressive language makes their thinking more accessible to adults and reveals how much is going on in their heads. Developmental researchers say that by the second birthday, "many of the essential foundations of social and emotional understanding have become established."[27]

Transformation of the relationship will be a theme throughout life as your child grows and eventually becomes an adult. Each phase of your child's development produces new challenges, which present opportunities for new closeness and growth. Transformation can only occur when parents engage with the *reality* of their child rather than with a fantasy image or a child perceived through the filter of parents' own needs. The challenge of later toddlerhood is to embrace and celebrate the real separateness and individuality of the child. Frustrating your toddler's need to assert his selfhood can lead to crankiness, whining, or angry outbursts.

No one can talk about older toddlers without addressing the label of the terrible twos. This issue will come up repeatedly throughout this chapter, but the label usually refers to toddlers' proneness to having tantrums. Rather than seeing tantrums as inevitable, we look at them as a toddler's last-ditch effort to regulate his "too big" feelings. This is a problem shared by parents and children who are challenged to find better solutions. Parents' task is to know your particular child well enough to anticipate when he will be overwhelmed from inside or outside to the point where he dumps his self-control outside in a tantrum. You need emotional muscle to stick with the task and not blame your child since it is a joint responsibility. When you can fulfill your task, you will be better equipped to help your toddlers find more adaptive ways to regulate their feelings.

This is a formidable challenge because toddlerhood is when aggression can take center stage, with children and parents clashing over autonomy. Parents and children are learning together how to use anger constructively, manage aggressive reactions, and find ways to resolve conflicts. In this chapter and all that follow, we will be tracking the emotional muscles parents and children develop to use their anger as a signal, to regulate their impulses toward aggressive action, and to problem-solve to find alternative realistic and creative solutions, using their love for each other as an ally in this endeavor.

What parents learn

EMBRACING THE INDIVIDUALITY OF YOUR CHILD

*Respect and tolerate the uniqueness of
your child as a separate person.*

We have talked about this in earlier chapters, but each phase carries its own version of the child's uniqueness and separate identity. Many parents who have developed emotional muscles from their child's infancy are able to gradually come to terms with and enjoy their child's separateness. They have emotionally integrated the difficult idea that separateness is not the same as separation and loss. But this is not easy, and all parents continue to struggle with these issues.

When children are between two and three, we see parents struggling with the task of truly acknowledging the child as an individual with whom they can learn to negotiate differences. For some parents, loving has meant being the same, and differences are experienced as a loss of love, or even as hostility.

Salman's mother, Nadia, was intensely impatient with his playing with the same toy for long periods of time. She wanted him to be just like her, including exploring the activities she was invested in, wanting him to work on what she wanted him to learn. It was hard for her to see him as having his own sources of motivation, need, and pleasure that were appropriate to his age.

Nadia sounded worried that the difference of his interests indicated that he didn't like or approve of her. It helped her to relax when teachers at his university day care, with support from the Allen Creek family consultant, explained why it was important to validate Salman's curiosity and described the steps to more mature functioning that were being consolidated in each of his self-chosen activities.

The teachers modeled being interested in Salman's choices and enjoying what he was getting out of them. It was hard for Nadia not to get bored when Salman worked with the rice in the sensory table for the whole free-choice time. His father's support was also recruited to reassure Nadia that Salman's persistence was a sign of growth and a result of her good parenting. As she understood more clearly what Salman was actually learning and saw his pleasure in the process, she too began to tolerate his repetition and even appreciate it was consolidating his skills. She was developing more emotional muscle in relation to Salman's separateness.

Abby was just two when she began to defy her mother frequently on small matters throughout the day. Her mother, Sarah, had always kept Abby very close, following an attachment parenting style and enjoying the special close relationship they had. Sarah was confused and hurt by Abby's new contrariness. Abby screamed about putting her outdoor clothes on, wouldn't get into her car seat, and so forth. Sarah worked closely with family consultants and teachers to understand what was going on; she applied her devotion to Abby to the task of finding a bearable way to interact with her increasingly independent daughter. They helped her differentiate separation from separateness. Much of Abby's fussing and fighting had to do with wanting to assert her own ideas, feelings, and wishes.

After a few months, Sarah proudly brought a story about a conversation with Abby to the parent group. They were looking together into the mirror, when Abby said, "I Abby, you Mommy." Sarah said, "That's right. I'm Mommy and you're Abby." Then in a conversational tone, as if giving an example, Abby put up her hand toward her mother and said, "No, no." Sarah understood Abby to be saying that she knew she was a separate person by saying no, that is, having different wishes from another person. Sarah felt relieved to finally understand how important it was for Abby to be able to say no to her beloved mother.

Sarah worked very hard to revise her vision of her relationship with her daughter and to come to a realistic understanding that genuine closeness comes from acceptance of separateness. This was a crucial strand in her developing the emotional muscle needed to transform her baby relationship with Abby to one that now had the potential for lifelong growth without losing each other.

DISTINGUISHING ASSERTION FROM AGGRESSION

Reexamine your attitudes toward aggression.

Every day parents of older toddlers are faced many times with a child who wants fiercely to "do it myself." Drive is the distinguishing quality of toddlers. This is assertion. The drive to explore, repeat, master, and discover is located in its own part of the brain. It is a different part than where aggression is located.

When assertion is blocked, toddlers become frustrated. If they cannot overcome the frustration in order to continue the blocked activity, they get angry. If, as parents, we find their constant high-driving activity wearing, exhausting, and annoying and then try to deal with our own feeling by stopping them, toddlers get furious. Grown-ups are challenged by that anger and can easily respond with anger themselves. Thus the whole assertive sequence can turn into an aggressive face-off.

Parents are not helped by the cultural confusion of assertion with aggression. Much that is really assertive is labeled as aggressive. Aggression and competitiveness are also equated and seen as highly desirable, especially in men. To further complicate the situation, aggression is the impulse everyone has the most trouble with. Everyone has conflicts about aggression and has tried to deal with it in a variety of ways, some adaptive, and some very maladaptive.

This is an area where self-reflection, frequent discussions with spouses or friends, parent groups or parent coaching, can be very helpful. At Allen Creek, we make a point of engaging with this topic for grown-ups and children alike. Much of what we have written in this book represents interesting possibilities or suggestions for parents to explore or consider. In the area of assertion and aggression, however, we have a definite position. Our general aim is to promote and facilitate assertion while learning useful ways to manage aggression and limit anger to a useful signal.

We have found repeatedly that blocking assertion leads to aggression; allowing aggression just leads to more aggression. The first strand of emotional muscle for parents in this area is to differentiate assertion from aggression and respond appropriately.

Mariana was often late to school with Hannah, just two. Mariana complained in parent group that getting dressed had become a terrible battle; she said, "I don't know what's gotten into Hannah. She used to be easy to dress and now she fights me every step of the way. And that's not the half of it. She seems to say no every other minute. Now I know what people mean by the terrible twos." The other parents nodded, sharing stories of angry and frustrating battles that left them feeling helpless and shocked at the intensity of their own angry reactions. They talked about feeling ashamed, guilty, and embarrassed at the fierceness of the battles. "It's no fun anymore." Several of the group noted that their pediatricians had sympathized but basically just told them to live through it and hope it passes soon.

The family consultant clarified that assertion was pleasurable activity related to exploration and mastery while aggression related to anger when the pleasurable urges were frustrated for whatever reason. He suggested that the group go over with Mariana exactly what the sequence was with Hannah. By examining it closely, we might be able to differentiate the assertion from the aggression.

Mariana realized that the morning now generally started with Hannah, saying, "No no, Hannah do it!" Everyone agreed that this was Hannah's enthusiasm about her own newfound capacities to do all kinds of things herself. The battle seemed to start when Hannah rejected her mother's clothes choices: "Not red shirt!" Then it continued while Mariana tried to get Hannah's shirt on her. It escalated when the mother imposed her own timetable so as not to be late to school.

The discussion clarified the issue and then many parents and the family consultants could offer a range of suggestions. One parent said she had willingly given up an extra half hour of sleep when she realized that the whole morning went cheerfully when she allowed time enough for the toddler's pace. Another suggestion was to choose the next day's outfit together the night before and lay it out. When Hannah had made the choice, she would probably happily put it on, especially if the morning already included talking about how she chose her own clothes and could help dress herself. All agreed that the goal was to have mother and child enjoy Hannah's growing capacity to dress herself.

Over several months, with some ups and downs, Mariana and Hannah worked on this issue, not only in relation to dressing but also at many other moments of the day. Mariana reported to the parent group that they had rediscovered lots of fun together since she had taken a step back as a parent and worked on dealing with her own frustration by better understanding Hannah.

This mother and the members of her parent group were engaging in the hard work of differentiating assertion and aggression. This was not just an intellectual or theoretical idea. They also had to deal with their own strong wishes to keep doing everything for their children and stay in charge.

Isidore, a tall three-year-old, often ran around his mother, Deanna, and butted her in the behind with his head. She laughed uncertainly when he did this but passed it off as his exuberance despite the concerned looks she got from other parents and teachers. When this and similar behaviors were talked about in the regular parent conference with the classroom team, the staff gently suggested that Isidore was being aggressive and wondered what he might be expressing. Deanna and her husband were upset by this label; they had trouble with the idea that their adored son could harbor angry feelings.

It takes emotional muscle for parents to face the reality that toddlers experience the whole range of feelings, including the ones parents have conflicts about. But appropriate limit setting can't happen unless the feeling is correctly identified.

We saw above that it can be counterproductive to take assertion as aggression; it is equally unhelpful to see aggression as assertion. When assertion is accurately labeled, it can be facilitated, channeled, and enjoyed; and it will evolve into new levels of capability. When aggression is not recognized or limited, it tends to intensify, escalate and continue unchanged.

ENGAGING WITH THE REALITY OF AGGRESSION

Face the consequences of aggression in yourself and your child.

With the cultural confusion about what constitutes aggression and the idealization of aggression in sports or politics, some parents, consciously or unconsciously, promote aggression in their children. This can begin to appear during toddlerhood.

Uri grabbed whatever toy he wanted, whether or not another child was using it. He seemed not to notice or care about the other child's feelings. He laughed when other children couldn't do what he could and generally was intimidating to the other children in the class. His devoted mother was constantly apologetic to the other parents but never stopped Uri. The staff was puzzled because it did not seem that his aggression was fueled by either anxiety or by traumatic events in his history.

In discussion over time, Uri's father stated that he firmly believed that men are and should be aggressive and that women's attempts to control men have to be resisted. "Boys will be boys," he said proudly. He linked Uri's precocious physical skills and his aggressive behavior to the boy being a chip off the old block.

It was very hard for this father to see the harm done to his own life and the potential damage to his son by his equating aggression and masculinity. As complex as this situation was, there was an opening for dialogue in the idea that Uri's dad was not making the useful distinction between assertion and aggression. Teachers could see that he was not adequately supporting Uri's pleasure in assertion when Uri could use his good physical skills to play ball, use the slide, ride a trike. Nor was he responding optimally to Uri's avid curiosity and questions to channel the boy's intellectual energy into learning. Uri was feeling strong from bullying others rather than drawing real power from his physical and mental prowess. He was feared and disliked by other children and falling behind in his school skills.

Uri's dad continued to insist that his son's obvious aggression was a masculine attribute that would serve him well in the jungle of the real world. His male family consultant set up an individual meeting and they connected initially on a shared interest in sports. The family consultant, who had been a college athlete, talked about the tactic of getting opponents angry so that they lose control over their skills. Rather than being assertive, with the goal of playing one's best and winning, the angry athlete wants to hurt or humiliate the opponent. This usually leads to loss of skill, penalties, and being benched by the coach. This turned out to reflect the history of the dad's own athletic efforts in college. His was a typical story of someone with a serious anger management problem. He told the family consultant that he had been physically abused by his own stern, demanding father; he himself had been a bully at school, had few friends, and despite his current success, still had few friends and a wife who was clearly intimidated by him.

Uri's dad said, "As we talk, it takes me back to feeling really lonely and miserable as a child, and I don't want that for Uri. It's hard to believe, even harder to say, that my father was wrong, that I have been wrong too. What you say about the difference between aggression and active assertion makes sense. I wish I had known that difference when I was a boy."

This father developed emotional muscle to face his own personal assumptions and reexamine them, including the role his own aggressiveness played in his son's development. All parents and teachers can usefully apply the distinction between assertiveness and aggression to every area of life, learning from the experience of this Allen Creek dad.

Differences between partners regarding aggression are quite common and can be a major source of friction. The issue impacts children if parents don't have the confidence that their relationship can withstand the pressure of examining real disputes about managing aggression and promoting assertion.

Steven's father was concerned that his wife was a doormat to Steven, allowing him to order her around constantly. Steven was controlling, often hit his mother, or kicked her if she kept him waiting while she spoke to a teacher or another parent. At the same time, the father recognized that she discouraged any genuine assertion on Steven's part as she tried to keep him a baby with no interests or skills beyond her own. She often described Steven as needing her for everything and very clingy. The issue became more intense as the older toddler year unfolded and families were preparing to go into preschool.

Family consultants encouraged Steven's father to sit down with his wife and discuss their different perspectives on Steven's assertion and aggression. They offered special meetings, but these were somehow never possible to schedule. By the end of the year, the father had still not confronted his wife; she had not changed, and Steven was still treating her badly. Eventually, the parents decided to keep Steven at home for the next year as his mother felt he was not ready to separate for preschool. It seemed as if Steven's dad had felt unable to engage his wife in constructive dialogue around this crucial issue in Steven's development.

Rather than develop the emotional muscle to address the differences between the parents around aggression and assertion in Steven, they denied and evaded the issue and chose to withdraw. It is important to face that emotional muscle is not easy to develop. Just as there are outside limits with physical muscle, so too people can only go as far as they can bear emotionally. Steven's parents found themselves unable to go in the direction of building the muscle to look at the issues of aggression and assertion in their child.

Many toddlers go through the arrival of a new baby in the family. This event is full of feelings for all involved, and parents anticipate and worry about their toddler's reactions. Nowadays, most people understand that older brothers and sisters will have mixed feelings, but there is a danger of a kind of complacency about the presence of jealousy and aggression in the older child. When the older child acts on his feelings and hits or pokes or pinches or scares the baby, it should not be dismissed as just sibling rivalry. Toddlers need help to develop emotional muscles to contain and manage their feelings, but parents also need the emotional muscle to set protective limits for both children.

Two-and-a-half-year-old Angela made the grown-ups laugh when she remarked that it was time to send the new baby back to the hospital. But her mother described how she also was pinching her baby sister, Caroline, and rocking her seat too hard. Her parents felt they couldn't stop her as they understood that she was bound to feel somewhat displaced, but they were also angry and felt protective of the baby. Angela's behavior did not improve with time and was reaching levels dangerous to Caroline. Her mother felt afraid to leave the baby alone in the next room with Angela, even for a minute. The toddler parent group had several parents with new babies, as well as a mother with two older children. How to handle sibling rivalry became the focus of discussion for some time.

First came the distinction between feelings and action. The parents did not realize that their toddlers could understand this difference. Feelings, even strong negative ones, can be respected and accepted, but they cannot be acted upon or inflicted on others. Secondly, parents can suggest and reinforce assertive behavior, where the toddler can show everyone what she is capable of doing for the baby or to help parents. One parent described her son who brought a toy over to his baby sister every time she began to fuss. The baby usually rewarded him with a big smile. Noting that the baby had stopped crying, he felt wonderful about his competence at taking care of the baby and helping her feelings.

Lastly and most importantly is to immediately stop the aggressive behavior. There have to be firm, consistent, and explicit limits. "You are never allowed to hurt (pinch, hit, bite, poke, and so forth) your sister." This will probably need to be said repeatedly since the toddler's angry urges will recur. She needs your help to contain them. The more pleasure the toddler can get from being an active caretaker, the easier it will be to set these limits.

Toddler parents need continuous practice to maintain the distinction between assertion and aggression, recognize aggression for what it is, distinguish feelings and actions, and address aggressive actions promptly and firmly. We will see that the challenges of supporting assertion and managing aggression continue throughout childhood. The muscles needed to handle these feelings are established in the years covered by this book.

HOLDING ON TO LOVE

Recognize that you have enough love to go around.

Just as anger and aggression have to be dealt with at every level of development, so it is with love. We talked earlier, in the chapters on babies and one-year-olds, about the muscles parents need to keep joy and love in the picture, to tolerate sadness, and to hold on to love even in the midst of anger. With two-year-olds, parents are faced with the continuing challenge of ensuring that love prevails. At this point, children are ready to understand that love is not finite. But parents have to feel that conviction first in order to be able to present a consistent, authentic stance to their children.

Many people operate as if love is a finite quantity, living according to an assumption that you can only love a certain number of people, that there is only a certain amount to go around, and that it will run out. This is one source of intense envy and jealousy, often between siblings. During the toddler period, which is often when parents have another baby, parents have to work hard emotionally and psychologically to maintain and nurture their love for the older child. There is also a physiological tide to swim against as the oxytocin hormone released during labor, childbirth, and breastfeeding not only serves to strengthen the bond to the new baby, but also to wipe out the feeling of biological connectedness to the older child.[28] This is why it is important to transform the relationship with the older child.

Parents can focus on the joy and appeal of the capacities of the older child, the fun things the older child can now do, rather than leaving the child longing for the old biological tie represented by the things mother and new baby are doing. The prior infantile ways of connecting with the older child are no longer appropriate. Parents can develop the emotional muscle to work at maintaining the new level of loving with their toddler.

Contain mixed feelings

No one finds it easy to handle mixed feelings, in themselves or when faced with their impact on toddlers. Younger toddlers could contain only one feeling. Older toddlers are just developing the capacity to experience more than one feeling at a time, and it can be a rough transition for them because it is uncomfortable to love and hate the same person. Parents have the simultaneous challenge of their own mixed feelings in relation to their child, as well as containing the increasingly strong reactions the children struggle with.

Marcia eagerly began the parent group by saying, "I couldn't wait to get here. I had the absolutely most awful day with Nat, and I was ready to kill him! I felt terrible, like I was the worst mother in the world." When everyone smiled, she said, "No really, I've never felt like this before. It scared me." The family consultant noted that she was already demonstrating strength and love for Nat by recognizing the feeling and sharing it to get support.

Several other parents then spoke up and described how they had not realized before how very angry they could get with such a small person. One mother talked of hauling her child out of the supermarket, leaving the whole cart full of food behind, because he wouldn't stop throwing tantrums. One of the fathers described his complete rage and bafflement when his son wouldn't let him brush his teeth.

The actual coexistence of loving and angry feelings became clear as the parents described their internal conflicts. What could they do with this? The family consultant noted that the group had talked earlier about these issues when their children were one. Then we were teaching the children that, despite their anger, the grown-ups remembered and carried the knowledge that they still loved each other. This laid the groundwork for the more complex tasks of the two-year-old year. It is now not only the child, but also the parents, who have to frequently remind themselves about the constancy of their love for their child. Once the love is back in the mix, it becomes easier to restrain yourself from acting on the anger, limiting anger to an internal signal. Support from other people, like talking about the anger in the parent group, helps combat unnecessary guilt for having the feeling. The other muscle that comes into play at that point is to maintain the distinction between feeling and action.

Then the anger can do its work as the spur to problem solving about the situation at hand. This allowed the group to go ahead and look at what was upsetting about Nat's stubborn day and why the supermarket felt so overwhelming and what might be done about toothbrushing.

EMPATHY

*Call upon all your own internal resources to put yourself
in your child's shoes.*

Two-year-olds have developed a complex inner life. It takes effort, practice, and persistence for parents to imagine what and how their child is thinking, feeling, and desiring. Toddlers are constantly learning new skills. It may be hard for grown-ups to remember what that is like since we have probably not learned anything completely new since driving lessons in midadolescence. Mastery takes a long time and a lot of repetition. Mastery is unstable at first and even slight stress can lead toddlers temporarily to lose their most recently acquired skills.

Jim spoke to the parent group about how pleased he had been to see Jacob, two and three quarters, dry through the night for eight days. Then during a visit from his grandma, Jacob wet the bed and insisted on going back to nighttime diapers. Jim talked about trying not to let Jacob see how disappointed he was; he wasn't sure how to handle this step back.

The other parents pointed out that his grandma's visit may have been a bigger thing for Jacob, more disruptive, than his parents had understood. Jim realized that he hadn't seen how much energy and focus Jacob was devoting to toilet mastery. The change in mealtimes and sleeping arrangements for the visit interfered with the regular routine Jacob needed as background for consolidating his new skill.

Jim achieved a new level of understanding and respect for his little boy's efforts. What is taken for granted by a parent may not look the same way from the child's perspective.

Adults have a different view of the world than toddlers, because we have so much reality knowledge and experience to use to fact-check our conclusions. Toddlers don't actually think in a different way from us, but they often come to different conclusions because they don't have as much to check their ideas against. It is our job to teach them what we know of the world and respect their efforts to figure things out.

Abby had just begun to use the toilet consistently. One day the toilet overflowed. At first her parents thought someone had just used too much paper, and they tried to unblock it themselves. When that didn't work, they were upset and then called the plumber, who diagnosed a problem in the sewer connection to the street. Big diggers came to unearth the pipes and replace them and the whole thing took over a week to resolve. Abby's parents were stressed; they had to spend a lot of time and money dealing with this major household disaster.

Abby immediately stopped using the toilet, and she was very insistent that *no one* should use it again. She went back to diapers, and her parents were mystified and annoyed. A week later, when the repairs had been finished, Abby's parents could turn their attention to her issue. Why wouldn't she use the toilet now that they said it was all fixed and she had been so proud of using it before?

In the discussion, we realized that Abby had actually thought the same thing as her parents at first—something too big had been put into the toilet. Abby stuck to that hypothesis, whereas her parents could use their greater knowledge and capacity for abstract thinking to understand what was going on in a pipe, invisible under the ground, and come to the realistic explanation.

The family consultant suggested that Abby might need explanation and reassurance that it was not due to anything she had done. Her parents agreed to try and then reported back to the group the next time; their explanations made no difference, and she still would not use the toilet and was upset when anyone else did. Abby had insisted that she had indeed caused the trouble.

This allowed the group to think about another characteristic of toddler thinking; they put themselves in the center of events. This too is not actually so different from what grown-ups do when they feel powerless. It gave Abby some sense of control to feel that she had caused the event that made her parents so helpless and anxious. Grown-ups do this too, but we can often correct ourselves and gain a sense of agency and control through practical action. This avenue is not available to toddlers, who can't yet do much about anything.

Understanding this helped the group in two ways; first, it offered another idea to Abby's parents. They could talk to her about how upset they had all been about the pipes and how that had worried her, but how they all felt better now, because they had figured out how to fix it. They could tell the story over again and play it out with dolls and toys. (This turned out to work and Abby regained her toilet mastery.) The critical factor in the story was regaining agency and control. Neither Abby nor her parents was helpless anymore.

Second it gave a renewed sense of how much effort parents may have to make to imagine themselves into their children's minds, and how respectful they should be of the child's mental efforts. The crucial insight was to include more than the objective facts of the pipe problem in understanding what was going on for Abby. Her parents' feelings and reactions were integral to the reality of the situation for the little girl. This was a vivid example of how parents stand for reality for children. And it brought home to all the parents the empathic imagination they needed to factor themselves into the equation when they were trying to make sense of their children's experiences.

Jeffrey's dad brought an interesting anecdote to a parent group. He had told Jeffrey that his aunt would be coming to visit on an airplane. At a backyard barbecue with neighbors, Jeffrey heard an airplane. He pointed up to the sky and ran around, saying, "Auntie, Auntie!" Several of the grown-ups laughed. Jeffrey stopped and looked hurt. His dad wondered why he reacted that way.

Jeffrey was making an association that was important to him because his father had presented the connection to him. That made it real to Jeffrey since the majority of his knowledge and experience is still presented or filtered through his parents. He was doing the figuring out that is constant for toddlers making sense of the big world. This is a serious and dignified pursuit that takes up a lot of mental energy and commitment for the toddler.

The parent group agreed that it was sometimes hard not to laugh but that they could see why it was important for them to make the effort to respect the child's working to understand the world. They have to use the emotional muscles to take responsibility for what they say and what the implications are to help their toddlers build their knowledge of reality. If there is a misunderstanding, as there was for Jeffrey, parents can apologize and make a fuller explanation instead of laughing at the child. One mom suggested, "It sounds like Jeffrey needed more details and context for the connection of his aunt's visit and the airplane. Maybe you could have told him that there are lots of planes, and his aunt would let you know which one she was coming on so you would tell him the day before."

TOLERATING THE DIFFERENT PLEASURE NEEDS OF GROWN-UPS AND TODDLERS

Recognize that the source of your pleasure with your toddler is his pleasure and not the actual play or activity.

Play in the earlier years is generally in short bursts with instant feedback. This starts to change in two-year-olds. The play becomes richer, deeper, more complex. But it involves a lot of repetition while toddlers master the content and the skills and come to terms with the feelings that can be carried in their games. Play is essential to toddlers' growth, brain development, and learning. However, this can be an area of mismatch between toddlers and parents as adults tend to seek more novelty and stimulation in play. Many parents get very bored playing the same things over and over with their toddlers. It takes muscle to understand why your toddler needs to play through the same things repeatedly, to stay with her through the process, and to take pleasure in her achievement.

Parents in the two-year-old class asked the teachers why they couldn't add new toys and activities sooner, sing new songs, and take the children to play on the big kids' playground. They wanted their children to be stimulated to try new things. The teachers understood and agreed with the parents' wish to have their children feel good about new possibilities and challenges. But they pointed out that they had a very dependable criterion for judging when the children were ready for new alternatives.

Teachers assess when to introduce new toys or activities on the basis of the kind of pleasure the children are taking in the current offerings. As long as the children are experiencing a good level of pleasure, effort, creativity, and success, then what is available is just right. As soon as the toddlers seem to be repeating without getting distinct pleasure or satisfaction in mastery, it is a sign that they are ready for more.

At this age, you have to recognize a difference between parents and children that will persist, probably until late adolescence—your interests and level of involvement are likely to be different. Parents can use their empathy to recognize that toddlers are consolidating important steps in their play and will be ready to move forward at their own pace, which is often more slowly than adults'. When you have developed the muscle to tolerate the different pleasure needs you and your toddler have, you are likely to find more interest in toddlers' play. You can see what your child is accomplishing, enjoy that, and eventually introduce graded elaborations of the same game.

Polly's mother, Deirdre, spoke with difficulty in a parent group; she felt really guilty about not enjoying playing. "I know we're supposed to be playing with them, how important it's supposed to be, but I don't know what to do and she wants me with her all the time. I am really having a hard time with this. I'm embarrassed that I get so bored." Other parents thanked her for bringing this up, as they shared the feeling, but thought that good parents were supposed to have a wonderful time on the floor endlessly building block towers!

The family consultant also thanked Deirdre for providing an opportunity to open up an important topic—parents don't automatically know how to play and shouldn't get caught up in some mystique. Doing the same thing over and over is intrinsically tiresome unless a parent can find a different source of good feeling. Play is another part of parenting that takes practice to master, so it's a gradual skill acquisition. He said, "Toddlers play all day, whereas grown-ups can't and shouldn't have to. Some of you may want to start with a planned brief amount of time that you expand when you are ready. It is fruitful for children to play both with a grown-up and alone as they develop different skills in the two situations. But it doesn't have to be either/or. Grown-ups can be participants, audience, commentator, bystander, stepping in and out of the play as you do other tasks. All these roles are possible and useful.

But actually playing with your child is different and requires its own muscles that help you overcome boredom."

One of the dads said, "What I do is create a Zen moment. When I am playing with Jessica, that's all I am doing. We stay in our bubble. I don't talk on the cell phone or do e-mail or cook dinner. We just have a good time doing what she wants to play. So there are no distractions, and she doesn't have to compete for my attention. But I always build in an exit strategy. I find some point in the play, like when she has put the dolly back to bed for the tenth time, to say that I will soon go start dinner. Jessica can keep playing, or she can come into the kitchen with me. I tell her that I am having so much fun watching her play, and I'll remember that while I go in the kitchen." He went on to say that he feels his times playing together with Jessica without any other distractions do something really important for him in his relationship with his daughter. He feels really in tune and close to her, which gives him great pleasure.

Another mother said to the family consultant, "I'm struck by what you said about how important playing is for our kids' growth. It sounds like their pleasure is like gas in the car for their learning or mastery. I feel bad about how many times I say I'm too busy to play." A dad remarked that he had come home a few days before to find that dinner wasn't ready. His wife apologized as if she had done something wrong, spending time playing with their twenty-two-month-old. "I'm going to tell her again tonight that I would rather she enjoyed playing than having dinner on the table when I walk in the door."

The issues these parents were working on in an Allen Creek parent group give us insight into a conflict shared by most parents. The solutions they came to can be used by all parents in any situation.

ADVOCATING FOR YOUR CHILD

Maintain confidence in your own thoughtful choices for your child.

Parents often find that their families or neighbors don't understand or approve the parenting choices they are making. It takes conviction and persistence to withstand questioning, however well-meaning, when you are a new parent and are feeling your way into the job. When the challenge is not so friendly, it can be even harder. This sort of pressure can reach a peak at two as many friends and relatives may say that you are letting your child "get away with murder" when you are trying to work with her to plan better solutions to difficult issues.

Louise came back very upset from a family visit with Sylvia. The grandmother had been angry when Louise insisted on following Sylvia's bedtime routine, which pushed the grown-ups' dinner an hour later. When Louise tried to tell her mother why she felt it was important to maintain Sylvia's home patterns, her mother told her that she felt Louise was ruining her child and that she found it hard to listen to the ways Louise talked with Sylvia.

All the other parents in the group sympathized with how devastating Louise found this judgment from her mother. Several shared similar stories that they had felt reluctant to reveal, as they were so hurt and shaken by grandparents' disapproval. A moving discussion ensued, with parents describing how arduous the process was to find their way to parenting as they felt was right.

Family consultants and parents worked together to think about ways to talk with grandparents or to design visits to minimize friction. One mom said that she had phoned her mother to talk before a visit because she was worried about it getting ruined by just this kind of criticism. "I told her that I had learned from her that mothers know best about their own kids, so I wanted to plan together how we were going to manage the practical parts of the visit. For instance, I told her that James wakes up slowly and doesn't usually want to have his breakfast until about an hour after getting up. We would have a more pleasant morning if he wasn't pushed to come to the table right away." Other parents agreed that sharing the routine, and the rationale for it might help.

Jeannette, nearly three, was going to have a minor surgical intervention that necessitated a general anesthetic. Her parents contacted their family consultant to talk through how best to prepare her. They talked about how to describe the procedure and the aftermath with Jeannette. The family consultant also said that most doctors say they give children some "medicine to make them sleep" for the surgery. She said that it is important to differentiate sleeping from being anesthetized. She counseled the parents to insist that the doctor should instead describe anesthesia as some medicine that makes things not hurt. This is a realistic explanation that reflects the true difference between sleep and unconsciousness. The family consultant told the parents that children given that inaccurate label often had sleep difficulties after surgery, fearing (quite logically) that another something might happen to them during sleep.

Jeanette's parents conveyed their wishes about terminology to the surgeon. Nevertheless, during pre-op, the surgeon began to use the *sleep medicine* words. Jeannette's mother stopped him and insisted that he explain it accurately and usefully. The surgeon was taken aback at first but thought for a while, then said, "What you say actually makes a lot of sense. I am going to remember this in the future." Jeannette's parents were pleased that she had a good experience and were also proud to have helped other children by educating the surgeon.

It takes grit and determination to stick with your plans as a parent. Being an advocate for your child is a role that will be important not only in early childhood, but also in negotiating with teachers, principals, and doctors throughout her childhood. Practicing parental planning and decision making in the early years strengthens the emotional muscles needed for making sure that your child's needs are fully met in the way you know will be best. Speaking up may sometimes be hard, but it is up to you to take a deep breath and do it for your child's sake.

An Allen Creek family moved to a new city in the summer Frannie turned three. Her mom Gloria called to tell the following story: She had researched day cares near their new home and decided on the center attached to the church she and her husband were going to join. She was pleased at the overall philosophy and the director's willingness to have her stay for the first few days to settle Frannie in. But there was a center rule against bringing toys from home. The problem was that Frannie was very attached to her little teddy bear, especially since their recent move.

Gloria made an appointment with the director and presented her point of view that Frannie would settle in much better if she could have her transitional object, her teddy bear, with her in her cubby. It would help remind her of Mom and home and maintain her connection while she was at day care. Gloria talked about how nervous she was before the meeting. She was planning to challenge the director and her rules in a community she wanted to join. The discussion went well, however. The director understood why the teddy bear was important to Frannie, and Gloria felt encouraged that this flexibility confirmed she had made the right choice of center. Gloria told her old Allen Creek family consultant,

"I really learned to stick up for what I think my child needs. Thanks for the support!"

Parents in a group were discussing how differently they were brought up from how they were trying to raise their own children. Several shared their sense that their own childhoods were abusive, painful, or unnecessarily neglectful. They all talked about how difficult it felt to criticize their parents. The family consultant, in an attempt to lighten the atmosphere, remarked that "they had all turned out all right after all, hadn't they?" The parents did not accept this escape clause, saying that their insights had been painful and arduous. None of them enjoyed being critical, but they had felt impelled to face these issues to provide a better life for their own children. The teachers and the family consultants had helped them to reach this point, and they felt the family consultant was wrong to try to get their parents off the hook. The family consultant apologized and agreed that perhaps she too had found criticism of parents painful.

One of the dads said, "It's not that easy to disagree with our family consultant either since we get so much from your expertise and appreciate your help. But you're the one who has taught us that we are the experts about our own children and our own parenting. It feels good to have the opportunity to exercise our emotional muscles, even in the face of resistance, whether it's from our own relatives or an authority figure, like teachers or doctors or family consultants."

No one is immune to the internal struggle involved in differentiating ourselves as individuals throughout the course of life. These parents felt clearly and strongly enough to confront the family consultant they knew and respected, advocating for themselves when they felt she was undermining their hard-won insights and their commitment to thoughtful parenting, whatever emotional muscle that would demand.

Stephanie's mom, Helen, talked about the sustained effort she makes to maintain her confidence and authority as the parent. "Stephanie spends long hours every week at her babysitter's and with her teachers. It would be easy in some ways to abdicate and feel that the caregiver knows her better than I do. Also, Stephanie loves her so much and sometimes minds her better than me. This discussion is helping me hold on to my identity as her mom." George's dad said, "It feels like we're talking about an important loop. I feel confidence in my work self—I'm good at my job. But learning to be a parent adds a new aspect to my identity. Like Helen said, I can really feel like George's dad when I figure out what's right for him. The more competent I feel, the more confidence I have to stick up for what he needs."

The family consultant brought a story of a call from an Allen Creek alumna parent who had been concerned that her daughter's first-grade year wasn't going well. That mom had phoned to convey the good news that she had worked to find the right classroom placement to meet her child's learning style. The mom had said that she learned at Allen Creek how to work with teachers and other professionals to make sure her child's needs were met.

These parents learned to stick up for their kids and themselves from their parent groups, teachers and family consultants at Allen Creek. But parents everywhere can be inspired by their experience to do the same.

INCLUDING SOCIAL CONSEQUENCES

Have the courage to be honest: feed back the impact on others of your child's behavior.

A theme throughout this book is the need for graded change, consistent with your child's rate of growth. Toward the end of this year, when the children will soon be three, teachers and parents are thinking ahead to preschool, when the parents won't be there in the same way to mediate and filter interactions between the children and with other grown-ups. Even when a child has been in care earlier, preschool includes a new level of demands for functioning in a group with other children and grown-ups.

Infants and toddlers do not fully understand their actual effect on others. Children understand causes of emotions before they can consistently understand the consequences.[29] It begins to be appropriate at this point in your child's development to introduce the idea that she has an impact on others. Other people will have reactions and feelings about what she does and says. This has started earlier in the sense that parents react and set limits from infancy on. Now it takes on new dimensions as parents and teachers begin to demand that the toddler herself take responsibility for her impact on others.

This creates a new challenge for parents who have to feel able to tell their child that she has done something hurtful or unacceptable or disgusting. It is not easy to go from generally emphasizing the positive to including the negative.

Deirdre began a parent group by saying that she had something sort of embarrassing to talk about. Her daughter, Polly, was masturbating in various public places, and Deirdre was concerned to know what to do and say. She didn't want to inhibit Polly or make her feel that it was something bad, but at the same time, she felt it was socially embarrassing, and it made her feel uncomfortable.

The family consultant helped the parents frame the issue around using their own feelings of discomfort as a signal. A parent asked if the children were old enough to understand the idea of public and private. The parents liked that idea but weren't sure how to apply it to something sexual. The family consultant suggested that it would help the children, rather than harm them, to explain that you are glad they feel good about their own bodies and the good feelings they can get from them, but that this is a private pleasure with private parts of their bodies. Other people will be uncomfortable if these private things are done in public, so they may do this in a private place, like their room, but not in the kitchen or the supermarket. The same discussion would be applicable to nose picking, taking their chewing gum out of their mouths, and so forth.

Another social reaction to bring in at this point is disgust. This is usually not an issue in the first year or so. But by three, if a child has not yet mastered toileting, this may be a relevant dimension to communicate. One reason older children and grown-ups use the toilet is because poo smells disgusting. Parents and others don't like to smell it.

Nelly had moved into an autonomy battle with her parents. Toileting was no exception. She saw no reason to master toileting when she felt it was being imposed by her parents. At the same time, she valued her friendships and the positive response she generally received from grown-ups.

Nelly's parents were worried that they would be attacking her self-esteem if they told her that poo does not smell good. When they did, Nelly seemed genuinely surprised. Soon after, she decided on her own to use the toilet. Mastery was swift, and Nelly was proud of her new achievement.

Explaining these realities to your child is not easy. It feels awkward to feed back a negative social reaction to others. There is always a concern about hurting the other person's feelings. But we do not do our children a favor by shielding them from the reality of their impact on others. This social learning is critical to success in relationships throughout school and life afterward.

THE EMOTIONAL MUSCLES USED BY PARENTS OF TWO-YEAR-OLDS ARE:

EMBRACING THE INDIVIDUALITY OF YOUR CHILD

DISTINGUISHING ASSERTION FROM AGGRESSION

ENGAGING WITH THE REALITY OF AGGRESSION

HOLDING ON TO LOVE

EMPATHY

TOLERATING THE DIFFERENT PLEASURE NEEDS OF GROWN-UPS AND CHILDREN

ADVOCATING FOR YOUR CHILD

INCLUDING SOCIAL CONSEQUENCES

What do two-year-olds need to develop emotional muscle?

Two-year-olds need parents who have been able to develop the muscle to enjoy their children's increasing independence and autonomy while remembering how important parents remain. This is very often the age at which many parents have a second child or increase their work. Whatever the specific cultural, economic, and personal factors involved in parents' decisions and planning, there is often a powerful dimension of parents' feeling no longer so necessary and useful to their children.

Older toddlers need to know that their parents are still emotionally available to them on a new level. Then the children are free to use what their parents offer them to develop the emotional muscle for responding most adaptively to the many challenges of this phase and entry into the next.

What two-year-olds learn

EXPRESSING FEELINGS IN WORDS
MAKING FEELINGS "JUST RIGHT" SIZE
CONTAINING BOTH LOVE AND HATE
BRAVERY
ACCEPTANCE OF REALISTIC POWER AND LIMITATIONS
STRIVING FOR MASTERY

How parents help two-year-olds build emotional muscles

EXPRESSING FEELINGS IN WORDS

Words are the main tool for children to understand,
master, and work things out.

Parents can promote this growth by

- **NAMING FEELINGS, LISTENING, RESPONDING, AND EXPLAINING**
  Now that language is in the foreground and rapidly accelerating almost daily, words become more available to both parents and children. Parents whose children have begun to talk relatively early notice a big drop in frustration and anger. They assure other parents that they will soon get the benefit of this huge leap forward. The big difference is that the children can now verbally communicate their desires, feelings, reasons, and ideas. Many parents use language comfortably from early infancy; those who named feelings accurately for their children when they were one-year-olds usually find that the children can often say how they feel as a step to solving the problem rather than moving right into action. These children have already learned that talking things through helps resolve conflict.

Kyle often said to his mom, "We need to figure this out." During tough moments Sylvia said to her mother, "Let's talk."

Parents who can work with their children in this way have already built up lots of emotional muscle as they persisted in verbalizing and naming for the two preceding years, when their children mainly had only receptive language capacities. We have emphasized the possibilities of this early nurturance of emotional strength, but parents can do this work at any point in their child's development to great benefit.

Parents who have not promoted naming feelings can now catch up and get immediate verbal feedback, which demonstrates that their children do indeed understand them. When parents hear other parents or teachers describing this kind of interaction they are encouraged to give talking a chance or even to insist on it.

George's mom, who often had to carry him screaming out of the room when he didn't want to make a transition, sat down with George and the teachers after class one day and said, "You're strong enough now to put your feelings into words instead of speaking with your whole body. When you tell me in words, we can figure out together how we can have more fun when it's time to go to the next thing."

This is the alternative to the terrible twos. Parents are helping their older toddlers become strong enough to manage feelings by putting them into words and then making the demand that their children participate in further discussion to find a solution.

Tassie's dad described running into her room in the middle of the night because she was crying hard. Unlike six months earlier, when he had often walked the floor with Tassie, he could now ask her what the trouble was and expect an answer. "Daddy, tooth hurts," sobbed Tassie. He was very relieved to know what was bothering her; he felt less helpless and knew how to relieve her pain. After some Motrin, as the doctor had advised, and a good cuddle, Tassie went back to sleep. He felt the talking calmed him down, which helped to calm her down, and with words, they could solve the problem together.

The new opportunity for dialogue between you and your toddler is the foundation for all the other emotional muscles we are going to describe. Words and interactions have been central from the beginning to your growing relationship with your child, but there is a huge leap forward when your toddler becomes an active participant in discussion, conversation, and emotional muscle building.

MAKING FEELINGS "JUST RIGHT" SIZE

Turning feeling states into internal signals.

Parents can promote this growth by

- **TAKING "TIME WITH" YOUR CHILD TO MAKE THE BIG FEELINGS MANAGEABLE**
Toddlers may be overwhelmed from the outside by events or experiences. They are also vulnerable to being overwhelmed from the inside, when their feelings get too big. These can be positive or negative feelings—it's the size that matters. Since toddlers have intense feelings and reactions, they are often flooded, particularly with anger or excitement.

All parents of toddlers dread tantrums. Children have tantrums when their feelings are so big that they feel overwhelmed. Then there is a ripple effect in which parents feel overwhelmed too. It takes muscle to subdue such big feelings constructively.

Jake's mother said she was at her wit's end since Jake kept melting down, and it made no difference when she gave him a "time out" on the stairs. So she had tried shutting him in his room, but he banged on the door and seemed to get more frantic. Another parent, who had attended the previous year, mentioned how helpful he had found the idea of "time with," instead of "time out" since the child was usually not able to draw on his own resources when he was overwhelmed with such big feelings.

Arabella's parents then chimed in because they really wanted the help of the group to find a solution to their little girl's tantrums. She was disrupting the household and spoiling the fun at school. Her mother dreaded going anywhere for fear that Arabella would ruin it with one of her unpredictable meltdowns.

All the parents could relate to their anger, frustration, and helplessness. The parents all talked about trying to reduce the amount of frustration in the day but recognized too that Arabella was a strong-willed, energetic child who was trying to master many things at once. The family consultant agreed that the idea of "time with" did seem relevant to these problems and suggested that the task during a "time with" was to help the child make the "too big" feelings manageable. Arabella's mom could stretch out her arms and say, "Oh,

Arabella, sometimes your feelings are just sooo big, this big, too big for anyone to hold alone. I'll sit with you and we'll make these 'too big' feelings just the right size for us to talk about them."

How can parents find a way to help their children understand the task? The first step was to describe the overwhelming feelings accurately for the children. Then parents could show them how to stretch out their arms to gather in the big feelings and make them just the right size to fit into their hand.

Another way to convey this was to suggest squeezing the feelings into a ball you can hold safely. Sometimes, it helps to have a child squeeze the grown-up's finger really hard to focus on the idea. This concretizes the effort needed to condense the huge feelings into a manageable size. Parents need not address the cause of the tantrum until the feelings have been brought under control. They could say to the children, "Once you are strong enough to press your too big feeling into one hand, then it will be the right size for us to talk about it, and find ways to make you feel good." Together they would then be able to look at the feelings and find a solution.

Jake's and Arabella's parents tried these ideas and reported back that the children had nodded in relief when they labeled the feelings as too big. Arabella's parents told her that they could see that it was too hard for her to manage those all by herself. They would help her make them the right size, so the feelings wouldn't feel so scary. All the parents decided to start experimenting with these ideas, activities, concrete actions, and words. In class and at home, we saw the children actually using their arms and straining with the effort, ending up with their hands clasped or their arms wrapped around themselves.

A few weeks later, one of the other children in class looked at Arabella, who was trying to take over all the play food in the kitchen, and said, "Your feelings are too big. You need your mommy to help you." Arabella brought her voice back down to an ordinary level and took her mother's hand, saying, "Please help me keep my feelings the right size." Her mother replied, "I see that you have already started using your muscles. You made your voice just right by yourself. I'll help you with the feelings and I know that soon you will be strong enough to do this all by yourself."

One of the most significant insights for this parent group was realizing that aggressive behavior was a sign that anger had become overwhelming. Aggressive behavior calls for an effort, the application of muscle, to turn aggression into a usable signal. When it could be brought back down to being a signal of not liking something, anger was a useful, even crucial, indicator to seek out the cause of the trouble and try to solve the problem.

All the parents, including Arabella's mother and father, found that they could make their children stronger by supplying them with concepts and tools to manage their intense feelings, especially of anger and excitement. Rather than being overwhelmed and breaking down into tantrums, the children responded with progressive moves. There is enormous pleasure from owning one's feelings, being in charge of feelings. This helped the children play more harmoniously with each other, as well as equipping them with a crucial internal tool for the lifelong task of managing strong feelings and reactions.

A few weeks later, Jake's dad reported a conversation with his sister, who had kids the same age. He had told her about making feelings just the right size and how well Jake was responding to that idea. She said, "Yeah, but you have that whole group and the teachers to help you. Jake's dad had said, "Sure it's nice to have their support, but anyone can use the idea. You just have to think about it and have the conversation with your kid."

CONTAINING BOTH LOVE AND HATE

The "too big" feelings of anger and hate can wipe out love and generate panic.

Parents can promote this growth by

- **REMINDING CHILDREN THAT THEY CAN HOLD MORE THAN ONE FEELING**
  Ruby's mother came to a parent group with a puzzle. She said, "I tried a 'time with.' I sat down with Ruby and she calmed down. I thought to myself 'Great!' and then I said we could now figure out what the trouble was and she got furious all over again. It was as if talking about it brought all the feelings right back!"
  The family consultant said that there was a step in between that might have helped. When Ruby was so angry that she couldn't feel anything else, particularly her love for her mother, she panicked. Most

tantrums have that scared quality along with the rage. It's not only scary to hate your parents, but little children assume that others have the same reactions they do—"If I hate my mommy, my mommy must hate me back." Once the angry feeling is brought down to the right size, the next step is to talk about the love that is always there inside parents and children, even when they are angry.

Another mom said she remembered doing this with her older child, and it really helped. She recalled saying, "When you're so angry with me, you forget that you love me. And you may even forget that I love you too. But I remember and I'll remind you." She went on to say that it then became possible to move to the cause of the anger, once the security of the love was re-established.

The family consultant agreed that this was the sequence that would help the toddlers become strong enough to regulate their big feelings. As they grow in strength to contain both hate and love, they become more able to remember on their own and tantrums diminish.

It is a lifelong challenge to scale and contain strong feelings. The tantrums of two-year-olds provide an opportunity to begin building up the emotional muscle of maintaining love despite anger.[30]

BRAVERY

*Another important strength is the capacity to recover
from a physical or emotional setback.*

Parents can promote this growth by

- **HELPING YOUR CHILD BOUNCE BACK**
  In the midst of a crisis, toddlers don't realize that it is bound to end. Much of the crying from a tumble is because the toddler is afraid the pain will go on forever. The same is true for painful feelings.

  Narmeen was very disappointed that she didn't like the snack in class. She cried inconsolably and angrily hit her mother in the chest. Her mother took her out to the hall to calm down and make the big feeling the right size to talk about, but then Narmeen didn't want to return to the classroom where she had been so unhappy. Her teacher came out to join them and said, "I am sorry that you are so unhappy about snack, but now that feeling is over and we would be very happy if you came back to circle to sing with us. We are going to dance today too." Narmeen took a deep breath, smiled, and came into the classroom, where she danced and sang happily.

Narmeen's teacher helped her to bounce back from a position of powerful anger that Narmeen was reluctant to give up. She was able to end her painful feelings, recover, and move on. The teacher's affectionate invitation helped Narmeen find the bravery to get over the hump and return to the scene of her unhappiness and frustration.

This is a well-known virtue of conventional wisdom. "Getting back on the horse" or "standing up when you're knocked down" reflects the understanding that resilience makes the difference. Research now validates these common-sense ideas, demonstrating that people who can bounce back go further.[31] We think that it takes the emotional muscle of bravery to be able to do that.

ACCEPTANCE OF REALISTIC POWER AND LIMITATIONS

*This is the beginning of wisdom. Finding pleasure in
real capacities and positive effectiveness in the
world is a resource for life.*

This emotional muscle carries the ongoing theme of realistic engagement with the world that threads through this whole book. One of our basic assumptions is that joy and strength can be found in the pleasures of reality. To find them, everyone also has to accept the limits of reality.

Parents can promote this growth by

- **BEING EXPLICIT ABOUT WHAT YOUR CHILD IS IN CHARGE OF, WHAT PARENTS ARE IN CHARGE OF, AND WHAT NOBODY IS IN CHARGE OF.**

Older toddlers, with their accelerating skills, want to do everything, even things that no one can do. Much as they have grown, their desires outstrip their capacities. They can do a lot, but they can't do everything. A major source of frustration between parents and toddlers is battling over control. "I want to do it myself" is the anthem of toddlers.

Nora was ordering everyone around about what she wanted to do and what she wanted them to do. She seemed desperately invested in being the boss. Her parents were frustrated and felt helpless and angry. They didn't want to squash her assertion or initiative, but her exasperated parents likened her to a dictator. In the context of the continuing discussion about who is in charge of what, the family consultant devised an activity for them to do with Nora and her older sister Katie.

They set up three buckets and threw balls of paper into them. One bucket was for what Nora and Katie were in charge of, one was for what their parents or teachers were in charge of, and the last was for what no one can be in charge of. Each person shouted something out in turn and decided, with the help of the others, which bucket to toss the ball into.

For instance, when Nora shouted bedtime, her parents said, "Bedtime goes into our bucket, but sleep time goes into your bucket because you are in charge of your own body." When Katie shouted, "Sunshine," Nora, nearly three, said, "No one is in charge of that. It has to go in the last bucket." Everyone cheered. Their daddy shouted, "Rain! I'm in charge of the rain!" The children laughed and contradicted him, insisting that his ball go in the last bucket. They also were learning from his joke that everyone may sometimes wish to be in charge of everything. And so it went.

This activity could be repeated over time since, as the children grew, there were changes in what they could be in charge of. One day, Nora said, "Let's play the buckets. I want to put in there that I'm in charge of riding my trike and using the potty." "Hurray" said everyone and they all enjoyed throwing in the balls for the new skills.

There is a particularly intense set of toddler wishes. Two-year-olds realize they are separate individuals, which pushes them to face that others are separate too, and therefore not under their control. This is especially true of their parents, on whom they are still very dependent and whom they can't control. Many toddlers react to these developments by wanting desperately to be in charge of everyone else, especially their parents.

Several parents complained that their children were being increasingly bossy with them. They found it embarrassing to be ordered around at the supermarket or the park. The family consultant asked if it were the same at home. "If anything, it's worse," said Pauline's dad.

"She sort of treats me like a dog these days." The family consultant suggested that this uncomfortable feeling the parents were having was an important signal that something needed to be addressed.

Someone remarked, "We need an Emancipation Proclamation!" That gave the family consultant an idea to add to the three-bucket game. He said, "How about telling a story about how a very good president said that it was wrong to force people to do things, to make them into slaves, as if they had no ideas of their own. President Lincoln and many others made a law that no one is allowed to have slaves. You can help your children understand what they are and can be in charge of, what parents are in charge of, and what no one is in charge of. You can explain that it's against the law to make someone a slave." Some of the parents decided to try it even though it sounded pretty ambitious.

In a couple of weeks, parents fed back their experiences of emancipation. Talking in this way had helped move the issue out of a control battle and into a shared topic of interest. The toddlers had responded well to the idea that their parents were helping them learn to be in charge of themselves so that they would never feel bossed around. But one night, one little girl, when going to bed, asked her parents if the good president Lincoln would change his mind. In a wistful tone she said, "Sometimes I wish you would be my slave."

The buckets became a shorthand way of thinking and talking for all the parents and children in this group. Through the active teaching of who is in charge of what the children had gained a sense of mastery through knowledge, not only of what they could now actually control, but also of the things they did not have to be responsible for.

When Nicky's grandmother was ill, his mother felt very sad one day. Nicky saw her crying and looked worried. Then he began acting silly, trying to make his mother laugh. She understood his need and reassured him, "It's all right that I am sad. It's because I'm worried about Grandma. You don't have to take care of my feelings, that's my job. But thank you for noticing. I'm still sad, but it also feels good when you give me a hug."

When his grandmother died a few months later, Nicky became very anxious. He eventually confided to his mother that he was scared because Grandma died after he had been angry with her. Nicky's mom could tell him that sometimes she too had been angry with Grandma, but that her feelings and Nicky's had not caused Grandma's death. No one was in charge of when that happened. Grandma was very old and ready to die. "Feelings are important to talk about, but they are just feelings and they don't make things happen. Remember the three buckets? Grandma's death would go into the bucket of what no one is in charge of."

The toddler Nicky was helpless in the face of his mother's sadness and the incomprehensibility of his grandmother's death. He fell back on a magical idea that he had caused it with his anger. Without his mother's helpful understanding and intervention, he might have carried this feeling of omnipotent responsibility and guilt forward to color his later development. Nicky's mother gave him an additional important lesson. She did not convey her experience of the grandmother's death as one of awful helplessness; rather, she presented it as a fact that can be encompassed. Acceptance of something that cannot be changed or affected is not the same as passive submission or resignation.

The mother of two-and-a-half-year-old Sylvia dreaded changing from a crib to a "big girl bed" because she was sure her daughter would refuse to stay in bed and go to sleep. She couldn't imagine being able to let Sylvia be in charge of herself. The family consultant suggested a gradual introduction of the new furniture, overlapping the presence of the crib and the bed, and that she talk to her little girl during the day about how bedtime would go. Sylvia usually put on her pajamas, then read some books with her parents before settling into her crib. The idea was for bedtime to have the same pattern, with the addition that Sylvia would be in charge of helping herself go to sleep in her new bed when she was ready. Her parents planned to have one of them sit with her quietly until she said she was ready for them to go downstairs.

Sylvia's mother wasn't sure this plan would work since she wasn't sure either she or Sylvia had the strength to do it but decided to give it a try. She told Sylvia that she would stay with her for a while at bedtime but that Sylvia would be in charge of when she went to sleep. Two days later, she wrote the following e-mail:

> I have to share this with you. Last night we had some of the usual happenings at bedtime. It took some strategizing to get Sylvia interested in pajamas and pull-up; even took some work to calm the mood down enough to get her to read books. But we eventually got there. I had reminded her that, even though she now had a "big girl bed," I was still in charge of bedtime, but she was in charge of going to sleep. We read

a last book and then talked with her little night light on. As she likes to say, "Let's talk."

And then we turned the light off and said goodnight and I told her, since this was her first night in her new bed, I was going to sit on the floor by the door until she was ready to sleep. A few moments later she turned her light back on and grabbed a book from the floor next to her bed and started reading—propped up a bit, the book held in both hands like a big person (a good size picture story book). She read that one, then got the next one. At one point I said quietly, "Remember that when you are tired you can put the books down and read more tomorrow." "Okay," she said. She read for forty minutes and I found myself wondering just how long I could stand to let this go on, but we had set it up so Sylvia was in charge of sleeping and I had undertaken to sit there. She didn't try to engage me; didn't try to get out of bed. Just quietly reading. And then she put her head down and went to sleep. The whole scene just blew my mind! Of course it might not happen again for a long while, but these messages do slowly get in, don't they?

The emotional muscle to take responsibility for oneself, cede appropriate responsibility to others, and accept the fact that there are things that no one is in charge of is a lifelong strength for parents and children. It must be nurtured and expanded throughout development as children become increasingly capable of being in charge of themselves. This is one of the central tasks and challenges of parenthood, and mastery of this task is deeply satisfying for parents. It also produces children who will be able to feel good about themselves functioning in the world.

STRIVING FOR MASTERY

Mastery is the goal of development. Pleasure is the fuel of emotional muscle. Pleasure powers the self-reinforcing positive cycle of challenge, competence, and mastery.

There are many externally driven methods to get children to do what grown-ups want. Children can be intimidated or bribed, and they will usually comply eventually. We feel there is greater gain and greater good from internally fuelled growth and change. Hence our emphasis throughout on the positive cycle of mastery.

Parents can promote this growth by

- **FOSTERING POSITIVE PLEASURE**
Competence and mastery are sources of profound satisfaction, which motivates efforts to master the next challenge. This positive cycle that begins in infancy unfolds throughout life in every area of functioning. Toddlerhood is an important phase for establishing pleasurable mastery of the body and feelings.

Play is a major way for toddlers to learn about their feelings and practice self-regulation. It is also where pleasure can connect with growing self-knowledge and confidence. Two-year-olds need their parents to make sure they have a safe space for play, both boisterous physical activity and quieter games and crafts. They need time to play on their own and with their parents and other children. Parents should stay alert to play that is losing its keen pleasure and strengthen it by adding some new element. Other ways that play can lose its constructive value are when it becomes either aggressive or overexcited.

Sally and Amy were very busy every class time in their center, playing with the doll strollers, putting baby dolls in and out, walking them around the room, taking them in and out again, walking around. The teachers noticed after some weeks that the girls were going through the motions, wheeling their babies around, but actually watching the other children and seeming distracted.

This drop in the active pleasure of the game was the signal to the teachers that the girls were ready to have their play stretched. One of the teachers asked if they were taking their babies to the park. Did they think it might be nice to have a picnic there with their babies? This small addition was catalytic. Amy and Sally went to the kitchen area and busied themselves putting together the picnic food, packing it in bags and adding it to the strollers. They walked purposefully around the room, saying to others, "We're taking our babies to the park for a picnic."

They passed Alan at the play dough table. He said, "I'm making pizza." They nodded and went on. At the next class, they stopped by the table where Alan was again making "pizza." Sally and Amy joined Alan.

They all enjoyed making pizza together, chatting about the ingredients they were using, and then all proceeded to go to the park with the babies and the pizza picnic.

These teachers chose the optimal moment to intervene to enhance the pleasure dimension of a game and revive it at a new level. The children added to their play repertoire and took a further social step in enjoying sharing their game with another child. The emotional muscle dimension, fueled by pleasure, was the reinforcement of the positive cycle of mastery.

If the teachers had not noticed the drop in pleasure and intervened, this game would have turned into a frustrating, empty and probably aggressive activity, where the pleasure might have resided in excluding other children. This would lead to a negative cycle, with pleasure arising from feeling powerful over other children, rather than competence and creativity in elaborating the play and including others.

Self-care is an area of great growth for two-year-olds. Toddlers become able to dress themselves almost entirely, brush their hair, put on outer clothes, boots, and shoes, click their stroller straps, use the toilet dependably, make food choices and feed themselves, convey if something hurts or they feel ill, and so forth. Any or all these skills can become a battleground unless parents help their children acquire these skills gradually, with the goal of the enormous pleasure that comes with competence.

Jeffrey and his mother had solved the problem of choosing clothes by putting them out for the next day in the evening before bed. She had gradually been teaching him to help getting dressed, reaching up his arms for the sleeves, pulling his pants up, and putting on his Velcro shoes. One Saturday morning, Jeffrey ran into his parents' room to wake them and he was fully dressed. "Mommy, Daddy, look! I did it all myself!" he proudly exclaimed. His parents were duly impressed and made a special breakfast to celebrate.

Many parents wonder why children would ever want to use the potty. Since parents are understandably reluctant to use shame or intimidation the only thing left seems to be external rewards like stickers, candy, or "big kid underwear." This kind of toilet training is a behavioral approach in which adults impose something on children. In contrast, we suggest to parents that they think in terms of toilet mastery.[32]

Teddy's parents described how pleased they were when he seemed excited to get a sticker every time he urinated in the potty. Accumulating five stickers was the goal because then he got a candy. But very soon, he seemed to be getting twenty stickers a day. They realized that he was running into the bathroom, peeing a little bit, then coming out for a sticker, and then peeing a bit more in a few minutes. He seemed more interested in the stickers and candy than in toilet mastery. His parents were perplexed since they felt they had run out of ways to motivate Teddy.

The family consultant reminded them that internal pleasure in success is the basic motivator for wanting to be effective and competent. Pleasure in competence is a crucial ally in all areas of development. Perhaps they could rekindle that motivation for Teddy in two ways. First would be to talk to Teddy about the strong muscles he has—they are strong enough to hold the pee inside and then strong enough to push it all out. Then his dad could tell Teddy about how good it feels to him to use his strong muscles to pee, and he knows that Teddy will feel good in the same way when he does that. "Let's stop with the stickers and do some fun 'man things' together when you've learned to use the toilet, like using our muscles shoveling the snow and going out for hot chocolate."

All the elements of development for two-year-olds have the potential for enormous pleasure. Most parents know that their child feels good about mastering new skills like riding a bike, but they may be less likely to notice that all the other developmental achievements, like mastering big feelings and taking charge of one's body also feel very good.

HOW PARENTS HELP TWO-YEAR-OLDS BUILD THE EMOTIONAL MUSCLES OF:

EXPRESSING FEELINGS IN WORDS
Parents help by
• NAMING FEELINGS, LISTENING, RESPONDING, AND EXPLAINING

MAKING FEELINGS "JUST RIGHT" SIZE
Parents help by
• TAKING "TIME WITH" YOUR CHILD TO MAKE BIG FEELINGS MANAGEABLE

CONTAINING BOTH LOVE AND HATE

Parents help by

- REMINDING YOUR CHILDREN THEY CAN HOLD MORE THAN ONE FEELING

BRAVERY

Parents help by

- HELPING YOUR CHILD BOUNCE BACK

ACCEPTANCE OF REALISTIC POWER AND LIMITATIONS

Parents help by

- BEING EXPLICIT ABOUT WHAT YOUR CHILD IS IN CHARGE OF, WHAT PARENTS ARE IN CHARGE OF, AND WHAT NOBODY IS IN CHARGE OF

STRIVING FOR MASTERY

Parents help by

- FOSTERING POSITIVE PLEASURE

THREE-YEAR-OLDS AND THEIR PARENTS
BUILDING EMOTIONAL MUSCLES

Three-year-olds emerge from the rapid growth and steep learning curve of toddlerhood to a delightful new plateau of consolidation. They are now busy coordinating and integrating the various emotional muscles that they developed in toddlerhood into a more organized personality. This sets them on the long path of mastery in the face of life's challenges. Three-year-olds are challenged to master separateness, separation, self-care, and their feelings.

Three-year-olds Nellie and Nora were standing by the fish tank in the classroom, each claiming it was her turn to feed the fish. The teacher watched as the feelings began to intensify but actively waited to see how the girls would work it out. Nora went over to the job chart and said, "Look, it is my turn today, but it's your turn tomorrow. So today I'll feed the fish and you can watch me, and tomorrow you'll feed the fish and I can watch you." Nellie happily accompanied Nora back to the fish tank, and they implemented their plan.

These little girls could put together several emotional muscles when they showed mutual empathy, the capacities to delay and persist, an ability to consider alternatives and take pleasure in the competent resolution of a conflict at a level that did not involve one person winning and the other losing. They could enlist their minds in discovering a creative solution.

These girls achieved a higher-order synthesis of emotional muscles they had been working on since infancy. This is characteristic of three-year-olds. Many of the skills and capacities for self-care and self-regulation that appeared intermittently over the previous year become more dependable. In the area of self-care, toilet mastery is one of the biggest tasks for parents and children between two and three and a half. We will devote a major section to this later in the chapter.

Preschoolers and their parents and teachers can increasingly rely on the availability of longer attention spans, greater tolerance for strong feelings, and more willingness to negotiate and compromise. This greater complexity means that the emotional muscles in this chapter have more components. There are more steps and more facets to developing each one.

Nevertheless, three-year-olds are vulnerable to feeling overwhelmed when they overreach their own capacities or too much is asked of them. They continue to need grown-ups very available to sustain their best level of functioning and set limits as they can't yet fully take inside the controls that ground them.

Whether or not three-year-olds have already had group experience separate from their parents, in day care settings or other child care arrangements, we are describing them as preschoolers to reflect an important developmental progression typical of three-year-olds. There is an *internal* timetable of separateness and a level of emotional muscle that can support this development—three-year-olds have a clear sense of themselves as people in their own right. They have good and bad feelings about themselves and care how others see them.

Exercising emotional muscles is a major source of positive self-esteem: By three, most children have mastered many skills of physical and emotional self-care and can therefore manage some parts of their day independently. Three-year-olds take conscious pleasure in their achievements and revel in their self-confidence. This is fundamental to establishing a positive self-esteem cycle. With those good feelings about themselves, they are ready to make loving relationships with other children and teachers in new ways, at a new level.

The separate identity of each child is no longer primarily an assumption but is now undeniably apparent. Three-year-olds carry the authority of their own feelings, thoughts, ideas, preferences, and personalities. Their words have begun to catch up with their feelings so that they can express and discuss experiences at a new level of sophistication and complexity. They begin to keep their experience private, choosing what to talk about and whether to answer questions or select what they want to talk about as part of their sense of being a separate self. A major challenge for parents of preschoolers is to engage positively with your child's growing separate self, transforming the relationship accordingly.

What parents learn

INTEGRATING LOVE AND SEPARATENESS

Work to understand and engage with the difference
between separateness and separation.

Separateness *is* a fact
            an opportunity
            a challenge.

                    Separateness *is not* an attack
                            a rejection
                            a denial of your importance.

This issue is a challenge for children and parents throughout development. It is especially vivid at three, with children's consolidation of their sense of self and their actual, separate experience of classroom relationships with other children and teachers. At three, the physical separation takes on a new meaning for parents, confronting them with their child's undeniable separateness as a person. When they are younger and more dependent, it is possible to avoid fully engaging with your children being separate people. But three-year-olds demand that grown-ups see them clearly as unique individuals. Engagement and mastery of these issues create solid growth and strength in parents and children. Avoidance can have negative effects that reverberate throughout development.

Nellie's mother, Nan, cried in the hallway outside the preschool classroom door. "I just can't understand why she would prefer to be with ten other children in school when she could have me all to herself." Discussion with teachers and in parent group reminded her that Nellie was enjoying school because of the solid foundation of security her mother had provided. Through her tears, Nan acknowledged that Nellie did not seem to love her less—maybe they could both enjoy her big-girl capacity to stay at school on her own.

Just as three-year-olds are putting together emotional muscles developed earlier, parents of three-year-olds are doing likewise. In order to bear her sadness at missing Nellie, Nan could draw upon earlier thinking about the nature of love. She realized that she had slipped back into thinking of love as a finite resource, as if it were a thing that could be used up. She was worrying that Nellie would no longer love her if she loved her teacher and her classmates. She told the teacher that she had to remind herself of the feedback loop of love she had learned about earlier—"The more I love Nellie, the more she'll love school, and then Nellie will have even more love to bring back home to me." Their shared enjoyment would enhance them both.

Nan brought up her feelings at a parent group where the discussion focused on the children's settling into their new classroom. She described her embarrassment at being so upset when Nellie went happily into the classroom. "I know I should be proud of her, but it sure was painful." Another mom exclaimed, "You should be proud of yourself too. Sometimes I think this may be harder for us than for the kids. Loving and letting go is a real challenge."

The family consultant pointed out that they were all following their children's lead in transforming their relationships. Rather than losing their children, they were loving at the new level and discovering how much love their children were capable of. One of the dads said, "It seems to me that love is the ultimate emotional muscle! The more you use it, the stronger it grows and the more you can love." Everyone left parent group that night feeling inspired by his observation. This insight was referred back to many times through the year as the parents engaged with their children's growth.

Parents are not always as ready as children to make the move forward into preschool, especially when circumstances have complicated the establishment of secure attachment between them.[33]

Orrin was adopted from another country in his second year. His mother and father had taken turns attending toddler group with him so that each of them could benefit from the support and guidance of the setting. They were faithful attendees at parent group meetings and really worked hard and successfully to weather Orrin's periodic flare-ups of fears and anger. They seemed to strike a helpful balance between taking his history into account and still not using his background to explain everything, perhaps facilitated by each parent's individual therapy experience.

Orrin started junior preschool functioning smoothly and made a comfortable transition to independent school attendance. After some months of school, however, two things happened: the first was that Orrin asked his mother why she didn't stay in class at the beginning of the day like one of the other mothers did, and the second was that he got angry and called her a mean mommy. Orrin's mother reacted dramatically, deciding to keep him out of school the next day and then planning to home-school him from then on.

There seemed to be a strong continuing impact of the adoption on Orrin's mother's sense of security about their bond, which in turn affected her feelings about her own competency.[34] It was hard for her to feel like Orrin still needed her if he was adjusting well at school without her. She herself had been adopted at birth and had only recently found her birth mother. Leaving and being left were powerfully mixed up with aggression and loss. When Orrin called her a mean mommy, she could not take that as the momentarily angry words of a little child but instead tapped into her deep worries about loyalty and the value of her love. She was devastated and struggled to feel like an effective parent while also feeling bad about being more capable than her own adoptive mother had been.

After another month, Orrin's parents met with his teachers and family consultants. Orrin's mother felt she had indeed overreacted but still decided to keep him home, saying ruefully that she needed more time to feel secure with him. She acknowledged that it had been too hard for her to use the help school had offered. She had been able to handle and absorb Orrin's toddler anger and set limits appropriately, but when his anger took the form of a judgment on her as a mother, it evoked overwhelming anxiety that she could deal with only by retreat within the phase of parenthood. Looping back to spend more time as a pair would allow Orrin and his mother to move forward together with more security in their belonging together as separate people. She was eventually able to try again for them both to have a successful school experience.

Orrin's mother had needed more support for the vulnerable circumstances of her parenting. When there are hard or complex factors in a child's or parent's past—like medical illness, deprivation, abuse, adoption, or upheavals from war, emigration, or natural disasters—each phase of the child's development challenges parents anew to rework and redefine the meaning of the issue. In situations like this, where deep, perhaps unconscious, forces are at work in the personality, we can see the limits of the concept of emotional muscle.[35] It is a powerful idea about conscious effort and change over time, but the force of unconscious conflicts and feelings demands a different intervention. However, the idea of emotional muscle is a useful first approach to change and can serve as a barometer of deeper issues. Orrin's mother was not at a place in herself where she could yet develop or use the emotional muscle to hold on to her love even while facing the separateness of her child.

RESPECTING YOUR CHILD'S PRIVACY

Distinguish between privacy and secrecy.

Three-year-olds' growing sense of their mental and personal privacy is not always easy for parents to tolerate. From knowing, or thinking that you know, everything in your child's experience, you now have to deal with her choosing whether to keep things to herself and respect her for the developmental achievement it represents.

Alan wanted to share a story about his son Colin. "Well, I guess in a way it's a story about me too," he said. "I have been wondering why Colin doesn't talk much about what happens at school, not like he used to. I came into school to pick Colin up and saw on the bulletin board outside his classroom that they were looking at birds today. It started me thinking about seeing an oriole that morning, which is pretty unusual where we live. When Colin came out, I just told him about it, and he started telling me about the red bird they saw in a story and how one came to the feeder outside the window. He said he and Jeff watched it together until it flew away. That was the longest story I have heard since the school year started. It was so great to get a sense of his enjoyment of a new experience at school."

Another dad said he still hadn't heard about any other kids in his daughter's class. The family consultant pointed out that Alan hadn't questioned Colin but had shared his own experience. It seemed as if respecting Colin's privacy paid off since he was happy to volunteer information when it was part of a conversation, not an interrogation. Parents sometimes react to the achievement of privacy as if their children are keeping secrets from them. They may then engage in a battle to extract information, which undermines a child's ownership of her thoughts and feelings, and creates more likelihood of hostile hiding, secrecy, and lying.

A mom said, "Yes, but that tells me that I have to bear not getting all the answers I wish for. It is painful to feel excluded." Other parents joined in, admitting they felt angry at being stonewalled and started to pepper their children with questions. One parent said, "Why can't we have a one-way mirror or a camera in there? Then we could see everything they are doing." There were a lot of strong feelings coming up. Alan said, "But it felt really different when Colin told me himself—it was a different tone of conversation than when he was younger. I felt almost like we were two guys together instead of me knowing everything my toddler has done."

The family consultant agreed—this is an opportunity to transform the relationship, staying in sync with the child's growth. "First of all, you never actually knew everything your child was thinking and feeling, but this year really brings that home. Your three-year-old now has a private experience and knows it. This is a great leap forward in mental functioning. It is his own experience to share if he wishes to. And we want him to learn that sharing with others feels good. Colin felt like telling his daddy his own story about a bird. This was a sophisticated and loving sharing of two separate experiences. Alan didn't extract the information from Colin, but he set the stage for Colin to choose to share. You and your child are working to learn how to be distinct people who love each other and feel connected even while different. This will be crucial when they are teenagers." The parents began to think of this issue in the context of the long path of development. They recalibrated their perspective in terms of their own wishes for autonomous self-respecting children, and then they could better hold on to love and respect their children's mental and emotional separateness rather than feel angry and excluded.

HOLDING ON TO LOVE THROUGH SEPARATIONS

*Organize separations in gradual doses; plan to think
about your children when you are apart.*

Separation is painful. Everyone develops ways to deal with that pain. Many people push aside the loving feelings that would make you miss the person and be sad to be away. It takes muscle to stay with the pain of sadness and missing, but this keeps you in touch with your love. Parents need practice to separate in a loving, positive way, just as children do. It is initially hard for parents to hold their children in their minds and hearts during absence.

If your child has been in some kind of alternate care as a baby or toddler, you have already been dealing with these muscles to bear all the mixed feelings involved. The easy way out is denial, shutting out your feelings and ignoring them. This works, but causes a huge loss to you and your baby.

Or you can take a harder but more constructive path, working in a gradual open-system way to strengthen your emotional muscles and keep your baby in mind. Love flourishes when you embrace both your sad and happy feelings away from your baby and enjoy the reunion. Trusting that your caregivers will take good care and keep your baby safe and that they will work to keep you in your baby's mind while you are apart can boost your emotional muscles. Life will bring many separations from your children, including the potential for living at a distance when they are grown up. That is why it is so important to learn how to say good-bye well.

In a parent discussion one evening at a large day care center, Dolores's mom talked about all the things she did at work to keep her children in mind. Her car keys had a keychain with their pictures on it; as she went through her day, she knew what the kids were doing at each part of the day in the center; she often found herself humming their favorite songs, and then she knew she was missing them. She said, "When my older boy started at day care, I tried not to think about him too much, and then we would fight when I picked him up. I was mad that he was busy playing and didn't want to come right away when I was wanting to get home. It's funny that, now, when the teachers have helped me think about their day much more, going home feels easier, and we are happy to see each other. Missing them makes it easier to love them."

SHARING YOUR CHILD'S LOVE WITH OTHERS

Embrace the importance of your
child loving her teacher.

New mothers and fathers work hard to support each other and to enjoy watching their child develop individual relationships with the other parent. As time goes by, your baby's circle expands to include grandparents, brothers and sisters, babysitters and more. This is a joy to see, but most parents also worry about whether their child will still love them best. Does she have enough love to go around?

When children start school, parents have to contend with a new set of relationships. Children will have significant relationships with teachers for at least twenty years beyond preschool and maybe even longer. How can parents position themselves to feel good about this?

Jose's mother looked unhappy when he threw his arms around his teacher at going-home time and didn't want to leave school. In parent group, she said, "I hate to confess this, but I felt really jealous when Jose seemed uninterested in greeting me. I didn't know what to think about myself. I mean, I'm supposed to be glad that he loves school, and I think his teacher is terrific. So it's not about her. I guess this is more about me."

As the parents and the family consultants shared their observations about the intense feelings the children had developed for their teachers, they realized that the parents were struggling with thinking that their children didn't have enough love for more than one or two people. The family consultant remarked that the parents were engaged in a deeply important step. They were developing trust that the love they have given their children had created a platform from which the children could launch into a lifetime of significant relationships. The intensity of the children's love for their teachers reflected this. Jose's mother said, "I hadn't thought about it that way—this is really about our trusting ourselves and what we have already done."

Being a parent often brings doubt. Am I doing the right thing? Is this good for my child? But there is also a need for trust in oneself and what has been accomplished. A child's love for her teacher is a tribute to her parents, not a rejection or betrayal. It takes muscle and also develops it further to be aware of this meaning of your child's crush on her first teachers.

SELF-REFLECTION

Increase your knowledge of yourself.
Take charge of the reality you model for your child.
Examine how you see your child. Take responsibility for
what you expect of your child.

There are many aspects of the phase of parenthood for adults. This is an important developmental stage for grown-ups. Overall, whether you have children or not, it means being able to create, love, and nurture something beyond oneself. There are many more detailed, practical aspects for people actually raising children. A major challenge is growing along with your child, changing in yourself as your child changes. Each year brings new opportunities for learning about yourself and transforming parts of your personality. If adolescence is a second chance to rework and redesign some of the patterns of childhood, parenthood is a third chance. Children evoke core feelings and issues in parents, and we can respond by looking inside ourselves honestly and bravely. Self-awareness is a part of thoughtful parenting.

Parents are each child's primary model. Your child wants to be like you. There are some scientists who think there is a deep neurological substrate in the "mirror neurons" of the brain that supports imitation and identification with important people in a child's life.[36]

Nora's dad described his shock one day as he watched Nora riding her trike around the driveway cursing and shouting at imaginary other drivers. She was swearing at delays, obstructions, stupidity and generally expressing extreme frustration in a very combative way. He recognized himself all too well—this was how he conducted himself while driving the car, and he had never stopped to think that his little girl was taking it all in from the backseat. He talked about facing his own problems with anger and tolerating delay. "I guess I can hardly expect her to learn how to wait if I blow up at every red light. I need to learn how to stand frustration. This may go way back since I remember my dad was always very impatient. I couldn't wait to be a grown-up so I could yell and curse too. Whoa. Now I realize that I don't want Nora to think that's how to be an adult. I better clean up my act. It'll take work, but I think it's worth it."

Nora's dad looked at himself and knew that he wanted to set a different example for her, just as parents of the nearly two-year-olds had done in another group. He also realized something more. From the positive side, parents are the source of all learning; character and personality structure derive in large part from important people in our lives. But the difficult aspect of this powerful connection between parents and children is the potential for negative aspects of personality to be perpetuated from generation to generation. As children get older, this complexity becomes increasingly evident. Late adolescence is a time for selection of those aspects of our parents we want to identify with. Parenthood is another opportunity for further refinement of the process, a second chance to change negative patterns that persist.

In order to see your child clearly in her own right, you have to clear away the filter of your own experience. This is not easy as it involves facing vulnerabilities and aspects of oneself and one's past that may not be comfortable. In theory, it would be optimal if everyone saw each other completely clearly, free of distortions. However, a husband may sometimes react to his wife as if she's his mother; a employee may react to her boss as if he's her father; a mom may see her son as her younger brother. Psychoanalysts describe this powerful psychological mechanism as transference, with the idea that people transfer some of their feelings and perception from past relationships into new ones, often without realizing it.

Another way relationships can get distorted is when people attribute a part of themselves to others, assuming they are just the same or, more problematically, disowning an aspect of themselves and seeing it in the other. This is called externalization, and it usually causes trouble in any relationship. Momentary externalizations often happen between parents and children, but a pattern of relating in this closed-system way can turn into a negative cycle. Part of thoughtful parenting is to be alert to times when you may be seeing your children through a distorted lens and attributing characteristics to them that don't really apply.[37]

Jennifer's dad said, "My dad was a pretty angry guy, but he was also a very hard worker. He cared about his customers in the garage and never completed a job until he felt he had done his best. It's interesting to think about how hard it's been for me to find a different way to express frustration, but I know I got my work ethic from him and I appreciate that."

Another dad in the group, who coached his older child's baseball team, remarked, "I wish some parents from the team would take a look at themselves this way! They yell and scream at their kids to play better, and I think they are really living vicariously. They are asking their kids to be successful for them instead of enjoying what their kids can actually do." The family consultant said that this was a really important issue since those team parents are robbing their children of their own authentic experience. Looking hard at yourselves and your child matters for sorting out whose feelings are whose and setting patterns for later. Now that the three-year-olds can participate so much more in conversations and interactions, it can be easy for parents to overestimate their children and start to lean on them for emotional support or supplies, which parents really should be getting elsewhere. When children are asked to meet emotional needs beyond their capacities, they can feel overwhelmed by a constant sense of failure, since they are being asked to do something they can't do. This is one basis for later perfectionism.

Janie's mom said, "I'm a single mom, and I know how easy it could be to unload my issues from work on Janie when we get home in the evening. I am constantly checking myself to make sure I don't lean on her. That's why this group is important to me and the friends I know I can call, to share whatever."

Kevin's mom, Jeannette, was really scared of dogs. She described her own mother's insistence on crossing the street whenever they spied a dog ahead. She was determined not to inflict this fear on her son. Accordingly, she asked friends with dogs if she and Kevin could visit to help familiarize him with how to approach, talk to, and touch animals. Nevertheless, she talked in parent group about Kevin's uncertainty on these occasions. The family consultant suggested that she bring Kevin into the dilemma and explain how she was trying to give him a different experience from her own. Jeannette said she would be embarrassed, and besides, hadn't they all talked about children's amazing ability to pick up feelings no matter what the grown-ups said differently?

As the group talked about Kevin and Jeannette's situation and added instances of other such transmissions of fears or conflicts between generations, an idea began to emerge. The group was uncertain whether it would be asking too much or if three-year-olds could truly understand, but the family consultant urged them to try talking with their children about sharing a problem, whether it was over anger or fear or something else. This is different from dumping grown-up problems on children, leaving them helpless.

The parents decided to enlist their children in working together on issues of vulnerability or difficulty. Jeanette planned to say, for instance, "I think you notice when I get worried every time we see a dog in the park. I am trying to feel braver and more comfortable and learn how to make friends with dogs since they seem very fun and interesting. I don't want you to think that you have to be scared just because I have an old worry about this. So we are going to learn together how to make friends with doggies."

Several weeks later, Kevin's mom described how she and her son had visited a farm where there were some puppies. They had petted the mother dog and played with the puppies and laughed about how surprised Kevin's daddy would be when they told him that they weren't scared.

Seeing her own fear reflected in Kevin's behavior, Jeanette had turned a potential negative into a positive growing opportunity for them both. She used the support from parent group to face her fears and change, strengthening her own emotional muscle in the process.

Facing the possibility that something is going wrong in your relationship with your child takes courage. It is sometimes easier to blame the child for difficulties or rationalize troubles.

Andy's mother, Sarah, asked to meet individually with her family consultant. She described with great distress, "I feel as if I can't find my love for Andy anymore. Everything he does irritates me—he's so contrary. And he's messy and provocative. I just don't like him." They were able to see that Sarah had accurately picked up danger signals in her relationship with her child. She and Andy's dad had tried to talk it through but felt stymied. Over a couple of meetings, they talked about alternative ways to see Andy's behavior. Sarah and her husband began to see that Andy had several reasons for being angry and worried; for instance, they had been talking about the possibility of a new job and a new house without thinking that Andy might have big feelings about these ideas.

In a few weeks, Sarah reported that things were going a bit better with Andy. She felt relieved about him but still struggled with her own waves of rage that felt excessive to her. Sarah hated the feeling of being so out of tune and out of touch with Andy. Together the family consultant and Andy's parents decided that they would seek some further professional help to sort out the situation further.

Sarah braved humiliation and self-blame rather than take out her feelings on Andy. She enlisted her partner as a strong first step in trying to address the problem, then turned to her school support system to find appropriate help. Admitting to needing help shows strength and is a quality that parents can model powerfully for their children.

TAKING PLEASURE IN YOUR CHILD'S NEW CAPACITIES

Acknowledge and adjust to change.

All the new skills of three-year-olds can take parents unawares; it is hard to keep up with rapid growth. Three-year-olds put ideas and experiences together in novel ways, integrating and understanding much more than earlier and much more than they are usually given credit for. Change, even when it's positive, always demands adjustment. The new capacities of three-year-olds are usually positive and carry wonderful promise.

Dan's dad described a stunning moment at a family dinner with his in-laws. Dan seemed to be busy eating his supper while the grown-ups and some adolescent cousins talked about a dilemma over choosing which team to join when two seasons overlapped. Dan piped up, "Choose the one you like the best." He had clearly been listening, understanding, thinking about the problem, and had a solution to suggest. Everyone at the dinner thought Dan had the best idea for solving the problem!

It's important to notice and appreciate the changes that show in positive ways; it's harder to notice and credit changes when they include troublesome behavior or negative feelings. Three-year-olds' new verbal capacities can feel like a mixed blessing to parents. When a younger child is upset, parents often fall back on, "He's tired or coming down with something." Now the child can tell you what he is angry about, say "I hate you" or "You're a mean daddy." New cognitive capacities are consolidated, so three-year-olds begin to compare parents with each other and with other adults, just as they compare themselves to peers or adults. Younger children can be distracted, while threes stick to their goals and repeat their point. We discussed earlier in this chapter the cognitive achievement of mental privacy and mixed reactions to it. Three-year-olds begin to feel rivalries with parents and others, feeling jealous or competitive, with newly conscious ambitions to be grown-up.

All these behaviors represent and spring from big forward steps in development, but they can have a negative impact in the moment. Parents are challenged to hold on to their own love, help their child remember her love, see this clearer window into their child's feelings as an opportunity, and deal with feelings of hurt or anger within themselves; this strengthening in your emotional muscle will become increasingly important with each year, finding its peak utility in adolescence.

With a longer perspective on the progressive development underlying three-year-olds' behaviors, parents don't have to take all this personally. The children are practicing their new abilities and will need your help and support to expand and strengthen them. It is crucial to retain that knowledge, for it can even allow for some humor in the situation. The emotional muscle to see issues in the longer view, face the present irritation, and perhaps share the predicament with a partner gives parents an important foundation for later tolerance of opposition and defiance. This year is a chance to practice and consolidate your own emotional muscle of tolerance and finding the positive, even in occasionally obnoxious behavior, and taking pleasure in the new capacities.

Torrey's parents talked about the dilemma they were facing around his new scooter. They had seen that he was ready and bought it for him with much excitement and pleasure all around. Torrey was thrilled and rode it skillfully for hours the first day. He then began to nag his parents to keep riding even when it began to rain and was getting dark. They felt increasingly annoyed when he would not accept their saying no. Finally, in desperation, they put the precious scooter in the closet. Torrey was devastated, and they felt awful.

There were various emotional muscles to foster for Torrey as we will discuss later in this chapter, but for his parents, the issue was how to modulate their own feelings to a constructive resolution. In the group, the family consultant and other parents pointed out the positives in the story—Torrey's passion, his persistence, his strong wish to practice and master a skill. His parents appreciated those reminders. His mother said, "It's so easy to forget the underlying positives when he's driving us crazy." Torrey's dad said, "We would probably have been able to find a better solution if we'd been able to keep those in mind. As it is, we will have to go back to the drawing board with him on the scooter situation. Stay tuned."

FEELING GOOD ABOUT YOUR ROLE AS THE PARENT

Understand the difference between stretch and stress.
Tolerate your child's inevitable frustration and distress.

With new skills come new ambitions. The sequence of practice, failure, repetition, and consolidation stretches your child to master new skills. Your child is bound to be frustrated, protest, and feel unhappy at times when she cannot do what she wanted to, when you set limits, or when reality just doesn't allow for success.

This is hard for parents, since you spend so much energy trying to protect your child from upset. It is also painful to feel that your child is angry with you. So far in this book we have emphasized the need for empathy and understanding of your child's feelings. Here, however, we begin to include the necessary balance, where your expectations are informed by, but not defined by, empathy.

How do you tell the difference between an appropriately scaled demand that challenges your child, stretching her capacities so that she grows stronger and more skilled, and one that is too much? Sometimes you don't know until you try making a demand and see what happens. It helps also to ask people who know a lot of children, like teachers, day care providers, or family consultants, what is a reasonable demand. Knowing that you can stand your child's temporary distress stretches your emotional muscles and gives your children the crucial message that feelings won't hurt them.

After several weeks of school and many cheerful days with her mom's company, Nadia whimpered the first time her mother, Maryam, started to carry out the plan they had made together for her to leave the classroom for a while. Maryam's eyes also filled with tears as she sat down on the floor next to Nadia, hugged her, and said, "Poor Nadia, it's just too hard, isn't it?" Nadia then started to sob and the two stayed locked in each other's arms, with Nadia unable to enjoy activities and Maryam trapped in the classroom.

When Maryam and the teacher discussed it during a quiet moment later in the playground, the teacher suggested that perhaps together they could differentiate a manageable stretch for Nadia's abilities from an overwhelming experience of stress, which would be destructive for them both. Maryam saw that she had some work to do to tolerate her own distress when she saw mild unhappiness in Nadia as this emotional muscle on her part would help her daughter in turn.

No parent likes to inflict distress; life inevitably brings many difficulties and sorrows without adding extra ones. It takes grit for parents to live with the knowledge that they can prepare their children better for life's downturns and adversities by graded stressful experiences. Thinking about one's own ability to manage challenging situations, whether they arise from internal or external sources, gives parents the emotional muscle to carry their children through hard times, making them manageable and constructive.

COMPETENCE, NOT DOMINANCE

*Take pleasure from your effective parenting rather than
seeking power from misusing your superior knowledge
and position of authority.*

Three-year-olds are often charming, funny, and quaint. They are rapidly acquiring knowledge, but they really don't know much about the world yet. Grown-ups sometimes take advantage of this naïveté, thinking it's funny to tease, ridicule, or laugh at children. It can be tempting to discount the impact of kidding around, tricking, or just messing with him, but it can be profound. It takes muscle to restrain oneself from the easy thrill of feeling good at the expense of a child and find good feelings in the longer-term, harder-won satisfactions of honest, competent parenting.

At a lunchtime parenting discussion at a local business, a mom brought up a concern about some of the interactions between her husband and their three-year-old, Sean. She said, "I know my husband really loves our boy, but sometimes I catch a bewildered expression on Sean's face when his dad is joking around with him. Something feels off, but I don't know what it is." Other parents joined in, contributing stories of times their children had joined in shared fun and others when there was a meltdown that completely surprised the grown-ups.

The family consultant conducting the workshop agreed that parents were picking up something significant to think about. She described how literal three-year-olds still are. They can make simple jokes that involve their new knowledge of what really goes together and what doesn't. A dad spoke up, "The other morning, my kid and I were rolling around laughing when I tried to put his pants on my head. Was I asking too much of him?" The family consultant said there were two significant elements that demonstrated how appropriate the level of the joke was for that child.

One was that the knowledge was within his range of experience; he has had three years to learn that pants go on legs and that his pants are smaller than his dad's. Second was the shared level of the joke. Both dad and son were on the same page. Dad was not operating from a superior position, putting him down with an ambiguous message and then laughing at him. They were enjoying the ridiculous idea together. Compare this with a visiting uncle who, when asked how he got there earlier than expected, said, "I have special powers and I flew here with my wings." The grown-ups laughed and the three-year-old looked puzzled, then joined in nervously. He later asked his uncle to show him how he flew, and everyone laughed again. The child looked tearful and was further laughed at for not understanding that the uncle was just fooling.

In the early nineteenth century, an influential children's book called *Struwwelpeter* was published. It contained stories that banked on little children's literal thinking, for instance, one about a child who sucked his thumbs, which were then cut off as punishment, or a girl who played with matches and was burnt to death. These tales were intended to make children obey and behave. They exploited knowledge of how children think and had the impact of terrifying children into submission. The adults invoking such tales used their superior knowledge of possible consequences to bully children. Despite the book's continuing in print and various derivative stage productions and adaptations, most modern parents would avoid such blatant methods. But the impulse to intimidate and overwhelm children persists.

Many parents can be heard in public, if their children are dawdling, to say, "Okay, I'm leaving." They turn and walk away, frightening their children into obedience, fooling them with the idea that they would truly desert them. Parents often allow older children sadistically to fool younger siblings with tales of adoption, favoritism, and so forth.

A true partnership with your three-year-old involves joining the real strengths you each have. Three-year-olds can be enlisted in partnership for many enjoyable and constructive experiences. It takes muscle for parents to do the work of defining their own values of collaboration with their children to build shared muscle based on real capacities of each.

In the parent workshop, the story of the "flying" uncle was discussed further as the parents wanted to figure out what response would have been helpful for the child. The mom who had told the story offered her solution. She said she had contradicted her brother-in-law, saying in front of everyone, "Don't be silly, Uncle Fred. People can't fly by themselves and they don't have wings. But you're from North Carolina, where the Wright Brothers figured out how people could make airplanes to fly. Johnny doesn't like to be fooled, but he's old enough to learn about what really happens. Please tell Johnny all about the Wright Brothers." She described feeling a little worried about whether Uncle Fred would be offended, but decided that her own good feeling as a parent and her boy's self-esteem were more important. To her surprise, Uncle Fred wanted to connect with Johnny; he had thought teasing was a good way to make friends but was actually pleased to be given another avenue for connection. Everyone felt competent, including Johnny, who later went to look at the birds flying with his uncle.

Then there is the issue of the lies grown-ups tell. Three-year-olds don't lie very much yet, but they are exposed more often than we think to adult lies. Parents lie about their children to others in their hearing, for instance, "Johnny is tired, that's why he is fussy," instead of saying that Johnny is angry about something. Parents lie in front of their children when they answer the phone and say the person who is at home is not. Parents lie with their children when they enlist them in secret conspiracies—"Let's not tell your sister we had hot chocolate this morning." And they lie to their children when they deny the real feelings they or anyone else is expressing, especially about anger or sadness.

What are these parents protecting with their untruths? There are various discomforts that can be avoided with these white lies. Parents can slide around embarrassment and take the easy way out. But they are then giving their children the message that lying is a viable alternative to facing feelings, assessing the situation and planning a course of action. They are acting as if they don't have those skills. Competent adults actually figure out what's going on and address it. Engaging with the real situation is almost always more likely to be successful.

In a discussion of white lies in a parent group, a mom brought the following story. In the kitchen before supper, Teddy was playing with his Legos, his dad was making the salad and his mom answered the phone. It was a call for Teddy's dad. When the mom said who it was, Teddy's dad waved his hands and whispered, "I'm not here." Mom took a message and then they had supper. She wondered about that pretty ordinary event; was that the kind of thing the group was talking about?

Other parents agreed that they often did the same. The family consultant asked if the group could come up with any alternatives that wouldn't involve lying since little children are strongly affected by how grown-ups handle reality and truth. Another mom suggested, "How about if you just said your husband wasn't available right then? Then he wouldn't have to answer the phone if he didn't want to and you wouldn't be lying." The other parents agreed that it seemed like a small change, but it would actually be quite different from the point of view of what the child would hear.

What we're describing is that, in both big and small ways, all parents can experience deep pleasure and satisfaction from the power of their real competence rather than feeling good from shortcut use of lying, fooling, teasing, and so forth to feel good from dominating children.

THE EMOTIONAL MUSCLES USED BY PARENTS OF THREE-YEAR-OLDS ARE

INTEGRATING LOVE AND SEPARATENESS
RESPECTING YOUR CHILD'S PRIVACY
HOLDING ON TO LOVE THROUGH SEPARATIONS
SHARING YOUR CHILD'S LOVE WITH OTHERS
SELF-REFLECTION
TAKING PLEASURE IN YOUR CHILD'S NEW CAPACITIES
FEELING GOOD ABOUT YOUR ROLE AS THE PARENT
COMPETENCE, NOT DOMINANCE

What do three-year-olds need to develop emotional muscle?

Three-year-olds need parents who have developed the emotional muscle to take pleasure in and respect their children's separateness. The greatest challenge for children in this phase is negotiating differences—between separateness and separation, between opposing wishes inside as well as with others, and between aspirations and real capacities. Adults who tolerate their own limitations and enjoy flexible problem solving with children as partners, as well as getting pleasure from competent parenting, provide the strongest example and support to three-year-olds.

What three-year-olds learn

> *LEARNING EMOTIONAL CAUSE AND EFFECT*
> *TAKING PLEASURE IN SHARING EXPERIENCE*
> *PERSISTENCE AND COMMITMENT TO A GOAL*
> *ASSERTION AND EXPLORATION*
> *MAKING CHOICES*
> *USING ANGER AS A SIGNAL*
> *DISTINGUISHING BETWEEN REAL AND PRETEND*
> *TOLERATING FRUSTRATION TO ENJOY PLAY*

How parents help three-year-olds build emotional muscles

LEARNING EMOTIONAL CAUSE AND EFFECT

Feelings can be connected with experiences to build an internal sense of what makes people feel good or not so good. This is an important aspect of mastering feelings and a component of mutuality in relationships.

Parents can promote this growth by

- **TEACHING EMOTIONAL SELF-AWARENESS**
  This is a continuation of naming feelings begun in the toddler years, with the addition of the link to where it came from. The habit of looking for the cause of a feeling contributes to positive social interactions and strengthens the capacity to use feelings as internal signals for self-regulation.
  "What does it feel like when someone gives you something nice?"
  "How did it feel when Johnny rolled the ball back and forth with you?"
  "What was your feeling inside when Thea took the stroller you were playing with?"

- **TEACHING EMOTIONAL SELF-AWARENESS BY EXAMPLE**
  "I like how it feels when " . . ."
  "I felt good when Daddy helped me finish building the bookcase."

- **MAKING SENSE OF OTHER PEOPLE'S EMOTIONAL SIGNALS**

Children have registered other people's feelings since babyhood. What three-year-olds can add is the knowledge that other children's and grown-ups' feelings are caused by something. Then they will be ready to learn to figure out whether they themselves were part of the other person's pleasure or unhappiness, which sets them on the path to emotional responsibility in relationships.

"I can see that Joey's eyebrows are frowning, and his hands are squeezed tight—that's what people sometimes do when they're angry. I wonder what he's angry about."

"Look, Sarah is smiling at you. She was happy that you gave her some of the playdough."

"I notice that Tom is putting his body in between you and the truck. His face is looking unsure. Maybe he doesn't know that you will wait for him to finish his turn."

Three-year-olds can understand and think about the feelings of characters in books, using them as models for themselves.

The teacher in a three-year-old class read a story about a dog who ran away from home because he didn't want to take his bath. The children eagerly joined in when she initiated a discussion of how the dog felt when he saw the towels and the water running and so forth.

Younger children learn what behaviors are acceptable and unacceptable, along with all the other categories they master. But until children consciously understand emotional cause and effect, they won't grasp *why* they shouldn't do something. The golden rule starts to have real relevance as children develop this muscle.

- **TEACHING AND MODELING EMPATHY**

This puts together what your three-year-old has learned about knowing her own and others' feelings and what contributes to them.

"I am very happy to see how good you feel about learning to put your coat on by yourself."

"I notice that Joel is sad that his friend George isn't here today. I understand how he feels since I am sad when I miss someone too."

"I am sorry that I didn't listen when you said your boot wouldn't go on. I didn't notice that your sock was bunched up. I can understand why you got mad at me. Let's fix your sock now."

Altruism,[38] which has been found to be a major strength for adults at times of stress, begins here, with empathy in the three-year-old.

Parents can begin to model and expect some helpfulness as a growth experience.

Karl was worried when a new boy joined his class. He asked his mother lots of questions about why Robbie's leg "didn't work right." His mother explained that Robbie had an illness that made some of his muscles weaker than others. She reassured Karl that he himself didn't have that illness and wouldn't get it and suggested that Karl might sometimes help Robbie if his leg made it hard for him to play a game.

Their teachers had also explained Robbie's condition in the same matter-of-fact way, sometimes asking children to shift in circle time, for instance, to make room for Robbie to put his leg in a more comfortable position.

One day, the class planned to play the running game Red Rover outside. Karl and one of the girls spontaneously said, "We're going to be the Robbie team," as they took Robbie's hands on each side and ran together at a comfortable pace.

The empathic responses of three-year-olds are more complex than when they were younger. They are able to see others as different people from themselves while simultaneously understanding the other person's feelings and the impact of feelings.

Dion watched carefully as George ran too fast in the classroom and ended up bumping another child. He said, "George, use your stopping muscles." Dion was seeing George as having an impulse, just as he sometimes had himself, but differently from him; at least on this day, George was not controlling it. Dion imagined a different solution and offered it to his classmate.

TAKING PLEASURE IN SHARING EXPERIENCE

The achievement of mental privacy is balanced
and complemented by broadening and deepening
connections with others.

We talked earlier about the emotional muscle parents work on during this year to respect their children's privacy and the effort it takes to give your child space for her own experience. Here the developing counterpart from the child's side is to grow toward sharing, fuelled by the pleasure that comes from feeling that others are interested and caring listeners. This is part of a long process that will need patience from parents as they wait for their efforts to bear fruit.

Parents can promote this growth by

- **CREATING TIME FOR RESPECTFUL LISTENING AND MODELING SHARING**
  Three-year-olds need help to enjoy their own privacy without turning it into a stubborn fight to retain secrets as a power struggle with parents.

  Nico's mother said in parent group, "I can't get him to tell me anything about school."

  Elena's mother described her method for finding out about Elena's day. Supper was not served until each child had said one good thing and one bad thing that had happened at school. Unfortunately, just as using stickers for toilet mastery can backfire by making the external reward something the child uses to manipulate her parents, this idea carried the risk that Elena would quickly say something, anything, to satisfy her mother. Then they would have supper, but both would both lose out on the pleasure of genuine exchange.

  The group talked about this for several meetings and generated many strategies for nonintrusive conversation starters with their children. For instance, the family consultants suggested that they ask their children what a different child played with at school that day. Or comment on the list of the day's topics that the teachers had posted outside the classroom door with a shared story of their own, like "I noticed that your class read a book about trains today. I waited at the crossing today while a really long freight train came through," without asking a question. Joe's dad remarked that they had a conversation about trains in the car and looked at the railway crossing when they drive past it. Joe hadn't said more that day about school, but it began to change.

  Tina's mother remarked with surprise, "It's become so automatic to turn on her music or a video in the car that we don't even use that time for conversation. I think I want to change that." Another idea is to develop a family dinner-table habit of people talking about their days. Sarah's mother reminisced about family dinners when she was a child. "We didn't have a television in the kitchen, so it was never on when my parents were making dinner, and so never was left on when we sat down, the way it sometimes is in my house. It seems as if I am missing opportunities for Sarah to share if I always have a competing source of talk in the room."

Joe's dad referred back to their conversation about trains in the car; he had mentioned it again at dinner, which generated a whole conversation among everyone about train trips. Then Joe had said, "We read a book about trains today. There were all kinds of train cars in it." His pleasure in having something to contribute was visible, and his mom could then also feel part of what Joe and his dad had enjoyed together. His big brother talked about his middle school trip on the train to Chicago and how cool it was to walk through the cars. Joe said he was going to tell his teacher how his brother went on a passenger train. From these discussions, all the parents felt clearer that they had to take responsibility for creating a pleasant context for sharing, but then wait it out until their three-year-olds felt confident enough in their newfound selfhood to begin to make the choice to share. Over the next few months of the school year, Elena and all the others gradually opened up, often chattering about school in great detail, to their parents' delight.

Teachers in the three-year-old class regularly allot time for the teachers and children to say something about the school day, sharing with each other something that mattered to them. The open-ended request allows for them all to reflect on their own experience, enjoying connecting with each other as they recall what they played together or the book they heard or the snack they ate. This practice models and strengthens the emotional muscle of taking pleasure in sharing.

PERSISTENCE AND COMMITMENT TO A GOAL

The strength to stick to a task and practice is the secret of success.

Work is part of life. Life is richer when there are pleasure and satisfaction associated with effort and achievement. Pleasure is the intrinsic motivator for persistence and commitment to a task. We all want children to develop the capacity for enjoying hard work and self-motivated learning. It begins in early childhood when grown-ups give children opportunities to develop good feelings from trying and succeeding. Children develop the emotional muscle to keep trying and work at developing new skills when parents and teachers make sure that they succeed and feel effective. Three-year-olds are adding new skills in all parts of their personalities. Their intellectual and physical skills are accelerating; they can be responsible for body skills of self-care; and they can handle many strong feelings with minimal support from adults.

Parents can promote this growth by

- **BREAKING TASKS DOWN INTO MANAGEABLE STEPS**
  We would not expect a child to learn to read all at once. They first have to learn to listen and talk, recognize letters and sounds, combinations, words, and so forth, building the component skills that will be combined later. If the scale of a task is too large, the only options are total success or failure and the stakes are too high. But, if the task is structured with small steps, there are multiple opportunities for success, enjoying the process, and the self-reinforcing pleasure that comes with it. Toilet mastery, a central achievement in self-care, which we will discuss in more detail, offers a good example of breaking a big task into manageable steps. Successful learning in steps is closely connected to owning one's body and self and feeling good about being a separate person.
  Ruby cried when she couldn't throw and catch a ball like her older sister. She said she never wanted to play ball again. Her parents did not want her to develop a pattern of avoiding activities where she wasn't immediately successful. So they did several different things to help her feel motivated to work at the new skills.
  They bought some balls that were textured for easy holding and catching, small enough for her hands. Then they devised a throwing and running game. Ruby could throw the ball toward the fence in the backyard and then run to bring it back for her dad to have a turn. Then he would throw it and bring it back to her. Ruby's dad talked to her about how he could remember his own dad teaching him—"I didn't know how to throw and catch until my daddy and I worked at it. I was three just like you." Next they threw the ball into the corner of the yard, and Ruby's aim gradually became more accurate. With each step, her dad enjoyed and praised the effort she was making.
  Ruby's dad next became the target; when he caught the ball, he rolled it back to her on the ground. She picked it up, then threw it again. Eventually, he moved close to her and began to toss it back to

her, starting with nearly putting it into her arms. Over the summer, he moved back further and further until, by the fall, Ruby was both a competent thrower and catcher. Even more importantly, she loved to play this game!

Ruby's dad told this story at a parent group in the fall. He said, "It may sound like a lot of time and energy to help a three-year-old girl learn to catch and throw, but her delighted face and her wish to 'practice' told me I was on the right track. Maybe she will be able to feel good about how long it takes to learn other things."

This dad had understood that pleasure that comes from persisting in learning a physical skill would generalize to other areas of achievement. One of the best illustrations of the importance of the emotional muscle of persistence and the parental technique of breaking the big goals down into manageable steps comes in relation to achieving toilet mastery. The overall goal is for your child to own her own body and be responsible for taking good care of it as she grows toward adolescence and adulthood.

Janine's parents were frustrated and baffled that they could not get their capable little girl to use the toilet. She seemed to understand the idea, but when they suggested that she sit on the toilet and go, she refused and resisted, seeming angry and scared. They wanted to give her choices but felt that she should be able to do this at three and a half. Yet they didn't feel they could force her, which had never been their parenting style. The whole situation was making them angry and helpless, which colored their daily interactions.

As they discussed this in parent group, it became clear that several of the parents were struggling with similar situations. Most children are actually ready to master toileting around two or two and a half, and it is easiest to catch the window of opportunity. By three and over, toilet mastery can be pulled into other issues and become a battleground. Many parents bend over backward in worry about pushing their children, afraid to damage them or make them feel bad about themselves. Janine's parents had waited for her spontaneously to accomplish toilet mastery, had held back the year before from explicit goal setting, and skipped many preparatory steps so that Janine did not have the component skills or confidence she needed to move forward in this important area of self-care and ownership of her own body.

Parents and family consultants shared ideas about how to talk about each step, to help Janine feel good about achieving them one by one. Because Janine was already three and a half, with all the physical capacities needed for toilet mastery, it was likely that she would move quickly through the whole sequence of steps. These are the steps that can be applied at any time from around two on. As the parents talked this through, they realized that it was easy to jump to the goal without giving their children the chance to master each step in turn, enjoy the process, and feel good about it.

Step 1 was for Janine to be aware of feeling the body sensations of urinating or defecating. So the first goal became noticing when she was in the middle of the act. Praise and pleasure in the child's pride in noticing should be established before moving on to the next step.

Step 2 was enlisting her intellect and related experiences to give her the idea of what she was trying to accomplish. This second step is setting the goal and talking about it with low-key conviction and confidence that it will be achieved. One technique described was to play with a bowl of dried beans, putting ever greater quantities into the child's hand and having her hold the handful of beans, talking with her meanwhile about her strong hand muscles that hold the beans in her fist. When her hand feels too full, she can use her muscles to open her hand and let the beans come out into the bowl. Or one can use a balloon with some water in it; the child holds the water in the balloon with her hand and then decides when to let go and let the water out. This is just like the muscles she uses to hold in her pee and poo. She uses those muscles to hold it in, then to feel when there's getting to be too much, and then to push it out. So the second goal was "localizing the sensations" and knowing she could control her muscles.

Step 3 was feeling the pressure *before* urinating or defecating. Parents can praise the child's ability to recognize and report the sensations to self or others and describe them as important signals.

Janine's parents reported back that she was enjoying letting them know before she wet or dirtied her diaper. Step 4 was to move on to make use of Janine's impatience with the diaper-changing process to suggest that using the potty or the toilet would mean she didn't have to deal with that anymore. They said, now she knew before the pee or poo needed to come out, she had time to go put it into the potty. This fourth step is offering the potty or the toilet as a solution to the child's problem.

Step 5 is dealing with whatever worries or theories the child may have constructed about the noise of the toilet or the water or where the contents go. With a three-year-old, such explanations are usually straightforward. Persistent anxieties need focused attention to find the source and clear up the problem, but most children can be reassured fairly easily.

Several parents mentioned their concern about making their children feel ashamed or bad in the process of toilet mastery. A lively discussion about disgust and self-esteem ensued. The family consultant reminded the group about parents being the ones who present reality to their children; the reality is that most older children and adults find bathroom smells unpleasant and that each culture finds a way to dispose of waste matter. These are social realities that underlie the goal of toilet mastery for small children. The group discussed how to convey disgust without humiliating their children and concluded that the simplest was the best. They felt they could just say that poo doesn't smell very good and that's why we put it into the toilet. The family consultant added that it helps also to talk about how good it feels to be in charge of your own body and to feel nice and clean like a grown-up. These ideas place toilet mastery into the long line of development toward being a grown-up, which is increasingly interesting to three-year-olds.

Within a couple of months, Janine's parents were happy to report that she was using the toilet independently and had proudly informed her grandparents about the achievement during their recent visit.

- **PRAISING THE EFFORT**

With younger children, there is almost no distance between the process and the achievement and the goals are relatively simple. Three-year-olds are reaching for harder and more complex things, and need more time to put together different components in order to master skills. The challenge is to maintain pleasure as the motivator through the sometimes long process of mastery.

Alina's mom Julie described how Alina loved to watch ice-skaters on TV. They decided to try skating lessons at the local rink. When Alina took to the ice and promptly fell down, she burst into heartbroken tears, not because she was hurt but because she was devastated that she couldn't skate like the pretty ladies on television. Her mom told the group what a painful moment it was seeing Alina so disappointed in herself in a way that her mom couldn't have anticipated since it never occurred to her that Alina would expect herself to do spins right away.

She said to Alina, "Oh my, you knew about the skating part from TV, but you didn't know about the trying part. The trying part is what comes first, and you will do that very well. You are already very good at trying. I'll help you begin, and then the skating teacher will show you more things to try and practice." They stood up together on the ice, and Julie said, "Look at you. You are trying so hard to keep your balance and you are standing! That's pretty hard to do on the slippery ice—good work!" Alina sniffed and smiled and said she was ready to try having her mom pull her along the ice. When they got home that night, Julie made a point of telling Alina's dad at dinner all about how hard Alina worked to stand on the ice and how happy they were that she was a "good tryer." Alina beamed.

Doug's father, Tom, who had two older children in elementary school, joined in with the idea that little ones are always watching grown-ups and older kids more than we realize. "My middle kid seemed so ready to learn to read, and he just wasn't doing it. One day, I peeked into his room and he was sounding out the words in a book. I went in and asked him about it and he said, 'No, I can't read like you and my brother, so I can't read.' I never realized that he would think he was supposed to just pick up a book and be able to do it immediately. But that's what he thought from seeing us functioning that way."

The family consultant and other parents thought Tom's example was very helpful in reminding parents to be explicit about all the steps there are to learning anything. How should little kids know that their parents went through a long learning process years before they were born? Tom said he told his boy a story about all the steps he went through to learn to read, just like his older brother did. And he said he was pleased and proud to see his son trying so hard.

The family consultant confirmed the importance of noticing and praising effort rather than only the results. He cited research that demonstrated that older children who received praise for being smart did less well on tasks than those who were praised for being hard workers.[39]

- **OFFERING RESOURCES TO SUPPORT MASTERY**

Important research in several fields has established that intense, too big, or chronic negative experiences generally overwhelm children and can cause lasting damage to their personalities. This is what is often called trauma because it renders the child helpless, unable to tap into his internal resources and use his emotional muscles. Smaller amounts of stress, on the other hand, are positive growing experiences, helping a child stretch his capacities and develop strength and flexibility. Practice strengthens emotional muscle, just as regular exercise strengthens physical muscle.

This is what we were talking about when we described grading separation experiences for babies and toddlers. Three-year-olds still need graded challenges since mastery of developmental tasks happens best when they match your child's capacity. Then you can genuinely be confident that your child's emotional muscles offer him the strength to proceed along the path to mastery with enjoyment of the challenge. But three-year-olds still need assistance. With resources mobilized, they can rise to a challenge and grow from it.

Rasheef's mother knew she would be going away on a business trip for a week and worried that he might miss her too much. He had disturbed sleep for several weeks after her return from a similar trip when he was a toddler. Parents in the group offered many good suggestions about how to prepare him. Making a small album of photos of her and of them together, for him to be able to look at while she was away, spoke to the importance of helping him hold on to his mental image of her. Another suggestion was to make a book with a page for each day of her absence—on one side she could draw what Rasheef would be doing and on the facing page make a picture of what she would be doing. That way they would each be able to think about the other in a context.

The family consultant suggested that she organize these ideas for Rasheef by telling him the story of how she has always held him. Before he was born, she held him in her womb, keeping him safe while he grew big enough to be born. Then she held him in her arms for a long time while he was a little baby. Once he could walk on his own, she held him with her eyes, always knowing where he was so that he would know he was safe and cared for. Now that he is three and goes to school by himself, she holds him in her thoughts and feelings, thinking about what he is doing at school and feeling happy that he is having a good time. When she goes on her trip, she will do the same thing, and he can too.

The trip went well; Rasheef and his daddy had a good week together, enjoying many activities and quiet times; Rasheef was happy to see his mother and told her that he missed her, and he had no trouble sleeping through the night when she returned.

ASSERTION AND EXPLORATION

These muscles will serve in meeting all of life's challenges.

Parents can promote this growth by

- **PROTECTING AND VALIDATING CURIOSITY AND DRIVE**
As we noted in describing the major challenges of toddlerhood, differentiating assertion and aggression is an ongoing task. There are personal and cultural pressures that make it difficult. But assertion turns into aggression when it is frustrated. When aggression is not recognized, addressed, and resolved it can turn into sadism. Bullying starts in early childhood. It can be stopped there if parents help their children develop the emotional muscle to speak up for themselves with adults and other children. Parents have to promote trust that adults will welcome assertion. Then children do not need to feel good by putting someone else down. They can get their good feelings from their own real achievements.

Exploration goes along with assertion and is one of the major biological drives of human beings. All children are curious; they are busy making theories to explain their experiences, exploring the limits of their capabilities, and seem to have an inexhaustible store of questions.

In the preschool parent group, Taroq's father described his impatience every evening when Taroq peppered him with questions the minute he arrived home from work. "Why does he assault me this way? Why can't he give me a minute's peace and quiet when I'm tired?" Everyone sympathized, and then one mother remarked that Taroq actually sounded so happy to see his dad, almost as if he had been storing up questions, waiting for him to get home—his timing was just unfortunate. Taroq's father looked thoughtful and said, "If that's the case, it's not a good way for Taroq to show it."

The family consultant noted that Taroq's father had thereby redefined the problem into a much more benign and soluble one—how could he teach Taroq a better way to express his excitement and positive wish to reconnect with his dad? Instead of turning the situation into an escalating battle, wounding both of them and squashing Taroq's enthusiasm, they might be able to plan a different homecoming routine. The group tossed out ideas like planning a special place to sit down together before supper and have some questions. Perhaps the dad could talk with Taroq about having a big hug when he got home, then a quiet hello for the other members of the family, while Taroq fetched his house slippers. Another job that could be Taroq's own might be to bring his dad the mail as well as getting a book for himself; then they could sit quietly together, each doing "big man work reading" until time for questions. Then they could help prepare supper or tidy up toys together.

Two weeks later, Taroq's dad started parent group with a big smile when he described the pleasant evenings he was sharing with his son. He remarked, "Some of his questions are pretty intelligent too!" He had moved from experiencing the questions and exuberance as an assault to seeing clearly that Taroq was loving and curious, admiring his father's knowledge and hungry for time together. This enabled him to make the legitimate and manageable demand that Taroq meet some of his dad's needs, supporting the development of Taroq's capacities to wait, accept alternatives, and appreciate someone else's feelings. He didn't do this out of anger, but lovingly, in order to have a warm and close time together. He was reinforcing Taroq's emotional muscles to seek answers and strive for knowledge and connection to others.

These parents point the way for others to understand that questions are usually part of curiosity and the exploratory drive. Exploration and assertion are not rooted in aggression. But sometimes, a child's persistent questioning takes on a different feel and can indicate the presence of a difficulty. Children quickly figure out that grown-ups are more responsive to questions than other communications. If your child asks questions but doesn't listen to the answers, he may be asking more to secure your attention than because he's curious. That's a signal to consider what might be making him feel needy just then and to examine whether he really isn't getting enough of your attention.

MAKING CHOICES

Accept the reality that you can't have everything.

Three-year-olds, with their expanded knowledge and capacities, have a tremendous appetite for the world and everything in it. They really would like to be able to choose all the flavors in the ice cream shop. They find it hard to accept the reality that life often demands choices and that even choices between two good things mean you don't get to have the one you didn't choose. This is what is called an approach-approach conflict or two-way feelings. [40] It takes effort to develop the strength to decide what you want, bear the sadness over what you won't have, and enjoy the choice you made.

Parents can promote this growth by

- **SPELLING OUT CONFLICTING WISHES**
  Rachel's daddy was going to come to school to take her out to lunch. She was wearing a special dress and barrettes and told her teacher and friends about the plan with great excitement. Her dad came at the appointed time, just as lunch was being served in the classroom. Rachel got upset and finally told her teacher that she wanted to stay at school at the same time as she wanted to go out with her daddy. Her teacher said, "You're having a two-way feeling. You want two things at once, and they can't both happen. But you can go with your daddy today and stay at school for lunch tomorrow and tell us about your special lunch out with your dad." Rachel sighed with relief, smiled, and skipped out holding her daddy's hand.

- **KEEPING THE CONFLICT INSIDE THE CHILD**
  Three-year-olds are just learning to take some responsibility and control inside. Like all newly acquired skills, it isn't consistent or dependable yet. Children often deal with conflict, for instance, having two-way feelings, by playing the conflict out in a dispute with someone else. [41]
  Stefan's mother described what happened the night before. He was having a great time playing in the bathtub when she told him it was pretty soon time to get out for story. Stefan kept playing, enjoying his water toys. When she said it was really time to finish bath, Stefan began to shout and splash. "It was really hard to know what to do since I know he loves story. That's what I said first. I reminded him that story is a nice time too. Stefan said he wouldn't get out of the bath and he could have story later. I said that wouldn't be possible because there wouldn't be enough time for both. He would have to decide." She described how Stefan got angrier and angrier but didn't get out of the bathtub. So she said to him, "I can see how hard it is for you to decide, and you're fighting to make it be that there doesn't have to be a choice. But you've

already made your choice by staying in the bathtub through story time. That's all right. We'll have a story tomorrow."

"Whew," said one of the dads, "you were able to hang tough." Stefan's mom replied, "I don't know if I could have done that if it had been something more important or something he wouldn't be able to do again. But even though he was very sad about his story, I stuck to the idea that learning to make choices was an important skill for him. In a way, I was proud of him that he made a choice even if he doesn't yet fully realize that's what he was doing." The family consultant agreed that Stefan's mother had strengthened his emotional muscles for making choices and living with the consequences, a life skill well worth acquiring.

USING ANGER AS A SIGNAL

Anger that is more than a signal is useless; maintaining and reinforcing the distinction between feelings and actions leads to effective mastery of emotions.

Parents can promote this growth by

- **WORKING OUT WHAT THE ANGER IS ABOUT AND WHAT'S THE GOAL**
  Insist with your child on understanding where her anger is coming from. Don't downplay or disregard it; validate the feelings, and set limits for the behavior. Aggression is not an impulse that needs venting. Children do not need outlets for aggression. Aggressive impulses and behavior are almost always the result of anger that has not been modulated into serving as a signal, combined with a situation where something threatening or overwhelming seems impossible to remedy. Powerlessness, frustration, and lack of emotional muscle contribute to aggression.

  Peter's parents were distressed and increasingly alarmed at his pushing, pinching, and poking at his little sister. One day, when she messed up his train tracks, he jumped up, grabbed her, and threw her down to the floor. Peter's dad had removed him from the room and given him a pillow to punch, saying, "You can't hit your sister, but you can get your anger out by hitting this pillow."

  In the parent group, everyone grasped the problem and shared that all their children had been jealous and angry about new brothers and sisters. The family consultant noted that there was research evidence that providing substitute targets for aggression only made children more violent because it reinforced hitting as a solution to anger.[42] The idea that feelings have to be gotten out rests on old mistaken assumptions that feelings are like hot water in a kettle that needs a vent or an outlet to prevent explosions. This widespread idea has been disproven. The challenge is to find other ways of dealing with these strong and understandable feelings. The group talked about how hard it is when you see where the older child is coming from but how bad feelings don't justify bad behavior.

This allowed the group to underline the crucial distinction that parents can help their children understand—"I know you feel very angry that Nancy messed up your train tracks, but you still can't hit her." Someone suggested that maybe Peter needed a bit more help from grown-ups to protect his trains. Maybe it was asking too much of him to be patient all on his own, especially when he had worked so hard and Nancy had ruined it. How about keeping the trains in his room with a gate on the door so that Nancy couldn't get to them, but Peter would feel part of the ongoing activity, and parents could also see and talk with him?

A further suggestion was to talk with Peter about how his parents were going to insist with Nancy even though she was just a little toddler, that she was not allowed to hurt him or his things. The family consultant said, "This will help him see that you will protect them equally. No one will be allowed to hurt Peter *or* Nancy." The family consultant added that research has demonstrated that conflict between siblings is frequent and is usually about possessions. Being proactive in these situations will really support a better relationship between them.[43]

Peter's parents were very relieved as all these ideas felt more comfortable to them. His mom said, "I was afraid he was going to grow up to be an axe murderer, but it makes sense to me that he is only three and a half and can't fight this battle alone. And we can help it not be a battle. It's a genuine conflict to solve."

- **SUPPORTING JUST-RIGHT-SIZE FEELINGS**

If we go back to Torrey, who was passionately involved in riding his new scooter, we can see how his parents could help him strengthen this emotional muscle to deal with his too-big feelings.

When the parent group returned to consideration of how to solve the dilemma of Torrey's wish to keep riding his beloved scooter in the rain through the night, they had several new tools to apply. Torrey's parents could first step out of the adversarial power dynamic and say to him that they could see how much he loved his scooter and how strong his body muscles were for riding it. They came back to the parent group and described how it had all played out.

They had followed the suggestions about talking to Torrey about his passion for the scooter. Then they said, "But riding a scooter needs not just body muscles, but feeling muscles as well. We knew your body was ready for the scooter, but now it looks like you need our help to make the feeling muscles stronger."

They could remind Torrey of how they had practiced getting his feelings just right, not too big and not too small, but just the right size for talking and solving the problem. Now he has such big feelings about wanting to ride his scooter all night. Can he make his feelings the right size for talking? When he can, they will be able to make a plan to use the scooter again.

Torrey cried a bit more, then said he wanted to talk. His mom pointed out that he had said his legs were so tired before supper. She said his legs would be stronger with food and sleep, so that was part of the preparation for riding his scooter. "Oh, you're having a two-way feeling, like the time you wanted to go to the ice cream store and you wanted to play next door. Now you want to ride your scooter, but your body also wants to eat and sleep and get strong, for more scooter. If your feelings are strong enough to see that you can choose to do one now and then the other tomorrow, I'll know that we can take the scooter out of the closet, so it's ready for the morning." His mom said he then collapsed in her arms, and she carried him up to bed.

DISTINGUISHING BETWEEN REAL AND PRETEND

Competence, creativity, and security are anchored in reality.

Parents can promote this growth by

- **USING YOURSELF AS THE MAIN RESOURCE FOR YOUR CHILDREN**
  This is the time when preschoolers are often exposed to TV shows and videos directed to little children. Parents generally talk about

showing their children videos for three reasons: First, they want the children to learn from them; second, they need something to occupy the children while they do necessary tasks; and third, just as grown-ups enjoy a good movie or an evening of TV, there can be pleasure or fun for children from movies or games.

Videos for babies are a multimillion-dollar industry, marketed with claims that they will boost babies' intelligence and give them an advantage. Many parents, wanting the best for their children, waste hard-earned money on these products. Research has indicated that they are not only useless but also actually decrease the cognitive capacities of children who spend time with these nonhuman and nonresponsive sources of stimulation.[44] Starting with the very youngest, there is nothing more fascinating or instructive for babies than the face of a responsive grown-up. No mechanical stimulation can hope to get anywhere near the variety, detail, and customizing of interaction that takes place when parents and infants play peekaboo, make faces, sing songs, do finger plays, read books, or go for a walk together. Hearing music, having conversations, feeling the wind blow, moving rhythmically, and so forth all stimulate brain development and lay a foundation of pleasure and learning within babies' most important relationships.

As babies become toddlers and then preschoolers, all their developmental energy is harnessed to the enormous task of mastering the inner realities of feelings and impulses and the outer realities of the world of people and things. Never again will children make such rapid developmental strides in such a short time; there are literally millions of things for them to learn about. They drink in everything around them and reach out to explore and discover more. Figuring out what is real and what is not, working out what causes what, struggling to differentiate what they are in charge of and what they cannot control are all big jobs. Little children do not securely know the difference between real and pretend until they are seven or eight years old, and even then, they occasionally need reassurance from grown-ups.

In the context of these long developmental efforts, we can see that movies and videos that present fantasy worlds and characters are confusing to young children. No matter how convincingly they may assert that they know it's make believe, three-year-olds are usually confused by stories that depict unrealistic and frightening characters and events. Preschoolers are figuring out the realities of things like their own body intactness and integrity, loving wishes and aggressive impulses, growing awareness of death and dying, what it means to grow up and how to remain secure in one's family and still become a big person.

Stories about people who can fly, dying/sleeping and coming back to life/awakening, the scarecrow and tin man who are lifelike but are missing a brain and a heart, dinosaurs who are still alive, the witch who melts, people who have the power to hurt or destroy others by an evil curse or a flick of the wand, the animals who plan to leave their overly rambunctious friend alone in the dark woods to cure him of his bounciness—these all have so much potential for feeding confusion about the power of both thoughts and actions. Most importantly, such movies and stories give children unrealistic material and characters to try on, when what they really need to be doing is becoming themselves, becoming grounded in their own feelings: excited, happy, disappointed, loving, angry, jealous, curious. Children cannot fly, they do have a brain and a heart, they cannot melt, and sleeping is not dying.

Trying to make sense of this input when they are already working so hard to understand the real world is too big a demand for most three-year-olds. When they are overwhelmed by their powerlessness in the face of superheroes or monsters, they will seek magical solutions that undermine their own developing skills. There is plenty of time for fairy and fantasy tales in the school years when children have consolidated the distinction between real and pretend at more than a verbal level.

But sometimes, parents need time for themselves—to cook dinner, to regain calm, to make an important phone call that can't wait. Videos, when chosen with a child's developmental level in mind, can be welcome aids for a maximum of thirty minutes at such times. For instance, old-fashioned material, like *Mr. Rogers' Neighborhood*, is suitable for most children over three. What makes these appropriate is their realistic setting, the gentle pacing, helpful and understandable lyrics, the clear delineation between the world of people and the land of make-believe, and the ever-present attention to feelings.

- **REGULATING TV USE**

Television shows for grown-ups are very confusing and distressing to children. The television is a presence within the child's home, part of the space that is defined as safe and protected. Research demonstrates that children as young as eleven months register and react to the emotional tone of television commentary. Three-year-olds, with greater understanding of words and images, may be overwhelmed by the news. The further complexity that the news or dramas describe or depict real events is beyond three-year-olds, who have no framework to process the content.

At the times of the two Gulf wars, the events of 9/11, Hurricane Katrina, and so forth, many little children reacted with bewildered alarm and regressive symptoms, for instance, reverting to wetting the bed, sleep problems, or tantrums. At Allen Creek, we counseled parents about how to talk about such events to children of different ages and how to meet their own needs for information and reassurance without overburdening the children. Our major piece of advice was to turn off the television. This led to a startling, immediate calming for the children, most of whose symptoms disappeared right away. It also reinforced for parents and staff how powerful and intrusively overwhelming the television could be.

- **STRENGTHEN YOUR POSITION AS A TRUSTWORTHY GUIDE TO REALITY**

Three-year-olds are adding to their knowledge about the world at an amazing rate. They know so much more than even six months before, their language is expanding, and they are busy figuring out how to put all the information together. Parents play the central role in ensuring that children are not overwhelmed but have reality presented in a way they can master. You can use books and stories to help your children grow and not be overwhelmed. It is important throughout early childhood to read appropriate books together, but it takes on new dimensions once children are developing greater sophistication about real and pretend.

You can assess stories by prereading them or checking as you go along. How is your child reacting? Is he rushing to the end because the book is over his head? Because it is scary? Because he really wanted a different one? Or because he hasn't had enough practice in the component skills of waiting until the page is done, turning the pages, reading from the front to the back of the book, and so forth?

Isidore had always loved to read books with his mom. They often spent more than an hour together with old and new stories, rereading their favorites. Isidore appreciated the idea of books that he loved when he was little. The fall after Isidore turned three, a relative sent a Halloween book as a present. He was excited to have mother read the book, and it rapidly became the only one he wanted over and over. His mom mentioned at a parent meeting that she was wondering why this seemed so important to him. She herself didn't particularly like it as it had ghosts and witches in it, and she felt that those scary pretend things were potentially confusing and worrying for Isidore.

The family consultant described that sometimes children want to repeat a story, game, or song because they want to master it. It is stretching them in a good sense, and we can spot that when we see pleasure and growth. This mom's discomfort was a good signal that something different was happening. Isidore was stuck, trapped in trying to come to grips with content and ideas that were beyond him, too scary and unreal for him to understand. Other parents chimed in about similar experiences.

Isidore's mother was very relieved at the suggestion that she simply tell him, "We made a mistake reading this book. It was written for older children. I will put it away until you are older and can enjoy it better." She described in the next group how Isidore heaved a sigh of relief, was sleeping better, and had not asked again for the book. She had reinforced for him that she would protect him and make sure he was not burdened with more than he could handle. He could proceed to be stretched by appropriate books.

Three-year-olds can listen to longer books and take in more complex stories. They appreciate stories about real-life events, like children going to school or a trip to the store, beach, or playground or trying to find a mislaid shoe or the sights along a walk. They can also use their growing sense of what is real and practical to be appreciative of humor and mild fantasy, bursting into laughter at the idea of putting a jacket on as pants or wearing a shoe for a hat or enjoying animals interacting with people.

Stories that include feelings, simple frustrations, and resolutions become especially satisfying and allow for safe practicing of experiences and solutions in the convenient guise of an animal or character's predicament. Such stories also convey the pleasures of mastery and competency as the heroes and heroines feel good at the end when they have found what they were looking for, helped the doggie get used to his new bed or overcome his dislike of baths, made a new friend on the first day of school.

Samir had just moved into town with his family and started immediately in his new school. He spent much of each day sitting alone at a table, drawing what he said were maps. His parents were proud that he understood what a map was but worried about his not socializing. Samir's teachers and family consultants suggested that his parents talk to him about how his new house and school were very nice but that perhaps he missed his old town too. Samir did not want to listen to these explanations when his parents tried to talk with him.

At the next parent group, Samir's dad said that he had been reading him a book over the weekend about a little boy who goes out to find a cave in the woods with a flashlight. The little boy's parents think he is lost, but he finds his way home just fine, and they all have a splendid reunion. The following week, Samir began to join into other children's games while also showing his classmates how to draw maps. He had been too upset to take in a direct explanation but was able to use the slight distance of the story to think about the good feelings of being with his family wherever they lived. His worried preoccupation had been changed into a progressive skill, and the anxiety defused through his father's loving attention and the message in the story. Samir had used this experience to start to master his big feelings about moving.

The issues of real and pretend go deeper than parents sometimes realize. The opportunity to talk them through can allow for significant changes in what parents teach their children and how they think about the values they want them to have.

In a parent group before the winter holidays, Polly's parents commented on the commercial blitz of decorations, store windows, and advertisements. This led to a discussion of materialism and also about Santa Claus and other such creations, like the Easter Bunny or the tooth fairy. One of the parents questioned why people would tell children about Santa Claus in the first place. Almost all the parents became highly indignant. They said things like "It's part of the magic of childhood," "It's so lovely," "It fosters their imagination and creativity to offer them these ideas." Another pointed out that there are lots of invisible things he wants to teach his children about, like God.

The family consultant asked, "But do you really believe in Santa Claus?" When the parents laughed and said no, he could make a distinction between things parents truly believe in, like religious ideas and values, which they want to impart to their children, and fictions like Santa Claus. He invited parents to consider why they would depart in this one area from their general stance of telling their children the truth and introducing them to reality.

As parents began to think about how Santa Claus fit into their own lives, the rosiness of the initial picture changed markedly. Every one began to remember his or her own confusion, embarrassment, or worst of all, their disappointment that their parents seemed stupid.

Polly's father, now an engineer, described realizing as a child that a big fat man could not possibly fit down the chimney. But since his parents seemed so enthusiastic about the idea, he didn't want to hurt their feelings, so he pretended for a few years more to go along with them. It had not been good for his relationship with his parents that he felt as a five-year-old he had to take care of them—a little boy should feel safely taken care of by his parents.

Nora's dad remembered his humiliation when his classmates teased him in second grade for still believing in Santa Claus. He was furious with his parents for fooling him and exposing him to ridicule.

Aneer's mother remembered being puzzled by knowing that her parents gave her holiday gifts but that Christian children had someone else and their parents gave them nothing. This worried her—had those children done something that made their parents so angry that they would no longer give presents? Could that happen to her?

Over the next year, this parent group explored this issue and related questions many times. Eventually, the group decided what they felt most comfortable telling their children: "Santa Claus is a nice story that lots of people all over the world tell in different ways. It is about the loving feelings people express with presents at holiday times." Then they would not be lying to their children and could go on building their children's sturdy security in knowing the difference between real and pretend and trusting that their parents would faithfully represent reality to them.

This book describes how thoughtful parents can include emotional muscle in bringing up their children. The parents considering Santa Claus help us understand that it is a big challenge to put energy into examining ideas that have been part of own upbringing and the general culture.

TOLERATING FRUSTRATION TO ENJOY PLAY

*Various emotional muscles developed earlier can now
be put together for a purpose.*

Younger children have played with others at school, day care, classes, and playdates but are usually closely monitored or accompanied by adults. Their play is not usually very interactive, except at moments of conflict and friction. But three-year-olds are starting the long journey of independent friendships that demand autonomous social skills. How can parents and teachers help them master the big challenges this represents?

Parents can promote this growth by

- **STRUCTURING INTERACTIONS**
Jason's parents described his difficulties letting others play with his toys during playdates. Other parents in the group agreed and talked about how they often felt discouraged as if playdates were more trouble than they were worth, going through the refereeing needed to deal with such conflicts. The discussion gradually turned to what they might do differently to promote a better outcome—more pleasure and social experience for their children.

The family consultant suggested some role-playing before the playdate. Parents could talk with their children about making it fun for both host and guest and choose together which toys would be too hard to have a different child play with. The three-year-old host and the parent could put away the very precious toys and keep out only those the host felt comfortable sharing. Other planful conversations could include how to take turns choosing what to play, and asking for help if it became difficult.

Over the next few meetings, parents reported that playdates were becoming more harmonious, with their children volunteering which toys to put away first, and being less possessive with the ones kept available. But the kids still seemed to melt down pretty quickly, as if they couldn't maintain this new level of functioning. The parents wondered what else was needed since playdates were still exhausting them.

- **MONITORING PLAY**

The family consultant wondered if the parents' frustration came from pitching their expectations too high too soon. He thought there might be something to learn from the teachers at school, where he had seen a lot of growth in the children's capacity to play together. He told them about what he had observed in class the week before.

The Allen Creek toddler teachers had introduced the idea of a whole turn to good effect with very young toddlers. The toddlers were increasingly able to wait for a turn, using the emotional muscle of tolerating delay; they could feel secure in their own turns, using the emotional muscle of trust in the grown-ups to protect them and willingly hand over toys to the waiting child when they were done, able to use empathy to take care of others as they had felt taken care of.

For the three-year-olds, who might not want to finish a whole turn with the trikes until outside time was over, the preschool teachers scaffolded a new idea on to the old. They introduced the idea of a quick turn. It was a sign of the children's readiness and emotional muscle that they immediately understood how they would all benefit and enthusiastically implemented the new idea.

A group of boys in the three-year-old class had been very dedicated to digging a sewer in the sandbox, working over many days to develop a big system. It was a very elaborate undertaking with construction cones to mark the site and a huge pit where everyone was digging. Children took turns coming in and out of the sandbox, riding bikes or blowing bubbles or planting between sewer digs.

One day, Earl was the first to request the hoe. This was an item he was very fond of, often carrying it around from place to place. Kenny told Earl he wanted a turn with it when Earl was done. The two headed for the sandbox. When the teacher came over, she noticed that the two of them were taking quick turns, passing the hoe back and forth.

Earl said, "Can I have it now? Yes or no?"

Kenny replied, "In two minutes. I'm almost done."

The teacher told them they were both doing "good friend" things. Both boys smiled and looked at each other. Then they went right back to work on their sewer.

The family consultant suggested that one difference between the classroom and the playdates was that teachers were closely monitoring what was going on. The children probably sensed their attentiveness, and this support strengthened them. One of the moms remarked ruefully, "I guess I can't just sit in the kitchen and see a playdate with three-year-olds as a break!" A dad agreed but added, "There is a different distance that they need now, though. I've noticed that they like to be able to see me, and I admit I feel safer being able to see them, but I don't have to be right there in the game. They're often busy doing their thing."

These parents had worked their way to a balanced position that would support their children's growing emotional muscle to play constructively.

HOW PARENTS HELP THREE-YEAR-OLDS BUILD THE EMOTIONAL MUSCLES OF

LEARNING EMOTIONAL CAUSE AND EFFECT
Parents help by

- TEACHING EMOTIONAL SELF-AWARENESS
- TEACHING SELF-AWARENESS BY EXAMPLE
- MAKING SENSE OF OTHER PEOPLE'S EMOTIONAL SIGNALS
- TEACHING AND MODELING EMPATHY

TAKING PLEASURE IN SHARING EXPERIENCE
Parents help by

- CREATING TIME FOR RESPECTFUL LISTENING, MODELING SHARING

PERSISTENCE AND COMMITMENT TO A GOAL
Parents help by

- BREAKING TASKS DOWN INTO MANAGEABLE STEPS
- PRAISING THE EFFORT
- OFFERING RESOURCES TO SUPPORT MASTERY

ASSERTION AND EXPLORATION
Parents help by

- PROTECTING AND VALIDATING CURIOSITY AND DRIVE

MAKING CHOICES
Parents help by
• SPELLING OUT CONFLICTING WISHES • KEEPING THE CONFLICT INSIDE THE CHILD

USING ANGER AS A SIGNAL
Parents help by
• WORKING OUT WHAT THE ANGER IS ABOUT AND WHAT IS THE GOAL • SUPPORTING JUST-RIGHT-SIZE FEELINGS

DISTINGUISHING BETWEEN REAL AND PRETEND
Parents help by
• USING YOURSELF AS THE MAIN RESOURCE FOR YOUR CHILDREN • REGULATING TV USE • STRENGTHENING YOUR POSITION AS A TRUSTWORTHY GUIDE TO REALITY

TOLERATING FRUSTRATION TO ENJOY PLAY
Parents help by
• STRUCTURING INTERACTIONS • MONITORING PLAY

FOUR-YEAR-OLDS AND THEIR PARENTS
BUILDING EMOTIONAL MUSCLES

Turning four marks a surge forward in children's lives. Three-year-olds needed an adult to stand by so they could function independently. By four, they have stretched out in both body and mind so that they can invent their own games, cooperate with their friends to set them up, and negotiate new experiences with confidence. They still, however, need our help when things get to be too much, or they are tired or startled, hurt, or disappointed; and they will always need a snuggle when times are tough or just because it feels nice to touch home base.

Children's development doesn't always move forward evenly: their self-care may lag behind their cognitive development; or their fine motor functioning may be more developed than their language. Parents and children can also be out of sync, with parents sometimes expecting too much or asking less than their four-year-olds are capable of. Children often adjust faster to their new capacities than their parents can, so you may have some catching up to do.

Four-year-olds make enormous intellectual and emotional advances. They realize that they have a private mental life, that what's inside their heads is not the same as outside reality. They begin to be able to assess other people's statements for how true or real they are. They develop a sense of time that brings questions and worries with it, as well as new strengths.

Their major developmental task is to take ownership of the knowledge of reality that parents and teachers offer. Four-year-olds have a lot to encompass as they come to terms with understanding both their inner worlds and the vastness of the world outside. They are in the midst of learning how to manage their feelings and impulses. They have to organize new knowledge and capacities to solve the challenges and conflicts they face. With this new mastery, they can consolidate the difference between real and pretend and begin to set aside the magical world of wishes and enjoy the reality of their own competence. This means that, in order to interact effectively in the world, they will take inside many of the controls that have so far been exerted by adults.

Over this four-year-old year, children develop an "inside helper,"[45] a conscience that acts as a guide, a goal setter, a moral compass that helps them feel good when they solve problems and find solutions that mesh with their values. The inside helper will also have to make them feel uncomfortable when the consequences aren't good, eventually uncomfortable enough in anticipation to stop themselves before they act. This is the time when children begin to share responsibility for consciously building and maintaining their emotional muscles with parents and teachers who have, up till now, carried the bigger proportion of the task.

Four-year-olds are in the world, engage with the world, and make judgments about the world. They compare themselves with other children and with grown-ups like parents and teachers. They make comparisons among grown-ups, like between their parents, their own parents compared to others', their parents and teachers, and so forth. They know how to evaluate the trustworthiness of others, which will stand them in good stead later, if it is supported and reinforced by adults.[46] These new capacities not only contribute to their self-image, self-confidence, and self-esteem, but also allow for external forces to influence them for good or ill. Influences from the outside contribute to the kind of inside helper they develop.

All these changes are very gratifying, but, at the same time, confront four-year-olds with their real limitations. This leads to frustration, anger, and even rage at times. A major challenge for children and parents is to find ways to manage these big feelings and the aggressive impulses they trigger.

What parents learn

PARTNERING WITH YOUR CHILD

Work toward the transformation of the parent-child relationship at this new level of realistic relations to each other and the world. Think of your child as your partner in the new stage of life. Growing up doesn't mean growing apart; rather the closeness can be experienced on a new level.

Parents' responsibility to present, interpret, and make sense of reality is an even bigger component of the job at this age than earlier. It takes effort and persistence to learn together with your child what to expect of each other, when to help each other out, and how to do that. From a situation where you knew most of the answers and had to devise most of the solutions to problems large and small, you are moving into a time when you will increasingly enlist your child to participate. This effort is enormously rewarding when you can feel yourself and your child enjoying working together.

Jonah's mom, Noreen, talked about how startled her own mother was when she saw how Noreen had set up a special bench in the kitchen to make it easier for Jonah to cook with her. Jonah's grandmother thought it was a lot of trouble for nothing. Why was Noreen letting Jonah help when it made supper preparation take twice as long? "I told her because it's fun to do it together, Mom, and the look on Jonah's face when his dad says yummy is worth the extra mess."

Noreen was working to maintain her pleasure as her relationship with Jonah changed. She also exercised the emotional muscle of conviction in her knowledge of her own child when she stood up to her mother's practical objections.

Parenting offers many satisfactions in the early years of a child's life. It is very gratifying to be the person responsible for everything your child does and knows. Sometimes, adult self-esteem can get bound up in being the all-knowing grown-up. So it can be hard to begin to share that responsibility with your child. But there is enormous and increasing pleasure in the moments when you can authentically partner with your child if parents can develop the emotional muscle to give up the illusion of being in complete charge.

Dave was a big jolly dad who seemed to be able to fix everything. He always volunteered whenever something was needed at school. Everyone knew him; if something broke in class, the children would say, "Joey's daddy will fix it." It was unusual to see Dave morose at a parent group meeting. The other parents gently inquired if something was wrong. Dave said that he was feeling really bad. Joey had asked him a question at bedtime, and he told Joey to stop pestering him and go to sleep. Joey protested and they argued. Dave ended up yelling at Joey and scaring him.

The other parents commiserated with Dave and described times when they too had lost control. They talked a bit about how their children had pushed their particular buttons on those occasions. One parent asked Dave if he knew what the hot-button issue had been. Dave said he realized he couldn't stand not knowing the answer to Joey's question. He talked about how important it feels that Joey looks up to him and respects him, expecting him to be able to do everything and know all the answers. But when the question stumped him, he felt he was letting Joey down and left the room in anger. "Talk about stupid," Dave said. "That was the stupid thing, to blame the kid."

The group lightened up, and everyone told stories of being embarrassed but ultimately relieved of the burden of being idealized and expecting themselves to be perfect. Dave then said he thought he should have been strong enough to tell Joey that he didn't know the answer. One parent reminded the group that they had talked earlier about how important it was to be honest and realistic. She said, "I guess now we should include telling the truth about ourselves." All the parents agreed that it takes guts to admit not knowing.

One parent said she thought it was important to model not knowing since it had taken her years to face that her mother didn't do everything absolutely right and that she didn't have to either. If her mother had admitted to screwing up every once in a while, she herself wouldn't have been such a perfectionist and made herself sick over mistakes. She wanted to work on ways to model the wish to seek out the answer. The family consultant added that we can share not knowing with the child and then partner with him to find ways to figure out the answers. "I don't know why the sky is blue. Do you have any ideas about it? We'll think about that some more tomorrow."

HONEST APPRAISAL

*Stand back and look at your four-year-old; face the
reality of her strengths and weaknesses.*

This is a time of comparison and judgment for parents as well. It is a good time to take an objective look at your child to check if she is on track in various areas of social, cognitive, emotional, and physical development. Will she really be ready to move on to big school? How will you be able to tell? Many parents worry at this point about whether they have adequately equipped their children for the rigors of the big world of elementary school.

Recent surveys of kindergarten teachers report that over 50 percent of children entering school experience problems that significantly limit their ability to learn,[47] so parents have some reason to wonder if their children will be all right. There is a lot of growing to do in this year, and most children, with support from teachers and parents, will be able to manage well. Teachers have the knowledge and experience to reassure parents; it may take some extra emotional muscle of trust to accept their positive assessment and have confidence that your child will grow into the task.

But you or your child's teacher may discover some concerns. If there seem to be lags in any area of development, this is the time to note them and talk with your partner, other parents, a family consultant, or another professional about what is going on. Perhaps your child needs to revisit the steps in a specific skill. This is another arena where focus on emotional muscle can be helpful. Parents and teachers can look at whether your child is fully using age-appropriate emotional muscles and what is needed to support established muscles and develop new ones. If looping back and going again through the breakdown stepwise learning process doesn't solve the problem, professional assessment may offer solutions. Four-year-olds still offer an open window for change and influence from the outside. The brain itself is still plastic, able to alter its ways of processing and patterning experience. It is important for parents not to lose that opportunity for change through denial of their concerns or embarrassment over their child's troubles.

Four-year-old Stephanie had started sucking her thumb again during the summer before her second preschool year. She had been an avid thumbsucker through toddlerhood but had not done so at home or at school for over a year. She now frequently had her thumb in her mouth, even at school during activities she usually loved to participate in.

A month after the start of school, her teachers asked Stephanie's parents what they made of the renewed thumbsucking. Her parents said they had hardly noticed it but that their pediatrician and Stephanie's grandmother had both said she would outgrow it. Stephanie's teacher suggested that while the thumbsucking itself might not be a present concern, she wanted to call attention to Stephanie's going back to an earlier way of comforting or soothing herself. The teacher wondered why she might be doing that and what had made her go back instead of forward.

Soon after this conversation with Stephanie's teacher, her parents had a talk with the Allen Creek Early Childhood Outreach consultant at their preschool.[48] They had realized they wanted to avoid their worry and embarrassment and so had been ignoring Stephanie's signaling something. Parents, teacher and consultant made a plan to observe more closely when Stephanie turned to her thumb; they found that it was at bedtime and moments of transition at home and school that Stephanie was most intensely sucking.

A central element of the plan made by the team of parents, teachers, and consultant was to enlist Stephanie herself as a partner in the exploration and solution of this problem. Her parents had to feel strong enough to call the thumbsucking a problem, risking that Stephanie's feelings might be hurt. But they knew they could explain their concern that she was missing out on fun because she didn't have two hands free in school and that she seemed worried about something—they wanted to help.

Over some weeks, Stephanie gradually confided that she was very worried about her friend's cat. The cat had died during the summer. It was Stephanie's first encounter with death at an age when she had some understanding of time. She had begun to imagine what it might be like if someone she knew died. She was worried about losing her parents and had turned back to thumbsucking for comfort. After conversations about this through several weeks, Stephanie no longer sucked her thumb.

Stephanie's parents had been strong enough to push through their own and others' denial to look clearly at their daughter's functioning and had not avoided exploring and addressing the issue. They gained confidence in their own ability to problem-solve with their daughter and provided her with an important experience of sharing and mastery.

Parents can often use support from teachers and other knowledgeable adults to make successful interventions with their children at this age. It is important to see whether parents can solve the problem together with their child. If that doesn't happen, for instance, if Stephanie had not stopped sucking her thumb so much that she couldn't play at school, it would have indicated the need for a referral for broader and deeper assessment of the situation. If parents are afraid to seek professional help when their little child is struggling with something, there can be much needless distress, and precious time can be lost. It takes strength and courage to face one's helplessness and deal with feelings of failure, but the potential gain in your child's future happiness is worth it.

Louise had just turned four when her mother Joanne said she had a peculiar problem to talk about in parent group. She described how Louise had always seemed especially interested in music, learning songs very quickly even as a baby, listening intently to music on the radio or in the car, banging rhythmically and participating enthusiastically whenever it was music time at school. Louise was able to hum many songs of all kinds, as well as classical music and other instrumentals.

A few days earlier, Joanne was in the kitchen, and she heard piano music from the living room. She went in to find Louise sitting at the piano, picking out tunes. Joanne said she was flabbergasted since she had not taught Louise how to play, thinking she was too young. Now Louise's grandparents were pressuring her to put Louise into piano lessons right away, but Joanne didn't want to be a pushy stage mother. "But if she's a prodigy" Joanne said, "what should I do? I could listen to my parents and push Louise or give in to my worries and ignore her musical talent. My main concern is for her to be a regular happy kid."

Joanne's question generated a lively discussion about giftedness, pushing children, losing opportunities, skipping grades, and related topics. Many parents talked about their own experiences, some regretting that their parents had not insisted that they continue an instrument, others still feeling resentment at their parents' athletic or artistic ambitions for them. Everyone felt this was a knotty, but important, topic. And all acknowledged that having a gifted child brought challenges too even if it was potentially wonderful.

The family consultant suggested that the group think about this in the light of other discussions about learning in general; they had already established the importance of pleasure and relationships for effective learning, as well as the value of developing the capacity to persist and work at something even when it was hard. How could these apply to Joanne's dilemma?

Joanne said it helped to think that anything Louise did, especially at this age, should be fun for her. That way, Louise would have a combined experience of pleasure in the activity, as well as good feelings from success in mastering a skill; piano lessons should be taught by someone who understood these needs of young children. Then Joanne could see how it went. She didn't think Louise would have difficulty working since she could see that Louise was already motivated to try even on her own. Joanne said she and her husband would think seriously about getting some lessons for Louise.

Three months later, Joanne and her husband reported back to the group. Louise had taken to her piano lessons with gusto. Joanne said, "It was almost like she was relieved, like we had finally understood how important music is to her. I sit with her to keep her company while she practices, but I never have to remind her. She is so enthusiastic that she asks me in the car on the way home from school whether she can practice before lunch. We have said she can play piano whenever she wants to. We'll see if this continues, but the teacher says Louise is moving forward amazingly. We're really happy that Louise's teacher is creative and not pushy. It feels like good teamwork for us all. We'll see what happens as time goes by."

Louise's parents had seen her from infancy as a separate person, with her own strengths and characteristics, so they could resist getting themselves caught up in the tide of enthusiasm for her musical talent. They had the emotional muscle to perceive their daughter's own special gift realistically despite their preconceptions and concerns and meet Louise's particular need for creative expression.

CREATING A SUPPORT NETWORK

Develop relationships with other parents; you are not alone in your experience of a four-year-old who can be passionately independent one minute and need you like a toddler the next.

Many parents live far from extended family; even for those with relatives close by, support is not always most easily found with them.

The parents of your child's classmates offer a tremendous resource for exploring options, testing your feelings and thoughts and gathering ideas.

Bernhard's mother wondered if she were doing something wrong. He was often so helpful and pleasant that it was "really like having another grown-up around." But she also described how he could suddenly get whiny and demanding, struggling to wait and needing her right away. She was exasperated and concerned. Did this mean that he was actually immature or even troubled?

Another parent exclaimed, "I'm so glad you've brought this up. Clara is driving me nuts with her unpredictability! Just when I think I can rely on her to be okay while we do another errand, she loses it."

The family consultant described the many forces at work inside four-year-olds. They are trying very hard to be grown-ups, sometimes wanting to skip the steps and be in charge of everyone right away; they are also realistically alarmed at the prospect of adult responsibilities and scurry back to the apparent safety of younger ways. The emotional muscle needed from parents is to understand the many-sided conflicts, sympathize, but not get drawn in. For the first time, four-year-olds really have a choice to take charge of using open-system emotional muscles or to opt for a power play, using intense feelings to push others around.[49] It can help parents stay strong if they remember that their child is actually capable of remarkably well-organized functioning.

One way to hold on to adult perspective is to be able to talk about it together with other parents, to realize that neither you nor your child is falling apart. The unpredictability is frequent and parents can gain support from each others' experience, as well as creative ideas for exercising that muscle.

A father suggested taking a deep breath and reminding oneself of the child's best functioning; then it would be easier to say, "I'm sorry you're having a hard time right now and it's hard for me to stay calm too, but next time we'll be able to have big kid fun together." He added to the group, "And then I won't be freaked out that my son is not ever going to be a big kid!"

These parents were developing and exercising the emotional muscle to admit to needing support and help, that they can't do the whole difficult job alone, especially when there are inevitably difficult feelings aroused in interactions with their children.

REVITALIZING YOUR ADULT PARTNERSHIP

*Your partner is potentially your best support, and your
child needs a model of a loving, respectful relationship.*

The early years can too easily pass in a blur of interrupted nights and shared focus on the needs of the little ones. It is important to children that parents are seen to have a happy life as a couple; growing up and forming significant relationships have to be attractive and desirable prospects.

This takes on new importance in relation to a major four-year-old developmental step. As they have now developed a sense of time, four-year-olds begin to truly wish to be grown-ups. They are very aware of the sensations and anatomy of their own bodies and particularly interested in differences, between boys and girls, between children and grown-ups. While they are expanding their awareness of the world around them, they may also hold on to strong beliefs from earlier that deny these differences because accepting reality would mean accepting the limitations of being little and young. They want to continue to believe in the power of their wishes and feelings.

Girls often become not only especially loving and close but also flirtatious and demanding with their fathers, which poses the dilemma of what to do about their mothers. They want to step into their mother's shoes, but they also love and need them. The analogous situation challenges boys, who want to be big daddies with their moms, but know that they depend on their fathers and love them too. Children in families with same-sex parents also play out these feelings, struggling with their mixed feelings about both parents. It takes a lot of emotional muscle for parents to accept that the snuggly love of the earlier years has evolved into complex feelings of passion, rivalry, desire, jealousy, and exclusion.[50]

Samples from a parent group discussion:

Four-year-old Peter said, "I'm really sorry, Dad, but you're going to have to move out. I'll miss you, but I'm going to marry Mom now."

Eddie, four and a half, stood up on the kitchen counter without his pajama bottoms, his penis erect. He exclaimed to his mother with excitement, "I'm big enough to marry you!"

Mary's family was preparing for a trip; she cuddled up with her father and said, "I don't like Mommy anymore. She's grumpy and mean.

Why don't we just go on the trip together without her?" Mary and her mother actually had a strong and loving relationship, but Mary's new four-year-old rivalry pushed her to criticize and demean her mother.

As these examples accumulated, the parents in the group began to laugh with mingled relief and embarrassment. "It's hard to believe it, but this stuff is really powerful!" "I know I shouldn't be hurt, but it stings to be told I'm ugly or stupid or a useless, bad mom." Several parents talked about the temptation to retaliate in kind, to put their children down. "I just wanted to put her in her place and let her know who's the grown-up here."

The family consultant picked up on that feeling to underscore the useful direction it indicated. The task for parents in the face of such intense feelings from their children is demanding, for it means holding on to adult sources of good feeling about oneself and not letting a four-year-old's wishful opinion define you. Parents need the emotional muscle to stand for the realities that the child is only a child, is not sexually mature, cannot marry a parent, and will someday have someone of their own. That means that it is important not to confuse children by inadvertently validating their wishes.

A mom exclaimed, "Well, there's no way I'm going to be telling Jeff that he can marry me after all!" Her husband then said thoughtfully, "But I wonder what Jeff thinks now when he sleeps in our bed with you when I am away on business." Another parent noted, "Sounds like you two are rethinking what it means to your child." The family consultant agreed that it is really helpful for parents to work together to figure out when the meaning of something has changed because the child has grown into a new stage; that's another part of the parental partnership. Making time to talk together as adults rekindles mutual respect, allowing parents to be thoughtful. For example, it takes mutual support and trust to be able to present these tough realities in a loving way, rather than humiliating your vulnerable child.

George's mother said, "I was kind of thinking when we were talking about revitalizing our partnership that our relationship is fine. But this is about changing together along with George's growth. Since he's constantly changing, we have to keep up, checking in with each other and helping out when needed, since we may have different reactions to George's new stuff."

All parents find this phase trying as it represents a big change from earlier times, which is always hard to adjust to. It may also revive painful feelings from earlier in their own lives, especially adolescent experiences of rivalry, jealousy, disappointment, and loss. Four-year-olds try ingeniously to split the parental couple, using their newfound knowledge that people can't read each other's minds, for instance, to ask one parent for something the other has refused or flatter one parent with preferential requests for bedtime stories or outings.

Revitalizing your partnership can take many forms. It is important since you are each other's major resource and support. Parents we have talked with at Allen Creek and other schools and centers have generated many useful suggestions over the years. One is to talk through again your guidelines for discipline, treats, and so forth to make sure you are on the same page. Parents can also, separately and together, remind themselves what they enjoy and admire about their spouse as a person. Another idea is to plan a regular night out, a standing arrangement with a babysitter, another parent or a friend, to give parents time to be together as adults. Even if you spend the whole time talking about the children, it's still doing so as grown-ups!

With a close, strong, and active adult partnership, parents can absorb the intense feelings and wishes of four-year-olds and develop the muscles to allow themselves to enjoy the real pleasures of adulthood.

FINDING THE POSITIVE AND ASSERTIVE IN YOUR CHILD'S WISHES

This is an ongoing challenge at each new phase.
This muscle allows for transforming the parent-child
relationship.

Under the onslaught of the intense wishes of four-year-olds, with their passionate feelings of love and hate, it is easy for parents to lose sight of the wonder of these forward moves. We talked earlier about how toddlers' activity may be exhausting but represents his growing need to be in charge of himself, to explore, and have an effect on the world. Three-year-olds demand acknowledgment and adjustment to their big changes, with the realization that their forward surges may have negative impact in the moment.

It is a testimony to your four-year-old's experience of family life that she wants to grow up. Her wish to marry her daddy speaks to her love and regard for him; she is creating the model for the kind of relationship she will seek out as an adult. Parents can practice looking for the underlying progressive meaning in their child's current struggle and challenge and hold on to their knowledge that the long-term goal is a positive one.

Peter's father had been greeted on return from a long day of work by his son's declaration that he should move out. He laughed but was clearly taken aback since he was used to being met with a leap into his arms and eager stories about the day. His wife saw the look on his face and went over to hug him. She said to Peter, "I am very pleased that you love Daddy so much and feel so good about yourself that you want to be a big man like Daddy and have a wife as nice as me."

Peter's parents zeroed in on the positive aspects of Peter's wishes. They didn't scold him for asserting himself but also didn't validate his irrational belief that he could get rid of his daddy. They held on to their knowledge of the real generational difference, their own strong adult bond, and enjoyed his forward move as a step on a long road rather than being threatened, hurt, or angered by his intense wishes.

ACCEPTING REALITY LIMITATIONS

Consolidate your own sense of reality by noticing and putting aside superstitions, magical thoughts, irrational worries and actions.

Everyone struggles over choosing open-system reality responses to life's challenges. Parents may have an especially hard time since raising children is bound to evoke feelings of helplessness. When parents are scared, they may reach for magical solutions. Children are very astute and sensitive to other people's feelings and can easily take on their parents' responses to worries.

Children at four have many new strengths, but they are also challenged by their new awareness of real powerlessness, smallness, and lack of knowledge. They are actively struggling with whether to deal with those helpless feelings by invoking an irrational, magical system of control (shown in continuing temper tantrums, out-of-control excitement or activity, aggression, excessive fears or anxieties), what we call a closed system of self-regulation. The alternative choice is realistic, competent ways of feeling safe and effective, a system open to learning and growth (shown in scaling feelings, talking, asking for help, using feelings as signals, problem solving, learning skills, and so forth). They need the help, modeling and support of grown-ups to choose open-system realistic responses.

As we noted earlier, four-year-olds can frequently tell when people are lying or wrong. If they are often given untruths, unlikely explanations, or evasive answers, they won't trust parents and teachers even when they are telling the truth.

Parents of four-year-olds were sharing stories of holiday experiences and the conversation turned to visits with grandparents. Raymond's mother told of not knowing what to say when he asked why Grandma always "knocked wood" whenever she said something nice about him. He wondered if he should do the same. He remembered that Grandma had said he looked so healthy, and then she said, "Knock wood."

Other parents recounted family superstitions, some of which they themselves went along with, like "warding off the evil eye" by sewing a red thread into a daughter's skirt, throwing salt over a shoulder if some spilled, not walking under a ladder or stepping on a crack. The most frequent was to automatically follow a positive comment with the phrase or the action of knocking wood.

At first, most of the parents described these as funny habits, shrugging off any significance, but then Raymond's mother said, "We shouldn't dismiss this. I think I was bothered for a reason, and as we've learned, I want to use my feeling as a signal to figure it out." She went on, "Now that I think of it, I realize it's not just my mother. I say knock wood too, and I do it when I'm scared. There are things I can't control, like Raymond's health, so I use this magic I learned from my mother to feel in control. But it's a lie! I remember getting sick as a kid and thinking it must be my fault because I hadn't knocked wood enough."

Another parent said, "We want to help our children know the difference between real and pretend and then we act as if magic is real." A third joined in, pointing out how they had all worked on distinguishing what they could and couldn't control, but that superstitions are like avoiding the whole issue. He said, "If we don't model and teach our children how to live a healthy lifestyle, all the knocking wood will make no difference. But the truth is that there are still things we can't control, sickness may happen and we have to bear it as part of life, and not think of it as a personal failure or fault."

These parents were coming to grips with an easily dismissed or hidden area of irrationality and magic denial of reality in all cultures. When they put together various emotional muscles they had worked on, they could see that they needed practice to develop the muscle of accepting the limitations of their ability to control every possibility. Even though it was painful, it gave them a feeling of strength to face that truth and think about helping their children to encompass that reality.

DISTINGUISHING BETWEEN AN AUTHORITATIVE AND AN AUTHORITARIAN STANCE

Use your authentic competence and self-restraint
rather than falling back on the power of domination.

We have talked throughout the book about parents and children building emotional muscle in relation to reality, in the context of loving relationships and respect for each other as individuals, even from earliest infancy. We also describe this in terms of open-system functioning, which includes using real skills and knowledge to the fullest at any age. Closed-system functioning, on the other hand, operates with power dynamics, forcing and magical thinking. By now it is surely clear to readers that we do not advocate authoritarian parenting, which uses parents' superior strength and power arbitrarily to overwhelm or intimidate children into obedience, submission, and socialization. We would characterize authoritarian parenting as operating within a closed system of self-regulation.

What we do advocate is *authoritative parenting*. Parents are adults with experience, knowledge, thoughtfulness, support, and the intention that they will honestly offer their children their best love, guidance, and support. Their authentic authority comes from that base. Pleasure in the work of thoughtful, authoritative parenting is its own satisfaction. As Emerson expressed it, "The reward of a thing well done is to have done it."[51] Open-system authoritative parenting takes effort, persistence, and muscle and returns authentic good feelings of mastery and growth throughout life. Authoritative parenting includes acknowledging mistakes and imperfections and apologizing when wrong. Authoritative parents accept the reality of change and transform their relationship with their children over time while always retaining their identity as the parents.

Lily's father talked in parent group about his grandfather who had died recently. He shook his head as he described trying to talk about him with Lily and her older brother. It had been hard for him to change the parenting style he had learned from his grandfather and father. They had both been "no nonsense, do what I tell you" adults, who reinforced their stance with spanking. This had been his model growing up and he had struggled through a wild and troubled adolescence, dealing with rage and uncertainty about how to feel like a good grown-up. It had taken him years to move past those issues.

The other parents were respectful and quiet, moved that Lily's dad was sharing his story. As he talked a bit more about the differences between his family's old way and how he was trying to raise Lily and her brother, parents began to nod and smile. Several chimed in with anecdotes about their arguments with grandparents or in-laws about giving that child too much say or letting the child disagree with you. They underlined how they relied on their own good feeling to sustain their parenting choices and also shared how hard that sometimes was.

Lily's dad then took the conversation a step further by asking what the other parents thought about spanking. He and his siblings had been spanked as children, and there were times when he felt that a spanking would be a useful way to discipline Lily. Others agreed that they had felt the urge to spank, especially if they had been spanked as children. Some reluctantly admitted that they did occasionally spank their kids.

The discussion became heated between those for and against spanking until Lily's dad intervened, saying that he had just figured something out. He now saw that spanking was at the core of *authoritarian* parenting because it meant exerting physical power instead of the genuine authority that comes with maturity and experience. He thought that his childhood experiences of being spanked by his powerful father and grandfather had led to his troubled adolescence, where he tried to push other people around and muscle his way out of conflicts.

The family consultant agreed that there might well be such a connection as recent research has demonstrated the impact of spanking on later problems, showing that spanking is the most significant cause of aggression in children and is one of the roots of later relationship violence and mental health difficulties.[52] He noted that spanking is approved of by 72 percent of American parents.[53] Since most Americans do spank, there's going to be social pressure to do it. We also have to address the mistaken prevalent idea that there is a Biblical injunction to spank children. It is important to know that this comes from an erroneous reading of the Bible.[54]

Additionally, there is no evidence that spanking is a more effective discipline method than any other. Because spanking has negative effects, it seems important to develop alternatives. The group set itself to think more about alternatives to corporal punishment since the urge to react that way is unlikely to disappear.[55] The family consultant thanked Lily's dad for so clearly putting into words for all that evening the distinction between authoritarian and authoritative parenting.

The emotional muscles of judgment and restraint that everyone was working to build and maintain were part of an open ongoing growth process for the parents. This parent group went on to work over months on generating alternative methods of discipline. They increased their repertoire of constructive responses so they would not feel helpless when their four-year-olds were disobedient or defiant.

Parents in an evening workshop for a Head Start program addressed similar issues when they worked to differentiate punishment from discipline. Punishment stems from authoritarian parenting and mobilizes angry and frustrated parental needs to retaliate against children. Discipline, on the other hand, uses situations of conflict between parents and children to discover and teach alternative solutions. Children can then build on these experiences to do better the next time and parents can begin to trust their children's capacity to make good choices.

One mother described how angry she became when her four-year-old son Jared had a tantrum about a rained-out picnic at the park. She had mixed feelings; part of her wanted to spank him for the tantrum, and part of her wanted to find some way to comfort him and make up for the disappointment. As the parents talked, she said she realized she just wanted to get rid of the bad feelings in both of them. Punishing Jared would get rid of her bad feelings but probably give him more.

As the group continued the discussion, parents began to think harder about what "teaching the child a lesson" could really mean. A true lesson for Jared would be about how no one can control things like the rain; then he would be better equipped to manage his disappointment the next time. Jared's mom said that the next time it rained, she would tell him, "I'm disappointed too, but I'm not angry because no one is in charge of the rain. Instead, I'm going to figure out with you something else fun to do." If parents develop their emotional muscles of restraint and holding on to long-term goals, they can more easily help their children learn to regulate their own feelings.

ENGAGING WITH THE ISSUE OF AGGRESSION

Continue to differentiate assertion and aggression.

We discussed in the chapter on two-year-olds the need for parents to maintain the distinction between assertion and aggression, understand the multiple sources of aggression, recognize aggression for what it is, distinguish feelings and actions, and address aggressive actions promptly. As we turned to these issues with three-year-olds, we saw that when aggression is not contained and resolved, it can turn into sadism. Bullying and being bullied can start in early childhood and can be stopped there if parents help children on both sides of the interaction develop the emotional muscle to speak up for themselves with adults and other children, to trust that adults will welcome assertion, and to take pleasure in real achievements and learning. Then children do not need to feel good by putting someone else down or taking the victim role.

When we arrive at the fours, however, we are faced with an upsurge of new physical and emotional capacities, intense feelings, and strong impulses. Four-year-olds are not only capable of hurting each other's bodies but have learned the power of words to wound other children and adults. There is no way to avoid dealing with aggression in four-year-olds. But as discussed earlier, there is cultural pressure and confusion that gets in the way of clear thinking about this loaded area, as well as parents' own histories and assumptions.

Parents are likely to be faced with aggressive wishes and actions in relation to siblings, peers, animals, parents, and other adults. You will have to think about your stance in relation to games, videos and movies about superheroes, toy guns and other weapons, exposure to news and sports on TV, and so forth.

Melanie's mother laughed as she brought up in parent group her daughter's plans for her upcoming birthday party. Melanie was using her new writing skills to make a list of people to invite. The list included her whole class, except for one girl. Melanie's mother exclaimed, "It made me think of middle school, with all the cliques. Does it start this soon?" Another parent spoke up to say that it seemed like it was indeed starting early and that middle school could be pretty nasty. "Is this what we are facing already?" Melanie's mom said, "I never thought of it that way. It is mean to leave out one child in a small class. Now that we're talking about it, I don't feel comfortable letting Melanie do that."

One of the dads said, "But it's *her* birthday." Melanie's mom replied, "I think I was originally assuming that too, but now I'm realizing that I don't like to think of my little girl being mean. It's my job to teach Melanie about being kind to others, and I shouldn't let her be cruel to her classmate. If she really doesn't want this child at her party, I can offer her the option of a different, smaller group so that no one will be singled out as excluded. But I have to take responsibility for that."

These parents were realizing that they had an internal reluctance to face the fact that their little kids could be hostile or mean. But they couldn't help them learn how to be better friends and manage their aggression appropriately unless they engaged with the issue.

Another father, however, continued the topic the next time. He said, "I'm still thinking about our last discussion. I'm not sure that we should be legislating for every little thing. After all, don't the kids have to learn to handle hurt feelings or even to try to figure out why someone doesn't want to invite them? Kids have to learn how to sort these things out for themselves in the rough-and-tumble of the real world. We can't shelter them forever."

The family consultant remarked that there was a wide spectrum of attitudes about aggression in children, ranging from zero tolerance to "throw them in the deep end." People worry about their children being sissies or bullies. The important thing here was that the parents were thinking through their feelings and attitudes, realizing that there would be consequences from what they taught their children. The whole group might not end up agreeing, but all the parents would be in a different place because they had considered the task of helping their children learn how to deal with their own and others' aggression. The family consultant added that being thoughtful parents, they could take into account their own histories of experiencing and inflicting aggression and also look to research and expert opinion since this is a crucial area of life.

Thinking in terms of developing your own emotional muscles gives parents the opportunity to engage with the issue of aggression or go along with cultural denial and reap the consequences.

THE EMOTIONAL MUSCLES USED BY PARENTS OF FOUR-YEAR-OLDS ARE

PARTNERING WITH YOUR CHILD

HONEST APPRAISAL

CREATING A SUPPORT NETWORK

REVITALIZING YOUR ADULT PARTNERSHIP

FINDING THE POSITIVE AND ASSERTIVE IN YOUR CHILD'S WISHES

ACCEPTING REALITY LIMITATIONS

DISTINGUISHING BETWEEN AN AUTHORITATIVE AND AN AUTHORITARIAN STANCE

ENGAGING WITH THE ISSUE OF AGGRESSION

What do four-year-olds need to develop emotional muscles?

Four-year-olds are challenged to find an acceptable way to get what they want. When they find a good way to do that, they can achieve satisfaction from doing the right thing, as well as satisfaction from gratifying their wishes. This is a challenge that will persist throughout life although it has particular vividness in early childhood when controls are just developing and conscience is forming. Children in this stage need support from their parents, a vote of confidence that doing the right thing will result in a stronger and more dependable good feeling than giving in to the impulse without thinking of the consequences. For this, they need clear and empathic limit setting and respect for their experience of events.

In line with their growing understanding of reality, four-year-olds need to have realistic consequences for their actions and have the differences between real and pretend, thoughts and actions, wishes and reality, motives and consequences reinforced many times. Establishing the distinction between what goes on inside one's head and what is real action outside is a challenging teaching effort for parents. Four-year-olds are just becoming cognitively capable of understanding that wishes, thoughts, and feelings are inside events and that actions have impact in the real world. They may struggle against accepting this knowledge as it is easier to assume that everything outside is just as you wish it to be.

What four-year-olds learn

> *INTEGRATING AND CONSOLIDATING EMOTIONAL MUSCLES*
> *GENERATING INTERNAL CONTROLS*
> *REGULATING AGGRESSION*
> *DEVELOPING A GROUP CONSCIENCE*
> *USING WORRIES TO INITIATE MASTERY*
> *LIVING IN THE REAL WORLD*
> *INTERNALIZING REALISTIC STANDARDS*

How parents help four-year-olds build emotional muscles

> *INTEGRATING AND CONSOLIDATING*
> *EMOTIONAL MUSCLES*

All the emotional muscles developed earlier are there for four-year-olds to integrate into their developing character structure.

Parents can promote this growth by

- **CALLING UPON EXISTING EMOTIONAL MUSCLES**
  Younger children feel big and powerful when they have big feelings and may try to use the intensity of tantrums to force others to do what they want. When older children continue to use these ways to feel good or safe, they are often described as lacking self-regulation or being "dysregulated." Starting from the perspective of assuming that everyone needs to find some way to protect themselves from feelings

of helplessness, humiliation, anxiety, rage, and so forth, we see this differently. Children who continue at four to have meltdowns, panics, or rages—employing two-year-olds' ways to feel strong—are using the only way they know to regulate themselves. We call these closed-system modes of self-regulation because they cycle repeatedly without getting anywhere.

All the emotional muscles we have so far described contribute to open-system functioning, where the methods of mastery and self-regulation lead to change, growth, and creative solutions to life's challenges. Parents and teachers have the task of helping four-year-olds put together the various emotional muscles that contribute to flexible, adaptive, smooth self-regulation. Parents help babies develop the muscles of trust and competence. One-year-olds gain mastery by learning the names and sources of feelings. Two-year-olds extend their mastery by turning feeling-states into signals. Three-year-olds regulate aggressive urges by consolidating and enjoying assertion.

All these muscles developed earlier, as described in more detail in each chapter, are there for four-year-olds to integrate into a rapidly crystallizing personality structure.

Xavier's father, Cal, found him in the kitchen with the stove turned on one evening. Xavier was proud that he was tall enough to reach and turn the knobs, "Look, Daddy, I can turn on the stove now." Cal was horrified, both by the real danger and by Xavier's disregard of the long-standing rule not to go near the stove controls. But he tried to read Xavier's happy face and see it from the child's point of view. He realized that achieving a grown-up skill took priority for Xavier over other considerations but that the child still had to know not to turn on the stove himself.

Cal said, "Your body is big and strong enough now to turn on the stove, and your mind is strong enough now to learn what to check with a grown-up since it's not safe for children to light the stove by themselves. But I know how good it feels to light a fire and how that could make you forget for a minute that you are really not allowed to touch the stove." Xavier began to cry, and his dad said, "Oh, I can see that you have two feelings now. You felt good lighting the stove, but now you are feeling bad because you did something you know you aren't supposed to do. It will also feel good to be able to light a fire safely. Let's think how we can put those things together well so you won't get the bad feeling from doing something dangerous. How about if we light the fire in the fireplace together? And next fall, when you're older, we can make a bonfire outside."

At four, teachers provide important facilitation as the children experiment with integrating their different emotional muscles.

One of the teachers in the four-year-old classroom was leaving unexpectedly before the end of the school year because of her pregnancy. After this was announced to the children, there was a return of potty language, silliness, and physical aggression in the classroom. The teachers talked to the children about being angry, upset, and sad and that the reason for the silliness and other negative behaviors might be because it was easier than dealing with those big feelings. This seemed to calm the children. The teachers also talked about how much in school would remain the same. Most of the children did not seem to want to talk about the change. But the teachers watched closely, and these were some of the observations:

At greeting time when Mrs. B. shared her news, Karl said, "I'll write you letters." Evan said, "I'll never write you letters."

Fred made a book about how to take care of babies to give to Mrs. B. His advice included feeding the baby milk, buying a swing if the baby wants to swing, and don't give the baby coffee.

Matt questioned Mrs. B. about whether she was telling the truth. When she asked why he would even ask that question he explained in great detail about a *Berenstain Bears* book where the characters break a lamp but tell their mom that it was broken by a bird soaring through the living room.

As the end of the week approached, teachers saw the children using play and language that showed they were starting to accept and manage their big feelings about the surprising news.

Fred and Evan both talked about their younger siblings. Fred said his brother "is a cutie boy," and Evan (who had said he would never write letters to Mrs. B.) described his sister as a "smiley, smiley baby."

Benny told the other teacher that he would bring a book from home to share, but make a Xerox copy to send to Mrs. B.

Henry commented on how hard it would be to take care of eight babies as Mrs. B. was reading the story "Make Way for Ducklings."

Matt, Barbara, and Kyle took care of baby dolls in the classroom, gently tossing them in the air, feeding them milk and a little vegetable juice, and tucking them into bed.

Otto showed Mrs. B. a picture he made, calling her over and saying, "Come look at it! It's pretty amazing!"

Robert, who had been giggling uncontrollably at his own potty language, first became very quiet and then returned by the end of the week to his usual role as a leader, helping the others learn how to play a game.

These children illustrate the consolidation of previously developed emotional muscles. They used words to register, express, and own their feelings. They showed empathy and concern. They contained their anger and did not put it into actions. And they quickly returned to competent functioning, using their intelligence, imagination, and creativity for restoring good feelings about themselves and the teacher they loved.

The teachers facilitated this integration and growth by recognizing the meaning behind the disruptive play, not punishing them but gently offering an explanation and paying attention to the children's own efforts to find open-system solutions.

GENERATING INTERNAL CONTROLS

Forming a sturdy "inside helper" supports self-control, judgment, kindness, and empathy.

This is a central challenge for four-year-olds. It has multiple components and involves many different steps, so this will be a major section. Each step is an achievement to be recognized and celebrated. In order to generate an inside helper, a child needs to have a conscious sense of herself as a person, with the agency to make choices. The operation of conscience builds on and expands a child's capacity for making judgments and comparisons of options. It cannot operate in a vacuum; children need parents who articulate values and standards for making moral choices. This is sometimes a challenging balancing act as the goal is to help your child develop a conscience that is neither too strict nor too lenient. There are often pulls within children and within parents to lean too far toward the extremes.

Parents can promote this growth by

- **DESCRIBING THE INSIDE HELPER AS A PART OF THE SELF THAT WILL HELP CHILDREN KNOW WHAT TO DO**

No child wants to feel alone and helpless. Offering the idea that they always have an inside helper with them can be reassuring. When you can additionally explain that the inside helper is like having a parent there to help them stay on track, worries about loneliness and not being able to cope can be allayed.

Donato's mother heard him crying softly in bed. When she went in to see what was wrong, he crept into her arms and confessed that his teacher had sent him to sit with the principal that morning for a while. He had kicked his classmate John and didn't want to say that he was sorry. As they sat and talked quietly, he eventually confided that he had been angry because John wouldn't let him join the Lego game and he didn't know what else to do; that was what he really wanted to play with.

His mom said that she understood his feeling of not knowing where to turn; perhaps he had forgotten that he could ask his teacher to help. Donato said he hadn't thought of that and wished his mother had been there to tell the teacher what he needed. Then his mother suggested that he did have a way to help himself at such times. His inside helper could remind him of how to get his teacher's assistance. Maybe they could think of ways to keep his inside helper on the job so Donato would not feel so alone again. His mother promised to remind him on the way to school the next day that his inside helper was always with him and she would also tell his teacher that Donato was trying to remember that.

- **CONNECTING GOOD FEELINGS WITH USING THE INSIDE HELPER**

Parents and teachers can piggyback on the pleasure children feel when things are going well to notice and underline how the child created that good feeling by listening to her inside helper. Every time she listens to her inside helper, she is making it stronger so that it will always be able to help her make good choices.

Some four-year-old classroom examples of connecting good feelings with inside-helper choices:

When he stepped on Bettina's toe by accident, Freddy stayed with her until she stopped crying. He was largely responsible for calming her by asking her what her favorite color was and also her favorite animal. He then talked about his favorites. His teacher told him how helpful he was and how impressed she was that he understood that Bettina's upset came from something he did even though he wasn't trying to hurt her. He had listened to his inside helper and made a choice to accept responsibility. He tried to fix it and he had succeeded. What a good feeling!

At outside time, Ori, Kevin, and Frankie worked in cooperation to build a snow fort. Before flipping over the bucket, Ori turned to the others and said, "Where should I put this one?" His teacher made sure to say to him that she had noticed that his inside helper reminded him to give his friends a chance to have their ideas included. That choice led to a good game together where they built a super snow fort, bigger than Ori could have done by himself.

It's a momentous step to not only use internal controls but to also get pleasure from doing so. When children experience good feelings from following the advice of their inside helpers, it gives them a base from which they can confront the powerful dilemmas that arise from situations where pleasure may come from unacceptable or forbidden behavior.

- **TALKING ABOUT HOW GOOD IT FEELS TO DO THINGS THAT ARE FUN AND ALSO LEAD TO GOOD FEELINGS**

Parents can help children feel trust in what they say if they first acknowledge honestly that there are lots of different ways to feel pleasure. "Sometimes, it can feel really good to be the boss and push other people around, but that only lasts for a minute until the other children get mad, the teacher stops you, and you don't feel like a good person." The challenge for parents is to be able to describe the more dependable pleasure that comes from doing the fun things in such a way that the child also feels the pleasure of being a nice person. This parental skill will be exercised at each later phase in the child's life, for instance, when talking to schoolchildren about cheating at games or tests, or adolescents about drugs and dangerous sexual activity.

Sarita spent time each night at supper telling her parents and her three-year-old brother all about how she had been in charge of every game at school. She described deciding who could play and how she didn't let another child change the game. Her parents, after talking this through at parent group, began to question these stories in various ways. First, they noted that she seemed to feel very big and strong about bossing other people. When Sarita agreed, they said that could be a very good feeling, but they wondered how other children reacted. Sarita said nothing, but on the following day, she remarked in an offhand voice that her friends Margaret and Lizzie were only playing with each other.

Her parents remarked thoughtfully about how that good bossy feeling didn't seem to last long since other children didn't want to be pushed around. "What were your ideas? Do those ideas make you feel good?" When Sarita told them that she liked her ideas, they were able to reframe the problem by saying that it would help to get more pleasure from the ideas than from bossing others. The pleasure of bossing was spoiling the pleasure of her ideas. "You have two ways of feeling good, and they don't go together. When you're bossy, nobody listens to your ideas." They wondered if they and Sarita could come up with some ways to keep the good feelings that come from her ideas.

Over the next few weeks, Sarita's parents and teachers worked together to monitor her play at home and school and be there to support her being a leader instead of a boss. They took every opportunity to notice and remark on how her inside helper was getting stronger in supporting her "idea pleasure" and curbing her "bossy pleasure." Her inside helper was reminding her to share her own good ideas and also listen to other people's ideas and work together with them. Sarita seemed increasingly relaxed and happy and there was a carryover to home, where she began to play more generously with her little brother.

Research has demonstrated that social relations in preschool predict relationships with younger siblings at home and future relationships throughout life. Children can best learn positive social skills in preschool when they have developed a sturdy inside helper.[56]

Four-year-old Benny's mother sent the following e-mail to his teachers about the shift she observed him making, able to be strong and confident enough to include his little brother Tommy's ideas:

"Last night, Tommy (aged two) initiated another pretend game. He lined up all the kitchen chairs in a row and called it a diesel bus. He chose to drive the bus from what was obviously the back of the bus facing forward toward the passenger seating. Benny noticed and wanted to play too but proceeded to tell Tommy that he was driving the bus the wrong way. I interrupted and told him that was Tommy's idea and that he should let Tommy drive the way he wanted to. After Benny got a chance to be a passenger, he asked Tommy if he could be the driver. Benny then ended up driving the bus exactly the same way Tommy was driving—from the back of the bus and facing the passengers! I thought this was an especially significant moment for Benny because he was able to respect and follow someone else's idea. Up until recently, I had only seen him be very adamant about playing his own ideas."

This thoughtful mom was able to make a minimal intervention to promote the growth of Benny's emotional muscle to get pleasure from cooperating and sharing ideas rather than bossing, a shift that had recently appeared in his preschool class friendships.

- **REACTING PROPORTIONATELY TO MISBEHAVIOR**

Adults can help the child work toward having a kind, firm, and patient inside helper. When parents' reactions and the consequences of the behavior are proportional to the problematic incident, it gives your child a reality perspective on the seriousness of the infraction. This teaches judgment.

When an inside helper is too strict, it makes life miserable for the child, setting up an unrealistic standard of perfection. The child may try to solve that problem by tossing the inside helper outside, dumping the responsibility for standards, guidance, and judgment back on to parents or teachers.[57] It can be tempting for adults to respond by joining the battle, but this just offers the child someone to argue with and feel persecuted by instead of addressing the original situation.

When an inside helper is not strict enough, children feel uncertain and anxious; not knowing what is expected places them in a helpless position, where they may look for leadership to other children instead of identifying with adult values. Too lenient an inside helper may also set up a risk of children being ostracized by their peers as they can't play kindly or follow the rules of a game.

Inigo was surprised and upset to learn on Monday that Freddy's family was soon moving to another state and that he would lose his best friend. He followed Freddy into the bathroom that day and told him that he was going to pee on him. Freddy protested loudly, and a teacher intervened to take Inigo out of the bathroom and then talk seriously with him about his threat.

The following day, Inigo, who generally loved school, mystified his parents by begging to stay home. Eventually, he revealed that he was afraid his teachers would send him to jail for what he had done. His parents and teachers understood that Inigo was punishing himself more harshly than he needed to; they told him that peeing on another child was not acceptable but that he had not actually done it. They reminded him of the difference between a wish and an action. They talked with him about how his plan to pee on Freddy was an angry one and wondered if he and his inside helper could find a better way to tell his friend how angry and sad he was that Freddy would be going away. Inigo decided to write Freddy a letter about it and included a picture of the classroom so Freddy wouldn't forget him.

Sonya's parents talked about how very upset she became whenever one of them reprimanded her even a little bit. "It feels like a federal case! Then we end up having to comfort her and the original problem gets forgotten." Other parents agreed that this sequence often happened with them too. The family consultant suggested that there were two issues involved. One was Sonya's disproportionate reaction, and the other was the importance of following through on the consequences of the original action.

Parents talked about different ways to help their children scale their feelings, and the family consultant recalled hearing the preschool teacher say one day in class, "That's a very big feeling for a small problem." He reminded the parents about the work they had done since toddlerhood to bring too-big feelings down to a manageable "just right" size to think and talk about. This could now be linked for four-year-olds to the inside helper. The group talked about games they could play with their kids, for instance, kicking a ball softly, firmly, or very hard in relation to how far it had to go and talking about the parallel to feelings. "Just as you have to use your leg muscles differently for each kick, your inside helper has strong muscles for big issues, medium ones for medium, and little ones for the little problems."

A sister school to Allen Creek in the Alliance for Psychoanalytic Schools[58] coined an apt phrase used by teachers; at the Hanna Perkins Center they talk about sorries that are "too big, too small, or just right." A "just right" sorry feeling is one that motivates the child to make amends, avoid repeating the offense, feel good and move on as Freddy did when he cheered Bettina up after he hurt her toe. Freddy couldn't undo the pain he had caused, but he had spontaneously found a genuine way to make amends. His teacher noticed and commented on this and underlined how good it made him feel. Grown-ups can teach children to recognize a "just right sorry" by how it helps both people feel better.

The family consultant brought the group back to the second task of making sure that the original infraction is addressed. When the problem was something reparable, addressing it may also fix it. Jaime's dad laughed and said, "Yes, after the crying, we still have to clean up the spilt milk!" It made sense to everyone that the children needed the repeated experience of the natural consequences of their actions. Then they would be able to anticipate and stop themselves before doing something wrong. Their inside helper's reminder to use their stopping muscles would make them feel good.

When we base our standards for children's behavior on the real consequences of their actions, we teach them why we want them to behave in certain ways and not in others. We talked earlier about how three-year-olds can learn to understand emotional cause and effect. The four-year-olds are able to add to that knowledge. They can be taught about the internal mental sequence that starts with a wish or an impulse to do something. Their inside helper then makes a judgment about the likely outcome of the action and assesses how they will feel. Then they can decide whether or not to go ahead with the action. Practicing this sequence, making sure that the pause for judgment is included, becomes the basis for their independent capacity to do the right thing.

Stefan's mother, Janine, told his teacher that Stefan said he was going to paint at school. Janine wanted the teacher to know that there was some background to Stefan's plan. She wasn't sure if he would use the paints properly since he had been in trouble at home. The afternoon before, just when they had been preparing to go to a friend's house, she had been very upset to walk into the family room and find that Stefan had drawn with marker on the wall.

Janine felt like yelling at him, but she had taken a deep breath and just told him how upset she was to see that he had put marker on the wall. She said that it seemed like he hadn't thought beforehand about where the marker really belonged and how he and his mom would feel if he put it in the wrong place. Now they would have to stay home and wash the wall to make it all clean again and wouldn't be able to go on a visit. Stefan protested and ran into the other room. Janine got some towels, a bucket of soapy water, and two sponges, then fetched Stefan, and said they would do the job of fixing his mistake together. Stefan didn't want to, but Janine told him there was not another option. They washed and dried the wall. By the time they had finished and Janine exclaimed over how bright and clean it looked, Stefan smiled with pride. Janine underlined his pleasure, remarking, "It feels so good to make something right again, doesn't it?"

Janine made two additional steps to reinforce the lesson; she noted that it was hard not to be able to visit Stefan's friend that day, but that the time had been used up by needing to clean the wall. And she settled Stefan at the kitchen table with paper and markers while she started supper so that he could practice putting marker in the right place.

At the end of that school day, Stefan's teacher reported that he had not only painted two lovely pictures but had also done an especially good job cleaning his brushes and putting the tops on the paint pots. She had remarked on this to Stefan, and he beamed when he heard her telling his mother about it.

- **LABELING THE ACTION, NOT THE CHILD**

When something goes wrong or your child misbehaves, focus on the behavior or action as unfortunate or unacceptable rather than defining the child herself as bad or naughty. This allows the incident to become a shared learning opportunity instead of an occasion for excessive guilt or shame.

Bad behavior often leads to heated battles and humiliation for children. "Tommy, you're impossible! I've told you a million times not to do that." Four-year-olds have very delicate dignity; they have only just mastered many new capacities and feel vulnerable to losing them. Humiliation and shame are likely to provoke angry defiance or lying and sneaking. So they are not only demeaning to the child, they are also being counterproductive, like most closed-system responses.

Zachary's mother came to a parent group indignant about his refusal to mind her. She had told him to be quiet since she had a headache, and he kept on kicking his ball down the hall. "I don't know what will become of that boy. Sometimes I think he'll just go to the bad." One of the dads protested, "I've always thought he was a pretty good boy. Maybe he sometimes does well and sometimes has bad days." Zachary's mother was thoughtful, then said, "It's true, he isn't one or the other. But on those bad days, I can't stand the things he does."

The family consultant said that was a key to the situation—that we were talking about Zachary's actions, not the boy himself. The question was how to help him see which actions were good or bad. Maybe making him feel he was a bad person made that harder instead of easier because it made him want to fight back.

This is where the idea of the inside helper is useful; his mom could talk to Zachary about how he needs to call upon his inside helper to remind him when his mom has asked him to do something. Talking to his inside helper instead of blaming Zach protects his feelings from being hurt, which makes him more likely to listen. She could say, "Zachary, what happened to your inside helper? Did he fall asleep? Let's wake him up. Yoohoo!" Enlisting Zachary in a pleasurable interaction reinforces the good feeling of listening to his inside helper and doing the right thing, which in turn boosts self-esteem and strengthens the emotional muscle of learning from experience.

- **CREATING EMOTIONALLY SAFE CONDITIONS**
  Children feel safe when adults are competent and maintain routines and expectations even at times of stress. Children cannot be expected to fully regulate their own behavior unless adults calmly manage the situation.

Jim was impossible to control in his day care room, bossy and provoking to adults and other children, often unable to manage his impulses. When the director of the center explained to his caregivers that Jim's daddy was very ill and his mother worked long hours, they understood that Jim's current life was very stressful. This recognition that his bossy behavior reflected an effort to control a scary situation, where Jim was powerless, helped them to be more patient; his caregivers bent over backward to be kind and give him extra chances.

But Jim's behavior just got worse! The Allen Creek consultant to the center pointed out to the staff that part of Jim's anxiety came from life circumstances that even grown-ups were unable to control and protect him from. Perhaps Jim needed to feel that his caregivers had firm standards and expectations that they would enforce to protect him and other children from his wildness. His teachers had not balanced their empathy with his need for safety. The suggestion was to enforce the rules of the classroom consistently and remind Jim of how his inside helper was still there and knew what made him and his friends feel good. After only a week, Jim settled down and continued to make better progress. The caregivers had understood that Jim could be helped to become less bossy to others and more in charge of himself if they felt comfortable with insisting on and supporting him in implementing the clear rules of the classroom.

The director talked to Jim's mother about how his caregivers had been able to help Jim get himself more in charge of feelings and impulses in class. Jim's mother said that he had been telling her that she "wasn't the boss," that he had been defying her at every moment of the day, just when she had less energy and attention available. Together they understood that Jim was probably very scared at home by seeing his mother's worry about dad's illness. The director suggested that his mom explain to Jim that she was indeed very worried about daddy and that it was especially hard since she wasn't in charge of making him better. The doctors were doing all they could. But she was still in charge of the rules and routines of the day at home; she knew that Jim knew what she and Jim needed to do. They worked out a special word signal to remind him to wake up his inside helper so he would feel more in charge.

Just as Jim had calmed down at his day care, his mom reported that things at home soon settled. She and Jim could share their worries about daddy, and enjoy being in charge of what they could each control. As the weeks went by, Jim recovered his happy bounce and his mother was able to enjoy his good functioning.

- **TRUSTING THAT YOUR CHILD CAN DEVELOP AN INSIDE HELPER**

Four-year-olds who have worked on building emotional muscles usually have all the components they need to develop an inside helper. Helping them want to have an inside helper depends on showing them how good it feels and connecting that feeling with experiences of success and effectiveness. But it's also uncomfortable at times to have an inside helper that pushes you to wait or be kind or makes you feel like a bad person. So children need adults to persist and believe in their capacity to have internal controls.

Jane listened carefully to her teacher's reminder about staying in her own space before circle time in the four-year-old class at her school. She nodded and agreed that she would work harder on this task. But only halfway through the story, she was leaning over the next child's lap and wouldn't get off even when that child pushed her and told her to stop. When her teacher came to sit next to her, Jane got even floppier and silly, acting as if she had no idea what her teacher's gentle reminder was about. Since the teacher knew that Jane knew precisely what the expectations for circle time were, the teacher understood that Jane was feeling ashamed and guilty and trying to get the teacher to be the one with the harsh feelings. Rather than argue and escalate the issue, the teacher quietly handed the responsibility back to Jane, reminding Jane that her inside helper knew how to use her stopping muscles to help Jane sit properly for story. The teacher spent the rest of circle time next to Jane, to support her in taking the standards back inside where they belonged. She told her, "I'm here to help you remember that you know how good it feels to sit in your own space at circle time. When you show me you remember all the time, then I will be happy that you can sit next to other kids."

Jane's teacher was handing back to Jane the inside helper that she had tried to put outside. Teachers and parents can work together with children when the adults feel confident that the children will be able to take responsibility for being in charge of their actions.

Davey's parents said they had tried to introduce the idea of an inside helper without success. "He went along with it for about a day, but then he said, 'I don't want to have an inside helper!' so we kind of let it go. Now we don't know what to do when he gets wild and won't mind." One of the other parents laughed and reminded them, "Don't you remember when we learned that you have to introduce new foods nineteen times before kids will even see them as familiar? I guess new concepts may be the same. We have to keep at it." The family consultant noted that having a conscience can sometimes be uncomfortable, so Davey seemed to be opting for the path of least resistance. The challenge for parents is to help kids find the pleasure in having an effective inside helper with consistent standards. Davey's parents said, "Well, back to the drawing board."

• MAINTAINING CONSISTENT EXPECTATIONS

Being consistent in your level of expectation helps to develop the emotional muscle of dependability in the inside helper. If we want children to have a dependable inside helper that they and adults can rely on, we have to make sure that grown-ups are dependable. This means sticking with rules and expectations, not constantly making exceptions or leaving routines undefined.

Parents can examine together what rules they want to have and enforce for themselves and their children. If you want your child never to cross the street on a red light, you have to make sure that you never do. If you want your child not to hit his brother, you have to make sure that you never hit.

REGULATING AGGRESSION

The major challenge to four-year-olds' inside helpers and their parents is aggressive impulses.

Parents can promote this growth by

- **EXPECTING SELF-REGULATION**
Parents struggle with the legacy of their own histories of receiving or inflicting aggression, as well as the societal ambiguities, confusions, and pressures that promote aggression as a solution to problems at all levels. Aggressive impulses in children are generated in response to frustration, disappointment, maltreatment or abuse, and humiliation. Children are tempted to stay in a closed-system world where they can respond to helplessness in the face of these feelings by magically being in charge of everyone and everything. Emotional muscle equips children and parents to turn instead to mastery and competence to meet this challenge.

Research underscores the critical importance of coming to grips with the problem of aggression at this point in development. It is now established that children who interpret ambiguous situations as hostile are more aggressive toward their peers.[59] What makes children see others as potentially hostile is their own aggressive feelings put outside, when they have can't find a competent way to deal with the problem. This is associated with long-term troubles with peers and later conduct disorders.

So we have to find a way for four-year-olds to master and modulate their own angry and hostile feelings, to develop the emotional muscles to contain them, and to turn them into useful signals to have a real impact on their world. When children are failing in this realm, it has profound effects on all their future development.

Henry had apparently random outbursts of anger and meanness in his preschool classroom. His teachers and parents worked together to try to understand what was going on. As they tracked his good and bad days, they realized that he was apparently reacting to times his dad was especially angry and frustrated over not finding a new job after being laid off. Henry's dad was struggling with his own feelings of adequacy to provide for his family and was taking out his feelings of impotence by finding fault with his wife and children. He was sometimes viciously critical and couldn't be satisfied with what anyone did. At the same time, he wanted Henry to succeed and bravely thought about his role in the situation. Feeling like a failure in his family role, Henry's dad had not realized how important he was to his son. The teacher and family consultant helped him see a pathway out of the impasse.

Building on both Henry's and his father's strengths, the family consultant was able to suggest that Henry's dad talk to him about the good feelings of being a grown-up man and how frustrating it sometimes could be not to be able to access all those good feelings when he couldn't do all his daddy work. But it wasn't all or nothing, and they could work together to help each other when frustration felt too big. Henry and his dad agreed to say "too much" when either one's feelings seemed too big.

In a few weeks, Henry's dad told the family consultant about how Henry had courageously stood there when he was ranting about an interview and said, "Daddy, too much!" On another occasion, when Henry was yelling at his mother about wanting to go to the store and buy a model plane right away, his dad said, "Henry, too much," and Henry was able to call upon his internal controls to settle down and make a plan with his mom for an excursion another time.

With the support of teachers, family consultants, and his wife, Henry's father was able to shift a potentially dangerous direction in Henry's development and support Henry's inside helper to modulate his aggressive impulses. He was teaching Henry that losing his temper was not a grown-up thing to do and fostering the muscles of restraint and patience.

- **VALIDATING THE PLEASURE FROM SELF-REGULATION**

A goal of group day care or preschool experience at the four-year-old level is to learn from interactions with other children and gain active capacity to foster and maintain friendships with others. Whether the source is primarily external, as it was for Henry, or internal to the child, aggressive children are unable to take advantage of opportunities for this learning; rather they seek to block other children's goals for the satisfaction of making a powerful impact, however destructive.[60] They are getting good feelings from short-term, closed-system power plays in relationships instead of from the enhanced and enriched opportunities of collaborative, creative interactions.

Corey and Otto had both been quite possessive of space at the sensory table in their four-year-old classroom for the beginning part of the school year, each suspicious that the other would impinge on the space or the toys. Their teachers had worked with them, demonstrating in practice how much more interesting activities became when there was cooperation. One day in November, when the sensory table had only some empty bottles in it, Corey and Otto together developed an elaborate idea to see how many bottles of water it would take to fill the whole thing to within an inch of the top. After spending a long time carefully filling it up, they decided it was a factory making carbonated water. Their teachers underscored how much fun they had working together and trusting each other's ideas. Both boys beamed and threw their arms over each other's shoulders when the teacher described their "factory" to some other children.

Helped by their teachers, Corey and Otto were choosing to set aside the pleasure of hostile possessiveness for the pleasure of a richer, more creative, cooperative play experience. They were developing the emotional muscle not only to choose the real open-system pleasure, but the sturdiness needed to risk losing out by letting the other into the game.

• SUPPORTING ASSERTION

A major way to regulate aggression is to be assertive instead. We have talked throughout the book about the confusion that persists for many adults between the two. There is also a weighty social tradition that equates aggression with masculinity, and correspondingly expects girls to be passive. For four-year-olds, who are actively defining their social identities and self-images, these issues take on especial urgency.

Ned's dad was upset in parent group as he described his brother's derogatory remarks about Ned. The uncle had said that he thought Ned was a sissy since he was a quiet boy, whose favorite activity was painting and drawing. The other parents protested, saying this was a ridiculous stereotype. "If anything," one mom said, "I see Ned as a very passionate person. He is so invested in his creativity." The family consultant agreed, "Assertion takes many forms and it doesn't have to be loud. Focus, commitment, and practicing are all strong ways people of any age assert their desires and needs. Both boys and girls need support for assertion because it leads to better solutions than aggression."

DEVELOPING A GROUP CONSCIENCE

Children's powerful wish to feel good with other children fosters the creation of a shared internal moral compass.

Parents can promote this growth by

- **REMINDING CHILDREN THAT THEY ARE MEMBERS OF A GROUP**

By four, children have learned at home and in preschool how to manage their own feelings in the context of the group. They have learned to let another child finish a turn and developed the emotional muscle to wait or find a substitute. They have learned to share, to have the strength to assert their wishes in the group when appropriate or put aside their own wishes for the pleasure of cooperation, group projects, and play. These demands are a stretch, and the children have been building muscle to manage their own wishes in the context of social realities. They refer to other children as friends and care about their opinions and feelings. The shared intentionality we saw babies and toddlers experiencing as they clearly understood the purpose of parents' actions expands at this age to include "collective intentionality." [61] Four-year-olds can encompass the idea of a group goal and group norms. They begin to develop what we have called a group conscience.

Josie resisted her teachers' reminders to participate in cleanup in the classroom, preferring usually to wander or watch what others were doing. One day her teacher, reflecting on the morning in conversation at snack time, remarked on how it made all the other children do extra work when any one child didn't do her share. Josie looked thoughtful. At cleanup time the next day, as Josie hesitated, about to go into her usual routine of avoiding the job, her teacher said, "Everyone feels good and likes each other when everyone works together." Josie joined the group picking up Legos and worked happily until the room was tidy.

The teacher was able to enlist Josie's inside helper with an appeal to Josie's wish to be liked by her peers and feel a constructive member of the group. In this instance, she could use a four-year-old's new awareness of the shared values and goals of the group to reengage Josie in helpful behavior.

- **TEACHING FLEXIBLE ADAPTATION TO DIFFERENT GROUP NORMS**

Sometimes, a child's disruptive behavior in the classroom reflects a gulf between the norms at home and the rules at school. This creates confusion and a potential loyalty conflict for the child. However, it is also an opportunity for the child to stretch, to develop the muscle to adapt his behavior appropriately to different contexts.

Davey's parents dealt with his anxious excitement at home by telling him to run ten laps around the house. When he began to run around the classroom for no apparent reason, his teachers told him he was making it scary for his friends and that there was a school rule about no running in the classroom. They asked him why he was running. "I always run at home. That's what I do when I get too excited," Davey protested. His teacher said, "You can run outside here as much as you want at recess, but we have to keep the classroom safe for everyone. We'll find other ways for you to deal with excited feelings. The rule at school is different from at home, and that's all right. Everyone's house is different, but at school, everyone follows the same rules."

Alerted by this incident, the teachers talked with all the kids about the many different ways they did things at different places. Children talked about what their skating teachers required and how things were at grandma's house. The teachers saw this as a chance to stretch the children's new capacities to adapt and enjoy adhering to helpful group norms in various situations.

- **SUPPORTING THE AUTONOMY OF THE INSIDE HELPER IN THE CONTEXT OF PEER PRESSURE**

Four-year-olds also have the new challenge of holding on to their recently formed inside helper in the social context of other children who are behaving in ways that are clearly bad. One or two children in a classroom may suddenly become aggressive or overexcited. This can quickly infect the other children, who seem to jettison their inside helpers and become as out of control as the instigators.

Teachers in a class of young four-year-olds described to their consultant how contagious overexcitement became in their classroom. First they discussed various classroom structures and routines that might help, for instance, alternating active and quiet activities, reducing the amount of stimulation from toys and objects in the room, focusing on transitions as learning experiences with their own routines, and practicing ways to calm down both bodies and feelings. Then the consultant suggested that teachers talk with the children about their inside helpers and how they can call upon them to hold on to doing things the right way when others may have forgotten. They can even help wake up their friends' inside helpers by reminding them when excitement is getting too high.

Another form of peer pressure comes from children's common confusion of "like" and "being like." Most children assume that if they like someone, they should be like them. If George's best friend Johnny runs around in the classroom instead of coming to circle, George may feel he is demonstrating his love for Johnny by being just like him, doing the same behavior. The distinction can be emphasized at home and at school, with adults adding the idea that having a strong inside helper to manage their bodies and feelings is more grown-up and that other children will like them for this, appreciating that each person is himself.

Noah, who had been an active player in ball games and sandbox construction at the beginning of the school year, began to hang back, looking sad at outside time, when the other boys were playing a wild chasing game about dragons and pirates. His teacher asked him what he thought of that game. Noah said, "I don't like that game, because there is killing. But I miss my friends. I don't like it when my friends are saying scary words." His teacher told him that she thought he was saying something very important about how friends can play together in ways that are fun for everyone and that they should all talk about it together.

At circle time the teacher introduced a discussion about the kinds of games that make children uncomfortable and ones that make everyone feel good. Various children piped up with ideas. Jill said, "I like to be a superhero and do *everything*!" Pietro interrupted her to say, "Yeah, but it's pretend, remember?" The teacher agreed how important it was to keep the pretend part in mind during games and asked the children how they could do that. Noah bravely said, "I sometimes don't like the words about killing and hurting." The teacher agreed that the children now understood that words stand for something real, so scary words make it harder to remember when something is pretend. She encouraged the children to tell each other if a game felt scary so that their friends could change it. She reminded the children to ask a teacher if they needed help to find ways to make a game fun again.

Noah was wondering what to do. He wanted to be like everyone else, thinking that otherwise they wouldn't like him, but he also wanted to retain his own values, to rely on his own conscience within the context of wanting so much to feel part of a group. We all need strength to withstand the power of a group at times. This issue will follow the child through to adulthood. Because adults understand the potential distress and dangers associated with cliques, gangs, group excesses, and peer pressure to conform to stupid or risky norms, it is an important responsibility for parents and teachers to address this conflict explicitly in the early years.

Adults stand for reality and know what is right and wrong behavior at home and in school. It helps children to know clearly what is acceptable, strong and appropriate for a four-year-old. Children need to have feedback when they are operating with a strong inside helper, as well as when they seem to have kicked out their conscience and are ruining their own fun and that of others. It isn't helpful to make excuses for four-year-olds. We want our children to have sturdy inside helpers and strong emotional muscles to help them make the serious choices that come in later childhood and adolescence.

USING WORRIES TO INITIATE MASTERY

Just-right-size worries are spurs to problem solving.

Four-year-olds are strong and capable enough to bear a certain degree of worry. This signal can start them on the path to creative problem solving and mastery. Experiencing oneself as brave and competent enhances self-esteem and builds a sturdy self-image as someone who can manage anxiety.

Parents can promote this growth by

- **USING JUDGMENT TO PROTECT CHILDREN FROM OVERWHELMING ANXIETY AND TOLERATE MANAGEABLE WORRIES**
  Parents and teachers are quick to reassure younger children and correct any misinformation that might be contributing to distress. This remains a critical task, but with four-year-olds, it demands more complex judgment.

Felipe knew about tornadoes and tornado warnings because he lived in Michigan. Felipe's grandmother lived in Florida. When he heard that there was going to be a hurricane there, he was worried if she would be safe. He told his teacher he had decided to make a picture story for her and send it to her. He divided his paper in two sections and asked the teacher to label them Day 1 and Day 2.

In the Day 1 half, Felipe scribbled black and blue crayon everywhere and asked the teacher to write his words on it: "It was in Florida that the big tornado came and the ocean was scared and the fish knew the tornado would be here soon, so it swam deep in the water where it was safe."

In the Day 2 half, Felipe drew some blue water with a big smiley whale in it and the sun up in the blue sky. His words were, "The tornado had gone and the sun shone bravely over the ocean of Florida, and the fishies came out once again. The whales did too. They loved happily ever after."

Felipe was able to take his own worries about tornadoes and his grandmother's safety in the hurricane and use them as triggers for constructive mastery. In his story, he both expressed the fears and resolved them, with the help of his knowledge and an understanding teacher, who could see that his level of worry was manageable.

The situation was harder for Keith, a boy who had many medical interventions and emergencies throughout his earliest childhood. When his health stabilized, he started preschool at four but was too anxious to let his mother leave the classroom even for a few minutes. Ordinary developmental achievements, like holding on to a mental image of his mother, trusting in her return, having the emotional muscles to bear missing her, enjoying himself on his own, and relying on other grown-ups like the teachers had been delayed for Keith. But he also had all the cognitive and physical capacities of other four-year-olds; these could be enlisted to try to help him change his overwhelming states of anxiety into useful signals to spur problem solving.

After a few months of his mother staying in the classroom, Keith's parents, teachers, and family consultants decided that it was time to start helping him stretch to gradually push forward to develop the emotional muscles he would need to master enjoying school on his own. The initial plan was for him to stay in the classroom while his mother went to the hall for five minutes. Keith's parents talked to him about their confidence that even though his feelings were so big, they knew those feelings wouldn't make anything bad happen and that he would be able to manage eventually. The first time, Keith melted down, enraged, hurling himself to the floor. His teacher had to hold him tightly to keep him safe. The next time he was able to sit on the floor between her legs, and a few days later, he sat next to her on the floor.

The classroom team had identified the vicious cycle of helplessness, panic, and overwhelming rage that made Keith feel helpless again. The family consultant also said that Keith was old enough to realize that none of his classmates were scared the way he was. They didn't need their mommies there, and he probably felt humiliated by his anxiety. With the help of this insight, the teachers decided to introduce a general class discussion about worries, with the idea of making it clear to all the children that everyone has worries and finds ways to cope with them.

In circle time, when teachers introduced the idea of what people are scared about or worry about, the children eagerly shared worries—about the dark, strange dogs, being alone, about their parents, including the idea that their parents might die. The teachers shared some worries of their own, like that they might get a flat tire on the car or forget to buy bread. Discussion then spontaneously turned to the fact that everyone, young and old, had worries and that worries can be useful as a signal to do something.

All the children came up with ideas about what to do if they are worried. Bettina said she used to worry that she wouldn't get a turn on the bikes, but now she knows the teachers will make sure everyone gets a turn, so she doesn't worry any more. Danny turned to the child next to him who had mentioned being afraid of the dark and suggested that a person could use a flashlight. Another child said he still has a little worry about his mom going away, but he now asks her where she is going and when she will be back, and that helps.

Keith listened to all this with wide eyes but didn't say anything. A few days later the topic came up again in circle time, and Keith volunteered that he had a big worry about his mom leaving the classroom. The other children said that they could see he was getting stronger, that he can now walk away from her and have fun with them. Keith beamed at this endorsement from his classmates. He no longer seemed ashamed of himself. As the days went by, Keith was increasingly able to let his mother sit by the classroom door or on the bench at the side of the playground. Paul exclaimed to Keith in the playground one day, "Look, your mom is way over there and you're smiling!"

Putting these concepts into words helps all four-year-olds see the ways they are similar to each other even as they are learning how they are different and individual. These are fundamental to genuine empathy, where children can enter into another's feelings, without losing the distinction between themselves and others.

Hal noticed Bettina and her teacher inside the gazebo in the playground one day. He went in to see why Bettina looked so sad. Bettina explained how much she wanted to score in soccer and win. Hal, the best soccer player in the class, listened carefully; when she finished, he said, "Well, soccer does take a lot of practice." When Bettina further explained that she had practiced a lot, he suggested they be on a team together. She happily reentered the game with Hal as her teammate.

Hal was demonstrating the integration and use of many different emotional muscles as he expressed concern for his friend and understood that her feelings and situation were different from his own, appreciating his own skill without feeling he had to put down a less skillful child to feel good, thought about what was needed, and offered a constructive solution, enlisting his experience, imagination, and feelings to help Bettina with her worry. Hal used her worry as a signal to generate solutions he could offer a friend.

Keith did something similar some months later when, listening to a story in which one character "kept another character company," he defined the meaning of the term by saying, "It's when you sit by somebody so they won't get lonely."

LIVING IN THE REAL WORLD

The richness of life resides in the
full spectrum of reality.

Parents are the representatives, the interpreters, and the filters for reality throughout childhood. Many people talk about reality as if it only means something negative. There are hard things in the world, but reality is also the source of all our pleasures and opportunities. In the process of protecting children from being overwhelmed by harsh realities, we may forget to convey the joys.

Parents can promote this growth by

- **SHARING THE PLEASURES AND OPPORTUNITIES OF REALITY**
  In a lunchtime discussion at a large company, a mom described Mary startling her by saying she never wants to grow up and go to work. "You and Daddy always say you wish you had a day off." The mom said Mary made her realize that they never did talk about all the satisfactions of their jobs and how good they felt when they had worked hard and completed a project. All Mary ever saw was them tired and complaining at the end of the day. Other parents agreed that their kids were probably seeing the same thing. "Why would anyone want to grow up if it's a miserable prospect?" said a dad. The Allen Creek family consultant leading the discussion said this was important since their four-year-olds were forming their ideas about reality based on what they saw. If we want them to aspire to gaining skills and joining the world, we have to let them know how good it can be.

- **FACING THE DIFFICULT ASPECTS OF THE WORLD BRAVELY**
  Life is filled with difficulties, large and small. There are many real situations that impinge on children. Parents have the task of deciding how to talk about them. Making judgments about what to tell your child is fairly straightforward when they are very little. By four, however, they are capable of absorbing a lot of knowledge and their questions are deep and wide-ranging. They are astute in judging when a grown-up is evasive or uncomfortable, which challenges parents to explain difficult things honestly without overwhelming a still young child. Yet we want children to have a sound basis for making judgments and a fund of knowledge to use.

  If parents are afraid of the hard things in life, their children cannot develop the emotional muscle to stand up to ordinary and extraordinary challenges. This is an aspect of resilience that has lifelong importance and can make the difference between later success and failure or even affect survival in extreme circumstances.[62]

  Dave, the dad who struggled over his inability to answer his son Joey's question at bedtime, met individually with the family consultant to discuss the situation further because he was uncertain about whether it was all right to bring up the content in the parent group. He then related that what Joey had asked about was a child in a different class in the school, a girl with a leg brace. Joey had overheard some parents talking in the hall about CP. He wanted to know what that was. The question was outside Dave's own knowledge base and also touched off memories of his own childhood medical problems. Dave said he had no idea how to talk to a four-year-old about disabilities—wouldn't it just scare him? Would it make him focus on that child and upset her?

The family consultant acknowledged Dave's intuition that there were important learning opportunities for Joey and for him and his wife in this situation, which he wouldn't want to miss. They agreed to take back any useful insights to the parent group as a whole. They reiterated that it took emotional muscle for Dave to admit he didn't know an answer but that this gave Joey permission to feel it was okay for him to be a four-year-old who didn't know everything either. Otherwise, Joey might pressure himself unrealistically and walk around feeling like a constant failure. Dave's admission encouraged Joey's exploring, curious attitude, and the growth of muscle to tolerate uncertainty. Dave's active plan to work with Joey to find the answers to his questions sent a clear message that ignorance was not a failure, but rather a spur to active learning about how to find things out.

Dave planned to enlist Joey as a partner in the search. The first step was to find out what Joey's ideas were. Dave took the time to have several conversations with him. It turned out that Joey had a number of theories and ideas that had spurred his anxious, persistent questioning. Was CP catching? Could Joey get it? Was it a punishment for being naughty? CP meant "see pee" to Joey—did she pee in her bed or her pants? Did she play with herself the way he sometimes did? Clearly, CP was very loaded for Joey with his own age-linked preoccupations. After clarifying the issues and reassuring Joey that CP was not contagious and that no one got it by being bad, Dave remarked that seeing the girl with the brace made him sad too but that she was going to school and having fun. So how about if they learned together a bit more about CP, and then they wouldn't feel so worried or sad?

Dave asked Joey how he thought they could find out more. Joey said, "Uncle George is a dentist, and that's like a doctor, so we could ask him." Dave praised Joey for coming up with the idea of asking an expert, just like Uncle George always came to Dave with car questions because that was something he knew all about. They also talked about looking things up on the computer; Joey had seen his mom and dad do that before. By this time, Joey no longer seemed worried. He told his dad that he wanted to go build his speedway and play with his cars and that Dave could look things up and tell him what he learned.

Dave did pursue more answers by talking to the teacher in the other class, who also referred him to the girl's parents. Teacher and parents told him the simple words they had used to explain cerebral palsy to three- and four-year-olds. Dave was able to go back to Joey and report definitively that doctors knew that CP was not catching, that no one got it because they played with themselves or were naughty, and that the little girl was doing very well, having fun, learning, and doing all her school things even though one of her legs was too weak to work well without a brace to help.

Even more importantly for this discussion, he used the opportunity to share with Joey how good it felt to learn. Breaking the issue down into steps, Dave said that the first step is always a question, then thinking about what you know already, and being strong enough to say you don't know it all, and then finding other people and sources to ask about it.

When Dave brought the story of his search for knowledge back to the parent group, he said that he now felt closer to Joey even as Joey seemed more mature than before. Both father and son had increased their emotional muscles for tolerating uncertainty, frustration, and anxiety and had used their minds to solve the problem. Joey had noticed a real physical difference. If Dave had continued to reject his curiosity and worry, Joey would have gotten the message that hard realities have to be denied and can't be shared or worked on.

Sometimes, big events in the world burst upon everyone's awareness, like natural disasters or political cataclysms. Children are easily overwhelmed, especially when they see the grown-ups anxious or uncertain about what will happen. We have worked with families after catastrophes, from the Challenger explosion through the Atlanta and Oklahoma City bombings, to 9/11, Hurricane Katrina, the Pacific tsunami, the Haiti earthquake, and more. While each crisis has its own characteristics, there are common responses that help parents and children deal constructively with the worries, sadness, and helplessness.

Only days after the event, parents gathered for a group meeting, all preoccupied with 9/11 and uncertain how to talk to their preschoolers about the many difficult issues involved. One mother said she didn't usually watch much television but had found herself glued to the set.

Another remarked ruefully, "I think I feel as if learning as much as possible is like doing something. The more knowledge I have, the less helpless I feel." The family consultant agreed that this was a constructive response for grown-ups and pointed the way to how to help the children. She reminded the parents that they had often talked together about the importance of engaging with feelings and issues rather than avoiding them. Children can only develop resiliency and sturdiness of mind and heart by understanding, integrating, and mastering the realities of life around them. We can support those processes by presenting reality to children in manageable bits. Too much is overwhelming, leading to shutdown or anxious outbursts rather than learning and growth.

Sam's dad said, "Maybe it's connected. The past few days, he's been running around the house, jumping out at people, trying to surprise them and scare them. Maybe he's playing out how shocked we all were!" Other parents chimed in with anecdotes of unusual behaviors: "I haven't seen Sonya take her blankie all over the house since she was two." "Steven builds so much with blocks that I am only now realizing that he has exclusively been building towers for three days and knocking them down over again and again."

As the group talked, the family consultant asked if they had all been watching television as the first mom had described. Everyone agreed they had kept the TV on most of the time. The family consultant noted that four-year-olds are still working on concepts like distance. The television images come straight into their own houses, and they don't have a firm sense of whether the events are happening far away or in their own town. And they don't easily distinguish between reality and make-believe, especially if both come indiscriminately through the television. These combine to make television problematic for small children. The family consultant suggested a simple way to help calm down children and parents alike—turn off the television. If parents really need to find out what is happening when the children are around, they could try listening only to the radio. Children find radio much more manageable because it's less intrusive, but news overheard and not discussed or explained, for instance heard while riding in the car, can also be frightening.

Georgina's mother said, "Georgina keeps asking me questions about everything! Not that she isn't usually pretty curious, but she's been bombarding me with questions all day. Could that be connected?" Another mom asked if Georgina was worrying about the Trade Center disaster or something else. The family consultant agreed that was an important distinction to try to make, that the only way to know was to listen carefully to the questions to find out where the confusions are and what they're about. But if they all seem to do with people missing or getting hurt or things getting broken, then she probably needs her parents to clarify that she is safe and so is everyone around her in terms that are matched to her capacity to understand. It helps children to have their parents tell them explicitly that they know what to do to keep them safe, like going to the basement during a tornado warning.

Stephanie's dad said, "Stephanie asked me the biggest, hardest question of all—why did those guys do such a bad thing? I think I fudged the answer, just saying I didn't know, because I was really stumped. And I didn't think my four-year-old needed to hear about geopolitical issues!" The parents discussed this part for a long time, expanding the issue to include all the bad things that people do. "I don't want to tell my son about crime and murder and stealing. That's too much for a little kid. Can't he stay little and innocent for a while longer?" "But we can't pretend those things don't exist," said another parent. "If we're telling our children the truth and helping them digest what's real in the world, we can't block out the darker side of things altogether."

Parents and family consultants agreed that these were big philosophical issues that stump grown-ups too and that there wouldn't be an easy answer to offer the children. That didn't mean, however, that we had nothing to say. One possibility was to take the opportunity to reinforce the idea that adults don't have all the answers, but seek to find out what they can. Another useful aspect could be to talk about what we do know, which is that some people are very angry about certain things, but instead of using their anger to help them find a solution to the problem, they only use it to destroy and hurt others. This is why it matters to learn to use feelings as signals for thinking problems through and then creating good solutions.

Everyone also noted that feelings of security come from feeling capable; the definition of *trauma* is "feeling helpless." Talking about what people are doing to help each other helps children master the big feelings around these events. There is the work of firefighters and police officers; there are the people who drive diggers and trucks and construction people who make buildings safe and strong again; there are moms and dads who collect food and clothing for the people who need it. Children can work too, selling lemonade and collecting cans to raise money for the helpers. All these people teach us how much we can do to make things safe and good again.

After the cataclysmic earthquake in Haiti, Will went to his children's atlas and looked for the page with a map of where earthquakes happen. He searched to see if there were any earthquakes where he lived, where his daddy worked, and where his grandparents lived. He checked the information with his father. Reassured, he then opened his atlas again and found the Haitian flag. Setting the book open to that page on the floor, he enlisted his little sister to make a caravan of toy trucks and cars to transport food and supplies to Haiti. Will was using his curiosity and knowledge to quell his worry and then to find something active to do in the idea of helping. That evening, he asked his mother if he could bring cans of food to school, where they were collecting supplies to send in aid.

Money and economic conditions constitute another aspect of reality that adults rarely share with children. But we know that even very young children pick up their parents' feelings and thus can be profoundly affected by changes or threats to the family's situation.

Dorothy's dad Leon said that he had something to discuss in the group. Every day when he went to work, people around him were being laid off, and he was getting very worried that the economic situation was soon going to affect him. He and his wife talked about it a lot, at night after the kids were in bed, but he thought Dorothy was probably picking up on the tension whenever he came home and his wife and kids asked about his day. How could he shield his kids from these grown-up worries about money and security? Or did saying nothing when there was tension give the wrong message? "Maybe I can just tell her that I have been having some difficulties at work, and that's why I'm grumpy. Then she won't think it's her fault."

The other parents appreciated Leon's dilemma and shared their current experience of job instability and economic uncertainty. Another dad noted, "It does seem important to let her know that you're not mad or upset at her. We've heard lots of examples of kids taking it all on themselves and assuming they're at fault." One mom said, "Yes, and if you don't address it, Dorothy will get the idea that it is a taboo subject. It seems as if kids ought to learn both about money itself and that it's okay to discuss it. The trick is to think of how to explain it for a four-year-old! I can't understand economics!"

"Maybe we're wrong when we try to shield them too much," said Jennifer's mother. "Shouldn't they learn by this age that all the things they take for granted come from somewhere? I mean the house and the electricity for the lights and the heat, the food and the clothes? We want them to feel secure, but I guess I'm groping toward an idea of helping them understand that we work for those things. They don't just appear. It's why work is important and why we leave them to go to work."

The family consultant agreed that Jennifer's mom was helping construct a concrete and straightforward story about work and money that would make sense to children. The language can be simple: Grown-ups have gone to school to learn what they need to know to get jobs. Jobs pay them money for their work, and that money is used for all the things families need to be healthy and comfortable. If there is money left over after paying for a house, food, and clothes, families can decide to save some and use some for extra things like vacations, toys, gifts, and so forth.

A dad said, "That sounds good and it's easy to imagine saying all that to my four-year-old. The harder part is when that structure feels threatened. Then I guess we would have to say 'sometimes there is less work or the job stops, and then moms and dads have to figure out what we absolutely need and what we will have to wait for until there is more money coming in.'"

Dave chimed in, "That's where that other idea comes in, telling your child that you know how to find out what a solution might be even if you don't have it yet. That's the point where you talk about waiting for work to start again or looking for another job or that grown-ups can go back to school to learn new skills, so the whole thing isn't completely uncertain."

A mom noted, "I'm still thinking about you and your wife being worried because, of course, you are, and Dorothy is bound to pick up on that no matter what you tell her." Leon answered, "It's funny, though, that we are talking about how to explain to four-year-olds about hard times and scary grown-up stuff, but describing that real sequence of going to school, learning skills, getting a job, paying for necessities has actually calmed me down too. I feel challenged and the issues haven't gone away, but I'm not so tense and anxious about it."

Leon went on to say, "Of course Dorothy is pretty smart, and she tends to answer with 'Yes, but . . . ' kinds of questions. I can almost hear her, 'Yes, but, Daddy, what if you don't find more work?' So I'll tell her about savings and why we and the government set aside money for just those times when there may not be enough work. 'Yes, but, Daddy, what if you use up all your savings?' That would be a tough one, but then I'd talk about going back to school. And how we as a family would decide together what we can do without, what substitutes we can find, and about waiting until we can have extras again in the future. I can talk about working on my old car to help it go for another year instead of buying a new one. I can talk about getting out my old woodworking tools and making some toys for her and her brother."

Then Leon looked around and said, "Of course the late-night kind of thought is what if it turns out to be the worst-case scenario, with the job and the savings gone?" Jennifer's mom said, "Dorothy may herself have the answer to that one better than you even realize. The other day, at Jake's birthday party, the kids had all just gotten their pieces of cake, and Jake's fell on the floor. The dog immediately bounded over and ate it. Of course Jake was about to cry, but Dorothy said, 'Jake, you can have some of my cake.' My granddad lived through the Great Depression, and he told me about how everyone helped each other out. Neighbors and relatives and friends make sure that families can manage. Dorothy's already learned that and there are plenty of grown-up Dorothys. You would never be alone and Dorothy would not have to manage more than she is old enough for."

By the time most children turn four, they are comfortable with the idea of today, yesterday, and tomorrow and begin to understand the larger dimension of time. Their keen attention to similarities and differences has sharpened their interest in grown-ups and change. They enjoy comparing themselves favorably to babies and toddlers and wish to be able to do what adults can. This convergence of developmental advances brings them up against some complex and difficult ideas, like growth, aging, and death, and they wonder and worry about these things. Many children have also experienced actual events by this age, like the illness or death of a grandparent, with its attendant worries for parents or the death of a pet. They may also have been exposed to media stories about disasters, wars, killings, the death of famous people, and more. Although less frequent in Western countries, many children by four have gone through the death of a sibling or parent.

Death is an inevitable part of life, and there are many philosophical and religious ideas that attempt to make sense of this reality and encompass the related anxieties. Most grown-ups carry inside many of the fears and confusions about death that four-year-olds say out loud. "Will it really happen to me? Is it a punishment for being bad? What can I do so I won't die? Can my wishes and feelings kill? If so, how can I protect the people I love from my killing wishes? Can other people's wishes kill me? How can I avoid that? If I'm sad, will it ever end?"

At Allen Creek Preschool, starting with the nature walks and gardening that are part of each toddler and early preschool classroom's curriculum, death is talked about as a natural part of the life cycle. This is continued in the four-year-old class with the addition of the idea of a "full life." Each plant and animal usually has a full life—when we see a brown leaf on the ground in the autumn, we can talk about how it was first a little curled-up bud on the tree, then a tiny leaf, then grew larger and used the sunlight to feed the whole tree, then turned yellow and brown, then dried and fell to the ground, there to dissolve and become part of the soil. The leaf has been through its whole, full life. Teachers talk about pets, how they each have a different full life. This usually leads to children bringing stories of their pets; they have sad and loving memories of the pets that have died.

Josie brought a photo of her hamster and laughed as she told how he used to wake them all up at night, making squeaks on his exercise wheel. Her teachers talked about the hamster's full and enjoyable life and about how long most people's full lives are. They go through preschool and kindergarten, first grade, second grade, etc., middle school, high school, college, then work, and so forth. When teachers and parents spell out all the stages and ages, children concretely get the idea of a very long time, which they find reassuring.

At circle time, Kyle mentioned that his grandfather was in the hospital and that his mom was crying because she is afraid his grandpa will die. Kyle said he was worried and sad too because he and his grandpa used to do fun things like going to the coffee shop for hot chocolate and cookies. Then Kyle said thoughtfully, "He's very old and he's had a full life. He's gone to the coffee shop lots and lots of times." Lucy, another four-year-old, said, "Did you tell your mom that? It might help her not be so sad."

- **HELPING YOUR CHILD DISTINGUISH BETWEEN "INSIDE THE HEAD" EVENTS AND OUTSIDE REALITY**

The capacity to make this crucial distinction arises in brain development around the age of four. It builds on earlier developments, fostered by parents' work on putting feelings into words, establishing who is in charge of what, as we saw in the toddler chapters, and continuing work on the difference between real and pretend. Teaching your child about various mental contents makes sense of her experience, contributing to her emotional muscle of regulating feelings and impulses in an open-system way.

Dreams: Four-year-olds become very interested in their dreams. They can recall and recount them; their nightmares can be vivid and very frightening. Four-year-olds want to know what dreams are and where they come from.

Natasha's dad told the parent group that he was puzzled by her asking him in the morning to tell her his dreams. What should he do? He doesn't usually remember them, and if he does, they are often confusing or inappropriate to tell his little girl. After everyone laughed and agreed about this, the family consultant noted that dreams are usually the brain's way of processing leftover things from the day, consolidating new ideas or experiences and dealing with unfinished business or wishes. Given how much four-year-olds are taking in and experiencing, they have a lot to process. Perhaps Natasha's question about her daddy's dreams was her way of asking about her own. Are they real? Is she the only one who has these nighttime experiences? What will happen from them?

Natasha's questions are an opportunity to help her learn to distinguish between what goes on in her mind and what is real outside. Her dad could tell Natasha that everyone has dreams as a way for their minds to practice feelings and wishes, to figure out what can be done now, done when you're older, or never done because no one can do that! Dreams aren't real, but they are like stories we can talk about or share.

The next time, Natasha's dad told the group she seemed very relieved to hear that everyone has dreams. She then told him she dreamed her favorite doll got in the family car and drove away, never coming back. He said to her that it was only a dream, about the worry that someone she loves might go away and never come back; that wasn't real, it didn't really happen, and the dream won't make anything happen.

Stanley's mother described how he was too scared to go to sleep at night. He had been to a birthday party where, unbeknownst beforehand to his mom, they had shown a video of *The Wizard of Oz*. He was now convinced that the witch would come to get him when he slept. All her explanations that it was just a movie and not real did not seem to help and she was at her wit's end to know how to help him.

After some discussion of the unsuitability for preschoolers of most films labeled as For Children, the group turned to trying to figure out a different approach to Stanley's persistent worry. The family consultant suggested that they think together about how to use Stanley's new four-year-old capacities to help him make sense of his own experience and of the movie. If he could master the ideas involved, he might be able to master his feelings. As the group discussed the film in more detail, they realized that it is a story about a dream. Dorothy puts the people, feelings, and worries from her real life into a dream story: The mean librarian who dislikes her dog is made into a witch; the friendly farm hands are her faithful companions in adventure, and so forth.

The next time in parent group, Stanley's mother described his expression of wonder and relief when she talked with him about Dorothy's dream in the movie. "Oh," Stanley said, "now I see how angry she was at that mean lady and how scary the storm was. She made a big dream story about it all." After that conversation he seemed to have no further trouble going to sleep. Stanley's mother talked about how impressed she was that her little boy could take in her helpful explanation and solve an internal problem for himself—"I guess he's not actually that little anymore if he can use his head like that!" The family consultant added that it was her help that fostered Stanley's growth to a new level of emotional muscle, tolerating his own worry and using it as a signal to enlist his intellect.

Emotional Problems: As we saw with Stanley, four-year-olds often develop fears. They may also slide back or regress to behaviors that they had mastered earlier, struggling with toileting, having eating or sleeping difficulties, temper tantrums, being aggressive with siblings, peers, or parents, and so forth. There can be many different causes for these regressions, and it may take some sorting out. But one major contributor can be a child's holding on to the belief that his thoughts, feelings, and wishes are equivalent to real actions, that wishing can or does make it so. Even while they are busy developing the intellectual capacity to differentiate real and pretend, their realistic perception of their relative smallness and powerlessness in the world leads them to *feel* reluctant about setting aside their belief in the power of their wishes and feelings.

On the one hand, they would love to be able to get rid of the pesky little brother or the mother they feel competitive with, but on the other, they feel horrible and terrified that the wish might come true. This dilemma is especially powerful in relation to angry wishes. Some children try to solve the problem by pushing it out or sideways. Instead of saying "I wish you were dead," they may say "I'm scared of going to bed."

After Stanley's worries had led to discussing this tendency to put worries into dreams or other problems Dionne's mother, Eileen, described how her daughter had begun insisting that she lie down next to her so Dionne could go to sleep. "She hasn't done this since she was two. I sure don't want to go back to that."

Eileen asked Dionne if she were scared of something. Dionne said with great conviction, "There's a monster under my bed, and he's out to get me." Eileen told her she knew there was no monster in her room but that the creature Dionne had made up sounded very angry with her. "Yes," said Dionne "it hates me." Eileen, thinking back to the parent group discussion, said, "The monster is pretend, but the angry feelings are real, and we can always talk about angry feelings." She went on to say that everyone has angry feelings, even nice little girls like Dionne, and they may get scared if they think that their angry wishes could come true. "Anger is an inside feeling. It doesn't make wishes come true. It's just a signal that there is something you don't like or something you want that you can't get. We can talk about it."

Dionne threw herself into her mother's arms and said, "Sometimes I get so mad that I feel real bad, and I'm afraid you will send me away." After much reassurance and talk about other ways to address the things that made Dionne mad, Dionne went off to bed. Her mother heard her saying to herself, "I'll tell that monster that mad is just a feeling, and it can't hurt me or anyone else."

Feeling States: The emotional muscles needed to turn feeling states into internal signals have been worked on and exercised since toddlerhood, but really knowing the difference is a new and still precarious achievement for four-year-olds. When they feel very frustrated or helpless or inadequate, they can easily revert to believing that their intense feelings can and should make things happen.

Norman had been playing with the big digger, one of his favorite toys. After a while, he moved to the slide, and Tayshaun began using the digger in the sandbox. Norman ran back and tried to grab it away. The boys began pushing and shoving, battling over the toy. Their teacher intervened right away, saying that Norman had already had his full turn and now Tayshaun could have his. She was sure that Norman could have another turn when Tayshaun was finished with his whole turn. Now, however, she was going to make sure that Tayshaun could have his whole turn.

Norman threw himself on the ground, screaming and kicking. His teacher sat down next to him. After a while, she said she could tell he was having "very, very big feelings" about the digger. "Yes," Norman wailed, "I need it. It's my favorite toy." The teacher repeated the idea of full turns, but Norman would have none of that and wailed even more loudly that he "needed" the digger "now" and he "hated everyone else."

His teacher commented again on his very big feelings but added that even though big feelings make everything feel so powerful inside, they don't really change anything on the outside. Tayshaun will still have his whole turn, and she will protect it, and when he is done, Norman will still have his whole turn—nothing will change. Norman stopped writhing and wailing and looked at her with some surprise. Was it true that his feelings were just feelings and didn't change the world? Over the next few days, the teacher found opportunities to reinforce this idea with Norman and the other children, working to help them consolidate the distinction between mental life and the outside world of real actions, which is so important to developing the emotional muscles of tolerating and regulating their own feelings.

INTERNALIZING REALISTIC STANDARDS

Aspiration and persistence build on experiences of genuine mastery, so children are less likely to struggle with perfectionism or self-doubt.

Parents can promote this growth by

- **MAKING REALISTIC DEMANDS**

When parents and teachers stretch children but do not overload them, children appreciate the process of trying and enjoy "good-enough"[63] outcomes.

Salmah's mother e-mailed her teachers as follows:

> Driving home from school today, we listened to a CD called "One Little Sound." One of the songs talks about the difference that one little sound can make when combined with other letters. It tells a cute story using words that end with "og" and showing how changing the beginning consonant changes the word. Anyway, when we got home, Salmah went straight to a piece of paper and wrote down "bog, dog, mog." She was very proud of herself for having paid close attention to the song and writing down what she knew to be correct.
>
> Tonight when we were getting ready for bed she said, "Mom, do you know a sign that I'm growing up?" "No," I said. "When I wrote these words today," she said holding up the paper, "I made a mistake when I wrote this G, but I didn't say 'Oh no I'm the worst writer. I can't write a thing. I'll never learn how to do this!'" She whined as she spoke, imitating a tantrum. "You're right," I told her. "You just fixed the G. That *is* a sign you are growing up." In my mind I was thinking, "and the fact that you recognize that shows even deeper insight."

Salmah's parents and teachers had clearly worked with her, not only on learning to write letters, but also on being realistically kind in making judgments about herself, developing and using the emotional muscles of accepting imperfection and enjoying being good enough. As we discussed in relation to three-year-olds, they had helped her to stretch, without imposing stress by asking too much. Then Salmah made appropriate demands on herself and could feel pleasure in her success. She was self-reflective as she described the growth she had made in developing a kinder and more realistic inside helper.

HOW PARENTS HELP FOUR-YEAR-OLDS BUILD THE EMOTIONAL MUSCLES OF

INTEGRATING AND CONSOLIDATING EMOTIONAL MUSCLES
Parents help by
• CALLING UPON EXISTING EMOTIONAL MUSCLES

GENERATING INTERNAL CONTROLS
Parents help by
• DESCRIBING THE INSIDE HELPER AS A PART OF THE SELF THAT WILL HELP CHILDREN KNOW WHAT TO DO
• CONNECTING GOOD FEELINGS WITH USING THE INSIDE HELPER
• TALKING ABOUT HOW GOOD IT FEELS TO DO THINGS THAT ARE FUN AND ALSO LEAD TO GOOD FEELINGS
• REACTING PROPORTIONATELY TO MISBEHAVIOR
• LABELING THE ACTION, NOT THE CHILD
• CREATING SAFE CONDITIONS
• TRUSTING THAT YOUR CHILD CAN DEVELOP AN INSIDE HELPER
• MAINTAINING CONSISTENT EXPECTATIONS

REGULATING AGGRESSION
Parents help by
• EXPECTING SELF-REGULATION
• VALIDATING THE PLEASURE FROM SELF-REGULATION
• SUPPORTING ASSERTION

DEVELOPING A GROUP CONSCIENCE
Parents help by
• REMINDING CHILDREN THAT THEY ARE MEMBERS OF A GROUP
• TEACHING FLEXIBLE ADAPTATIONS TO DIFFERENT GROUP NORMS
• SUPPORTING THE AUTONOMY OF THE INSIDE HELPER IN THE CONTEXT OF PEER PRESSURE

USING WORRIES TO INITIATE MASTERY
Parents help by
• USING JUDGMENT TO PROTECT CHILDREN FROM OVERWHELMING ANXIETY AND TOLERATING MANAGEABLE WORRIES

LIVING IN THE REAL WORLD
Parents help by
• SHARING THE PLEASURES AND OPPORTUNITIES OF REALITY
• FACING THE DIFFICULT ASPECTS OF THE WORLD BRAVELY
• HELPING YOUR CHILD DISTINGUISH BETWEEN "INSIDE THE HEAD" EVENTS AND OUTSIDE REALITY

INTERNALIZING REALISTIC STANDARDS
Parents help by
• MAKING REALISTIC DEMANDS

FIVE-YEAR-OLDS AND THEIR PARENTS
BUILDING EMOTIONAL MUSCLES

Five-year-olds are at the gateway of a new developmental stage. They are no longer preschoolers and have set in place the foundations of a structured personality. They have internalized controls and take great pleasure in exercising their skills and experimenting with new challenges. They have developed the capacity for strong friendships and sensitive understanding of others.

Five-year-olds are beginning a long period of learning and growth that will culminate in the changes of puberty and adolescence. Appropriately, they and their parents are forward-looking, thinking with enthusiasm about all there is to learn at school, all the skills there are to gain, and all the fun awaiting them as they move into more independent functioning. The world of reality is increasingly familiar and fascinating to them. They surprise us with their wise observations and delight us with their mental gymnastics and imaginative inspiration. During this year, they will become able to take things to the next level—they can consolidate, synthesize, and integrate emotional muscles. Increasingly, five-year-olds take the initiative in mobilizing their emotional muscles.

At the same time, five-year-olds need their parents to work with them to get the most out of their new capacities; support remains essential to enjoying the exciting new possibilities. Recent summaries of work on self-regulation underscore the importance of adult support for the growth of self-regulatory competence, what we have called emotional muscle.[64]

As children move to elementary, middle, and high school and on into college and adult life, they will always need emotional muscle. They are going to need strategies to independently access and mobilize the appropriate capacities for self-regulation, dealing with feelings that are "too big." Researchers describe older children's (elementary and high school) "growing understanding of mental processes and the ability to manage them deliberately to accomplish goals."[65]

But our experience demonstrates that children even as young as five can learn strategies that they can consciously invoke to deal with challenges. Five-year-olds have built a strong set of emotional muscles that helps them keep their feelings at a manageable level. With adult help, they can begin to see that they have a choice of responses. They move from realizing the strategic options *after the fact* to being able to respond beforehand to their own internal feeling signals with effective strategies for keeping their emotional muscles in shape. Just knowing that they have strategies gives children confidence to meet internal and external challenges. Elementary school teachers consistently remark on the self-confidence and competence of graduates of psychoanalytic schools with their emotional muscle curricula.

What parents learn

STAMINA

Stamina comes from persistent effort, sustained over time, whether in the physical or emotional realm.

Many different parental emotional muscles have been built up over the past years, but it can be daunting to realize that muscle is not maintained without regular exercise. There is an authentic sense of achievement and relief when your child is launched into kindergarten. At the same time, however, the job is, by no means, finished; and it takes emotional stamina to be the parent of a five-year-old. Remember, practice and consolidate all previously developed emotional muscles to increase your parental stamina.

Charlie's parents started the parent group by saying, "We think we need help with Charlie. He has become impossible! At first we thought it was the run of colds and flu we've been having, but everyone's been well for a while now, and Charlie is still being mean to his baby sister, the dog, and us." Another parent said, "Welcome to the exclusive club of parents of five-year-olds. No initiation fee is necessary, just proof that you've experienced the roller coaster of five-year-old struggles."

A dad with a second family said, "I went through this with each of my older kids. At every big step, like into kindergarten, middle school, and high school, I thought 'Whew, now I can relax. The teachers will deal with him, and everything is pretty much in place.' I had to realize that there were new demands on me and that what I needed was to stay the course, use my existing skills, and figure out what the new level for my kid was about."

The family consultant said that it did sound as if the group was talking about stamina, facing the disappointment that everything wasn't now automatically on track, that there will always be parental work to do. For example, in this instance, Charlie seems to be reacting to his mixed feelings about growing up and going to big school by putting one side of the conflict out into the relationship with his parents and everyone else. The group could then think of various ways to help him get his strong inside helper back inside where it belonged.

But it was also important to notice a big difference between grown-ups and children. Adults have built the emotional muscle to admit difficulties and ask for help without feeling humiliated or like failures. Charlie's parents agreed that they felt better having brought their disappointment and anger to their comfortable and comforting group; this made them feel stronger, rather than weaker, and they felt confident that they would have the stamina to keep using their parental emotional muscles to help Charlie through his rough waters.

At the first parent group meeting for the kindergarten class after the winter holiday break, people seemed subdued. There was some conversation around things that people had negative feelings about, like a child who had left the school and the classroom pet that had died, but the bottom line was a general sense of the "winter blahs." The family consultant described his observation of the kids in class that morning doing their morning greeting circle. He had seen a good discussion of ideas and feelings around missing their friend and sadness about the dead fish. The teacher then directed them to the regular calendar task. It was Kenny's job that day. He had been very sad about the fish, but he stood up and told the day and date, pointed to them on the calendar, talked about what day tomorrow would be, and so forth. In other words, he owned his feelings and then moved on. One of the parents remarked, "Sounds like we could learn something from the kids. They are showing some stamina, not getting discouraged and fed up. They faced their feelings and then moved on."

The family consultant mentioned that he had recently seen some research that linked the 60 percent increase in shortsightedness in the general population to a lack of time spent in natural light conditions. The parents' discussion then took off. They began to talk about how things had changed since when they were little. "My mom was a teacher, so she came home when we did, and she used to give us a snack and then kick us out the door to play outside." They described how kids now are so scheduled and the world doesn't seem as safe, so they are never just running around outside. Even skating rinks are indoors nowadays.

Then they started brainstorming about all the different possible outdoor activities they could do with their kids, even in the winter. As they talked, they realized that each parent had some special skill, talent, or enthusiasm to offer the group. Kenny's dad was an expert snowboarder and offered to teach kids and parents how to do that. One of the moms had the idea of them all going maple sugaring in the woods, bringing the syrup home, and making a pancake supper together. Another parent was a naturalist who volunteered to lead a winter walk and talk about the plants and berries, the animal tracks, and how much can be learned from a winter landscape. They made a plan to meet at George's house where there was a big yard; parents and kids together could shovel up a big snow mountain to play on and slide down. The enthusiasm was palpable, and one parent exclaimed, "Now I feel all energized again. I can face the parenting task because this is going to be fun for us as grown-ups and with our kids." He was making the point that stamina is easier to build and maintain when there is pleasure connected to the work. The parents made a plan to e-mail each other with more ideas.

There is a potential tension for all parents between hanging on to controls and authority like when the children were little or pushing children out of the nest as quickly as possible now that they seem so much more independent and capable. Throughout this book, we have talked about transforming the relationship to stay close at each new level instead of experiencing growth only as a series of painful and increasing separations. Stamina is needed throughout your child's life. When your child is five, you can consolidate your position as the parent available for your child's needs at the new level. This isn't easy in the face of parents' own wishes to be free of responsibility, as well as a Anglo-American cultural pressure to promote separation as quickly as possible.[66]

This issue appears often in the context of changes in your child's physical and emotional needs. Each step forward creates new space. Parents have a crucial role to play in determining how that space will be filled and used. Routines were important for them when they were babies, but they continue to be just as important at five and beyond. Parents have the job of maintaining and advocating for their children's needs. It takes stamina and confidence to stand up for your child in the face of the demands of school systems, peers, grandparents, and your child's wishes to do what the other kids may do.

A prime example at five is bedtime and sleep. Once children are in kindergarten and seem like schoolkids, organized activities in the afternoon come into play. Two-career family life, where parents don't see their children until the evening, tends to push bedtimes later and later. It's all too easy for bedtime to be what slides. Yet there is definitive evidence that sleep loss or a variable sleep pattern (like later bedtimes and awakening on the weekends) have both immediate and lasting effects on intellectual functioning and emotional self-regulation. Since these correlations reach a peak in high school, parental stamina in maintaining authority over your child's bodily needs and health in these early years set a crucial pattern.[67] Your goal is to ensure that your parental input remains important throughout your child's development.

EXERCISING JUDGMENT ABOUT EMOTIONAL RESPONSIBLITY

Use your feelings as a guide to differentiate between your child's and your responsibilities in dealing with internal conflicts.

We have talked earlier about how parents are in the habit of easing the path for their children, solving problems and taking up the slack. In the first few years, it takes a conscious effort to assess what will be a manageable stretch for a baby or toddler and make the demand while always being there as a safety net. With the consolidation of an inside helper in four-year-olds, they are truly ready to carry some responsibility for their own feelings, impulses, wishes, needs, and safety. But what helps a parent know how to allocate that responsibility? What should you share? What should you retain as your parental rights and duties? This is a continuing emotional muscle for parents to work on.

We have described parents' continuing efforts to help children take controls inside to regulate themselves. Until now, children's struggles have been largely between their own needs and wishes and the external demands of parents, teachers, other children, and external reality. A toddler wants to eat all the cookies and a parent says, "No, only one, because it's nearly supper time." Left alone with the cookies, most toddlers will eat them no matter what the parent had said. By three, a child will have some conflict but probably still eat them. In the last chapter, we talked about the many aspects of developing and consolidating an inside helper. Parents play a crucial role in supporting that development and influencing the form and style of a child's conscience. By the end of the four-year-old year, most children find ways to gratify their needs and feel good about themselves at the same time. They can work out methods to help themselves succeed at the demand although it is hard work for them. In a famous study, Mishchel showed that the children who could wait for a treat grew up significantly more successful on every measure than those who did not have a strong enough inside helper to support their waiting.[68]

At five, most children have a relatively strong and adaptive inside helper and have identified with the goals and values of this conscience. Now if left alone with the plate of cookies, a five-year-old will either eat only the permitted one and feel good about herself or eat more and then perhaps lie or blame someone else for the missing cookies. The struggle has become primarily internal, between the desires and the part of them, the inside helper, that enables them to gratify desires in an appropriate way. It takes effort and muscle to say "I'll eat one now and save two for my lunchbox tomorrow." The inside helper may be saying no, but it is also saying that you'll feel better about yourself if you exercise self-control and still have some of the original pleasure too. This internal conflict is with all of us lifelong, but we see it emerging strongly in five-year-olds who are just consolidating the inner agencies involved. It will intensify again in adolescence, when the choices available to resolve conflicts take on new reality.

Five-year-olds are in the thick of this struggle, making such choices many times daily, experiencing the encouraging praise or reprimand of their inside helper. Parents can understand this as a "manageable stretch" that will further strengthen their child's emotional muscles.[69]

Parents can expect that their children will also feel tempted to take the fast and easy route of pushing their inside helper outside again, recreating a struggle with parents or teachers, rather than grappling with the discomfort and pressure of an internal conflict. It can feel easier to say "I want all the cookies and my mean mommy won't let me" than to sit with the dilemma inside.

Billie was a very competent and capable child who started his five-year-old class with gusto and zest. He enjoyed the new activities and routines. As the year continued, however, he seemed to be having difficulties mastering the stepwise reading skills. In class he became disruptive during these lessons, refusing to listen to his teacher and inciting others to join him in silly, loud "potty talk." Everyone knew Billie had a strong inside helper, that he knew how he was supposed to behave in school, but he seemed to be ignoring his inside helper the way he was ignoring his teacher.

His parents brought the problem to parent group, wondering whether this was particular to Billie or related to some five-year-old issue. His mother described her feelings as she talked with Billie about the school troubles. She had started off sympathetic and eager to find some external excuse, like the material being too boring. But then she had found herself feeling increasingly exasperated and helpless, annoyed, and angry that Billie was not using the controls she knew he had. As the discussion proceeded, she used her feelings to see that Billie was getting rid of some inside struggle by creating a battle with his teachers and her. The group could see that this dumping outside was in part a five-year-old issue but that Billie also needed help from the grown-ups to get his particular trouble back inside.

At the next group, Billie's mom related what she had done to address the situation. She said to him that she knew he was upset about something and she was sure she and his teachers could help him with it. But first he had to stop misbehaving in school. She said firmly that he had to listen to his teachers. Billie responded by saying, "I'll try." She placed her hands on his shoulders, looked him in the eyes and said calmly, "No, you won't just try. You will do it because you can do it." His conduct changed, which made space for his teachers and parents to perceive his internal feelings of shame at not being able to read as well as his best friend. Then they could help him enhance his own emotional muscles to tolerate his temporary lag.

The parent group was impressed that Billie's mother had been able to use her own feelings of impatience as a signal that responsibility belonged to Billie. She didn't turn it into her problem, thereby avoiding conflict with Billie. Rather than shouldering his distress and providing the solution as she would have done when he was younger, she had the muscle to tolerate his upset and anger, knowing that he actually had the internal controls to manage his behavior. The family consultant said that this indicated her knowledge that Billie truly now had a choice. He could address his shame by putting the responsibility outside, blaming others and digging himself in deeper, which would be a closed-system way of regulating his feelings. Or as his parents and teachers helped him do by refusing to take on the problem, he could opt to use their support and encouragement, an open-system choice, which led to his accepting extra practice reading words. Soon, Billie regained his confidence and began to enjoy book-time again. His mother felt good that her feelings were still an indicator of Billie's needs even now that they were at a new five-year-old level.

The same kind of fine judgment is called for when a child is struggling with other children, and it can be hard to know who is in the right.

Shawna's mother described how Shawna loved school but was complaining of being teased and excluded by some of the other children. The family had just relocated and Shawna was new to her school. Talking about the issue at a parent group, her mom said she wasn't feeling any signals herself of anger or annoyance with Shawna. She felt sad for her and set out to teach her some other approaches to try with her classmates. But she also spoke to the teachers and other parents. No one felt this was an inside problem of Shawna's. Rather, it was something that needed the active intervention of all the grown-ups.

Many adults feel that bullying is something children have to sort out for themselves, that a child should toughen up and confront the bully. Even though some children may do things that invite bullying, it is still an experience beyond a child's capacity to solve. It is the responsibility of adults to take a "zero tolerance" attitude to bullying or any form of abuse. They must intervene with schools and other parents to end violence. The parents agreed that this was a useful contrast to the kind of situation described by Billie's mother, and the family consultant underscored the importance of developing the muscle of self-examination. Then parents can read their own feelings to differentiate a problem internal to a child from a social situation that needs adult action.

Benedetta's mother came into parent group and said, "I know we've often talked about the hard things and the struggles in parenting, but I realized on my way here that I wanted to also say something out loud about how good it feels with Benedetta these days. Not every second, of course, but overall we're having fun and it feels really nice to trust that she and her dad and I can work things out when we need to." Everyone smiled. The family consultant remarked that it is important to use one's own *good* feelings as a barometer, to make sure that the good feelings of happy times are put into words, enjoyed explicitly together and appreciated for their true importance as motivators, reinforcers, and rewards for living well.

MAINTAINING SELF-ESTEEM

*Hold on to positive feelings about yourself as a good
parent and a competent adult*

Parental self-esteem derives from several sources. First is a person's own base level of good feeling about himself or herself. A feeling of competence as a parent, a sense of strength and mastery from developing emotional muscles, builds upon that base. Then comes the assessment of how your child is doing. Is his functioning good enough? Will he be ready for the next step when the time comes? All parents are deeply invested in their work as parents. They also have to face the limits of what parents can do. Other factors are part of the equation, for instance, your child's endowment of capacities and temperament, the occurrence of medical or physical issues, the fact that you are not the only influence; there is the other parent, grandparents, family, care providers and teachers, peers, and so forth.

Sivan's mother came to parent group looking frazzled. She said that she was fed up, that he was driving her crazy. He's picking at her, saying she's a stupid bad mom. All the other mommies are nicer and prettier. He hates her and won't listen to anything she says, yells when she tries to talk to him, and she's left feeling limp, helpless and stupid. She feels like going back to work full-time and just putting him in eight-to-six day care. The group was stunned. After a silence, one of the dads said, "Wow! You are one of the best moms I know. We've all looked up to you." The family consultant said, "What we're all experiencing is the power of a five-year-old's angry feelings and how these can seem to overwhelm reality. It takes muscle and support to hold on to positive feelings about yourself when you are the target of your child's anger."

The other parents joined in to wonder, not only why Sivan was so angry at his mother, but also to note that the anger of a five-year-old carries a certain reality very different from the anger of a toddler or a rivalrous four-year-old. Parents noted that, on their good days, the five-year-olds could be very sharp, discerning, and capable of very accurate and astute observation and judgments. "Why does grandma smell funny? Why is Uncle John always so angry at his kids? He's never having fun." So when a five-year-old turns his attack on a parent, it can hit a genuine vulnerable spot that takes the hurt to a deeper level than the momentary sting of a toddler's rage. One parent said that the angry remarks carry a certain "authority, as if you're being put down by another grown-up."

The next day, the family consultant called Sivan's mother to see how she was feeling. She said that she was feeling much better, but she had realized after the meeting that she still carries a vulnerability because of being Sivan's adoptive mother. "I need a lot of muscle to hold on to my self-confidence as his mother." She used her emotional muscles to step back and assess Sivan's overall functioning and her own momentary drop in confidence and consider what else might be going on with him, rather than take the whole issue on herself. Sivan's grandfather was ill and she had been spending a lot of time caring for him; she hadn't realized the impact this was having on Sivan. She also had the courage to recognize her own special vulnerability because of the meaning of adoption to her. The family consultant supported this train of thought and discussed with her the various options that might be helpful, like attending an adoptive parents' support group, or seeking counseling if that wasn't sufficient to restore her positive parental self-esteem.

In this situation, the family consultant was mindful that the mom's emotional muscles might not do the whole job. Emotional muscle is necessary and helpful, but it can't do everything.

SATISFYING ADULT NEEDS

Validate your own need for adult pleasure and self-care
without guilt

As the children become more self-sufficient, parents of five-year-olds turning six increasingly begin to think about activities for their own pleasure and self care. Parents who work either full-time or part-time begin to talk about joining a health club, a bowling league, taking yoga, going back to school or taking a more demanding job, and so forth.

At parent group, one mother, who worked full-time, talked about having joined a monthly book club. She giggled with pleasure and seemed a bit embarrassed. "Finally, I get to read novels, one of my lifelong pleasures. It used to feel as if I would never get to read a book again!" Then in a serious voice, she said, "But I feel bad, as if I am doing something wrong, as if I'm taking even more time away from my child." Another parent followed with her worry that her return to full-time work would harm her relationship with her child. A dad joined in to say how terrible he felt when his mom put him in fulltime care at four as she returned to work. Others seemed to be reacting to their children's growth by feeling left. The turn to adult pleasures as one parent said, "Sounded like tit for tat. You leave me? Well, I'll leave you first. No wonder we feel guilty since that's not a valid reason for doing our own thing."

The family consultant noted that it sounded like the parents couldn't find good alternatives. They felt guilt for satisfying their adult needs and equally bad if they were using adult activities as an angry reaction to their children's growing independence. As the group grappled with this issue, they eventually arrived at two ideas, which they wrote on the board:

1. Being a competent parent is the work of an adult. We have to take care of our adult needs to remain helpful, loving, competent parents.
2. Taking action to satisfy adult needs is an important model for our children. They can learn from us that to be able to take care of others, we first have to know how to take care of ourselves.

But then one parent said, "Remember when we had the 'January blahs.' We came up with a bunch of ideas that weren't either/or. At the time I was struck by how my little kid could now do the same things I enjoy. It wasn't a case of me sacrificing my adult pleasures to spend time with my son or him being dragged along for my sake. We were actually enjoying the same activity. There must be more things like that if we can just think of them and not feel as if we always have to choose between our kids and ourselves."

The parents became enthused. They made a list of activities they could enjoy together. One mom recalled, "When I was little, my parents and my sister and I went every Friday night to family swim at the Y. My dad would swim laps while my mom played in the water with us, then my mom had a turn for laps while Dad invented great games, then we all had fun together in the pool. Afterward, we always went for pizza. Those were such great times and everyone got exercise and spent time together. What a nice way it was to end the week when we had all been at work and school."

One of the moms remembered that before she was six, her dad started taking her to major league baseball games. This became a great pleasure they still share. Now the third generation could become part of that. She said, "I had forgotten how young I was. Of course my dad would walk me around and buy a hot dog and generally make it possible for me to last for such a long time, but it stretched me and it felt so special to us both." Another mom said, "It was very special for me that my mom and I always went together to see the ballet company when it came to town. I still love dance, and it is still a bond with my mom." These parents were consolidating the emotional muscle of enjoying adult pleasures without guilt.

This emotional muscle will not eradicate the reality that having children is a responsibility that changes your options. Your child turning six doesn't turn back the clock and make you a single young adult again who can take pleasure whenever available. There are bound to be conflicts, and children get sick unexpectedly, and choices continue to be necessary. Rather than crippling guilt or an irresponsible avoidance the family consultant in the above discussion suggested the idea of thoughtful parenting.[70] We have talked about this throughout the book. It applies especially in this context, where parents are working to find a new balance in their continuing relationship with their children.

UNDERSTANDING MISBEHAVIOR AS AN ATTEMPTED SOLUTION

Empathize with the illusory power and safety of closed-system magical functioning for your child

"Why does she do that?" asked Theresa's mother. "She can be so sweet and nice and smart and loving. Everyone adores her when she's like that. And then suddenly, for no obvious reason, she can become mean, irrational, out of control, and frankly, sort of stupid! There is no talking to her, no way of getting her out of that bossy, angry mood." Other parents joined in with similar bewilderment about how their children could switch so completely. "Is this a bipolar disorder? Should Theresa be on medication?" asked her mom.

"Whoa," said the family consultant, "let's slow down and not be reps for the drug companies. They are trying to push the bipolar diagnosis to younger and younger age-groups. Before we go to a biochemical solution, let's see if we can imagine ourselves into a five-year-old's shoes. Maybe then we'll have some inkling of why they can swing in this puzzling way. Let's see if there's a clue in your own feelings when she acts that way."

"I feel helpless," said one dad and all the other parents nodded agreement. He went on, "But look what we do when we feel helpless. We come here, we ask for support, and we get help."

"Yes," said the family consultant, "this is something you have learned to do. You have the muscle to admit when you feel helpless and you can ask for help and share the burden. Your children don't even know they need help or that it is available. If you didn't have the muscle to admit your feelings and ask for help from other adults, you too might reach for a quick fix like a diagnosis and a pill you could give your child twice a day."[71]

Another dad exclaimed, "Now I can feel the sequence of the helplessness and the wish for a quick fix. It's like wishing I would win the lottery when the bills are piling up, and I don't know where I'll find the money to make ends meet."

"But why should our children feel helpless? They don't have any bills to pay or any real responsibilities. I often wish I could be a carefree child again," sighed one of the moms.

Another mom said, "Be careful what you wish for. I don't know but it seems to me that a child might feel that she could be overwhelmed at any moment. Overhearing the news, seeing us stressed out, seeing a caterpillar crushed underfoot, having a pet die, hearing about Grandad's bypass surgery or Aunt Elsa's divorce, having to learn lower case letters after having struggled to learn uppercase letters, to be sick or to be told when to go to bed—any one of these things could mean to a child being helpless or vulnerable. Whew, I guess I really don't want to be a kid again no matter how much I love them!"

Theresa's mom said thoughtfully, "Maybe my thinking she's bipolar was me feeling helpless and reaching for a quick but irrational solution. Because when I really stop and think about it, I know she doesn't have a major psychiatric disorder. But I still feel helpless and don't know what to do."

The family consultant agreed, saying that children, with their limited reality experience and knowledge, are even more likely than adults to reach for a magical solution that seems perfectly reasonable to them since they have little basis for assessing it. It becomes clear that helplessness, real or imagined, is a basic motive for seeking self-protection. We all have to protect ourselves from feeling helpless and overwhelmed at any age. As adults, we can usually keep the irrational closed-system response in daydreams or fantasies, like winning the lotto when faced with bills.

Parents started sharing their daydreams, like winning big in Vegas, beating the golf champion in the Masters, eating a box of chocolates with no effects, quitting work and living in Tahiti, and so forth. After much laughter, one dad said, "So that's what our kids are doing. Instead of working hard to learn lowercase letters, it feels easier, faster, and more gratifying to be disruptive, disobey the teacher, and get all the other kids to be in awe of you for being out of control."

"Would it help if we said to our children that we know how exciting it feels to yell at me? It makes you feel like you're a big strong man in charge of everyone else instead of being a wonderful five-year-old who is working to learn to be in charge of himself."

Another dad, a former marine, summed up the discussion as follows—"I don't know what you would call this, my new emotional muscle or what, but now I feel ready to engage with the foe. The worst mistake a commander can make is to underestimate the strength of the enemy. Once you have made a correct assessment and have respect for the strength of the enemy, you can go into battle well prepared. I realize that my kid is not being a baby or a bad boy. It's not genetic or biological when he goes into this state. In fact, he is feeling a rush of power. He thinks there are no reality limits or consequences, and that feels good to him. I now have more respect for the strength and power of that state. Now I know what I'm dealing with and what a big job it is to help him find better ways to feel safe and good."

THE EMOTIONAL MUSCLES USED BY PARENTS OF FIVE-YEAR-OLDS ARE

STAMINA

EXERCISING JUDGMENT ABOUT EMOTIONAL RESPONSIBILITY

MAINTAINING SELF-ESTEEM

SATISFYING ADULT NEEDS

UNDERSTANDING MISBEHAVIOR AS AN ATTEMPTED SOLUTION

What do five-year-olds need to develop emotional muscle?

Five-year-olds need their parents and teachers to provide time and space for them to keep exercising their established emotional muscles while building even more complex new muscles and strategies to mobilize them. Researchers have begun to recognize the specific ongoing needs for social-emotional growth, but our society and its school systems lag behind in acknowledging both the need and the impact of the presence or absence of noncognitive factors or what we call emotional muscle.

As we noted earlier, parents may feel their job is done when their children go off to big school. Kindergarten classes that have more than thirty children and one teacher are clearly not designed to continue to promote emotional muscle development. Academic testing as the measure of effectiveness of such education misses the point. It doesn't assess the factors that will be more potent over the long run in a child's future success in both school and life.[72] Growth in self-regulation competency (emotional muscle) does not end in the brain or in the mind until well into young adulthood.[73]

We talked earlier about parental stamina, staying the course in thoughtful, active parenting at the new level the children have achieved.

Helping five-year-olds develop new emotional muscles and consolidate existing ones is an ongoing and exciting task.

What five-year-olds learn

USING EMOTIONAL MUSCLES

PLAYING COOPERATIVELY

WITHSTAND INTERNAL AND EXTERNAL PRESSURES TO BLUR THE DISTINCTION BETWEEN REAL AND PRETEND

RESTRAINT

EMBRACING THE RULES OF REALITY

PLAYING WITH WHOLEHEARTED PLEASURE

SYNTHESIS AND INTEGRATION

FLEXIBILITY

ENJOYING COMPETENCE

SEEKING THE SOURCE OF PAINFUL FEELINGS

KNOWING HOW TO HAVE A GOOD GOOD-BYE

USING STRATEGIES

How parents help five-year-olds build emotional muscles

USING EMOTIONAL MUSCLES

Five-year-olds have many established muscles they can call upon.

Parents can promote this growth by

- **HELPING CHILDREN REMEMBER THE MUSCLES THEY HAVE**
  There are different kinds of memory. Skills like feeding ourselves, walking, riding a bike, and so forth are muscle memories or what researchers call procedural memory. Once mastered, these tasks don't demand conscious, active remembering. Another broad category of memory is active working memory, where we call up our knowledge from memory of how something is done. For instance, "I remember

how to play checkers," said Tommy in the five-year-old class. "You can only jump that way."

Polly's mom wanted to hear about her older boy's day at school, but Polly kept whining to have her CD played in the car. After a few fruitless exchanges, Polly's mother said to her, "I think you know that you're strong enough to wait." Polly subsided, then reached her arms out to the side, flexed her muscles, and smiled. Her mom helped her to use her working memory to mobilize an emotional muscle, her waiting muscle.

Keith and his parents talked on their way to school for a class performance. Keith was worried and didn't think he would be able to manage it. His parents told him they thought his muscles were strong enough to remember his job and be part of the group performance. After it was over, and Keith had done beautifully, he beamed and said to them, "Well, I guess I was wrong."

Children resonate to the idea of building emotional muscles. They feel good when teachers or parents comment on their strong waiting muscles, thinking muscles, stopping muscles, talking muscles, or how strong their inside helper has become. As Polly's and Keith's parents did, adults can help children remember the muscles they have and praise them when they use them. Parents can also model how they remind themselves to use their own emotional muscles.

Rashiv's dad told the parent group how he had lost his temper and yelled at Rashiv. Later, he apologized to his son, saying, "I forgot to use my inside helper to remind me not to yell. I need to practice more and harder so my inside helper can get stronger." Rashiv had said, "I'll help you remember, Dad. I'll remind you."

PLAYING COOPERATIVELY

Five-year-olds can play independently and cooperatively, building lifelong skills.

Parents can promote this growth by

- **EXPECTING AND ALLOWING CHILDREN TO INDEPENDENTLY INITIATE, SUSTAIN, AND ENJOY COOPERATIVE GROUP PLAY**
  On the first warm spring day, the children rushed out to their favorite playground activities—bikes, slides, digging in the sand. Two children

were digging when one said, "Why don't we make a city?" "Yeah," said the other, "but we'll need help. Hey, you guys, we're building a city. Do you want to join us?"

Soon, all the kids were at the sandpit, everyone contributing ideas and each spontaneously taking on a particular task. "I'll dig the roads." "I'll make the canals." "I'll get the water. Where's the bucket?" "I'll find wood and make the bridges." There was a cooperative division of labor and easy trading off of functions and roles. They worked together without bossiness or submission.

At the end they were all proud of their very complex creation and took the teacher and visiting family consultant over to admire what they had done. It was indeed impressive—a little Venice—but even more impressive was how well and with what pleasure these five-and-a-half-year-olds could independently accomplish the task. The grown-ups were still needed as backup presences, but their main job was to stand by to admire.[74]

A teacher described Bettina, who was working on a project building with newspaper. After working for several minutes, Bettina said, "I need some teamwork here." She enlisted two other children to help complete her designs for a bow tie for her shirt and various pieces of jewelry they could all wear on their arms and necks.

These children were consolidating a critical set of skills for life. They were learning the importance of collaboration, cooperation, teamwork, and the increased pleasure available from working together. Some developmental scientists emphasize that "our survival depends on our ability to understand other people . . . to make alliances, construct coalitions, and form teams."[75]

Groups are not only important for learning about working together. They also serve as powerful social controls, with the development of what we could call a group conscience. We described the helpful support of peer pressure for four-year-olds working to strengthen their inside helpers. This continues for five-year-olds and throughout life. What is new at five is the coalescence of explicit group norms, conventions and values, which play a significant role in self-regulation. Adults and children can call on these ideas to remind five-year-olds to use their inside helpers effectively.

WITHSTAND INTERNAL AND EXTERNAL PRESSURES TO BLUR THE DISTINCTION BETWEEN REAL AND PRETEND

*Staying strong in the real world is challenging for
five-year-olds, who are pulled to magical solutions.*

Parents can promote this growth by

- **INSISTING ON REALITY-BASED SOLUTIONS**
Grown-ups are the interpreters and teachers about reality from the earliest times. We have talked throughout this book about helping children know the difference between real and pretend and the security that comes from knowing the difference. Five-year-olds have a great deal of reality knowledge and use it effectively a lot of the time. But they are still vulnerable to the assaults on their reality testing that come from media materials or books or the stories that grown-ups may tell. There is still a disparity between what they seem to know and what they actually believe. By five, children act as if they are secure in the difference between what is real and what is pretend, but they really aren't. Without continuing grown-up support, pretend media and scary stories overwhelm them. They may then reach for a magical solution, which undermines their emotional muscles and eventually makes things worse.

  Kevin's mom said that she was thinking about his fascination with dinosaurs. Kevin only wanted to play T. rex games, where he was the frightening dinosaur, at school and at home. He had a favorite video that was full of dinosaur cartoon stories. She was annoyed and somewhat bothered by his preoccupation but didn't want to inhibit what she called his imaginative play. Other parents agreed that their children seemed to get stuck in certain scary games, but they also were concerned about interfering with creativity.

  A month later, Kevin's mother said she wanted to tell the group about what had been happening with the dinosaur game since they last discussed it. Kevin's teacher had told her how he was frightening the other children with his fierce growls and attacks in his dinosaur mode. The other children didn't want to play that game and began avoiding Kevin. He insisted that dinosaurs still existed and ate children. His mom had originally felt this was such an imaginative leap to put dinosaurs into the present and hadn't wanted to contradict it.

Kevin's teacher questioned the mom's way of seeing his games, saying that Kevin did not seem to be elaborating an interesting play scenario. He was actually repeating the same frightening and apparently frightened story in his game of T. rex eating children. His parents began to see that Kevin might be using this game to try to deal with some worry rather than as a creative expression. The teacher said that she would focus on the distinction between real and pretend in the classroom and suggested that the parents do the same. She would encourage Kevin to share his actual enormous fund of knowledge about dinosaurs instead of frightening others with his dinosaur fantasies.

The teacher coupled this approach with consistent reminders that dinosaurs didn't eat children since there were no children around at that time, plus the fact that many dinosaurs were herbivores. Furthermore, there are no dinosaurs now. She emphasized how interesting it was to learn more real knowledge about dinosaurs. At snack time, she asked what was on the table that dinosaurs might have liked; all the children then joined in to share what they knew about dinosaurs. The whole class, including Kevin, seemed to relax. Instead of frightening the other children with his scary fantasies, Kevin could share his vast knowledge. In the reality context, they began to enjoy playing about what it was like in the time of the dinosaurs.

Kevin's mom said, "I think I had to understand the importance of the difference between real and pretend better to help Kevin finally get it. He had to be sure about reality before he could comfortably imagine things." The family consultant added that "reality knowledge is like the fence around the playground. Once you have that security, you can play freely with your imagination."

RESTRAINT

Keeping hostile thoughts to oneself is a
crucial social capacity.

Parents can promote this growth by

- **EXPLAINING, DEMONSTRATING, AND COACHING RESTRAINT**
  Parents and teachers have focused, since the children were little, on putting things into words, naming and articulating feelings and wishes.

But five-year-olds may use words like actions and need to develop the muscle of restraint, making an internal choice about what to keep to themselves and what to express.

The five-year-olds were calling names and saying things that hurt each other's feelings, like "I don't want to play with you," "That's a stupid idea," "You're not my friend." So the teacher and the family consultants devised an activity to help the children practice keeping their thoughts to themselves until they could decide whether there was a useful and respectful way to share them.

There was an aquarium in the classroom. The teacher asked each child in turn to stand in front of the tank and think a really nasty, mean thought about the fish. "But don't say it out loud and don't let it show on your face. That would hurt the fishes' feelings!" The children relished the permission to have nasty thoughts, but at first it was a struggle to keep the thoughts to themselves. Some made faces; others smirked or giggled. The teacher commented that they could feel how much strength was needed to hold the thoughts inside. She said that if it felt too hard at first, the child could whisper it to her.

Over several days, the children practiced and became better and better at empathizing with the fish and keeping gratuitous meanness to themselves. The name-calling, teasing, and putdowns in the class decreased. When Katie turned to Anna, she stuck out her tongue and said, "You're so stupid!" Anna said, "You should use your muscles to keep that inside." Katie apologized, and both girls felt better. The children had learned that it took muscle to have restraint, and they were proud of what they had practiced and learned.

EMBRACING THE RULES OF REALITY

Accepting that reality operates according to certain rules that apply to everyone is an enormous achievement.

Parents can promote this growth by

- **REINFORCING YOUR CHILD'S PLEASURE IN MASTERY OF REALITY RULES**
  When five-year-olds can enjoy learning the rules of a game it means that they have developed the muscle to withstand the wish to ignore

reality and force everyone to obey their imperial orders. The queen in *Alice in Wonderland* represents that closed-system wish to be in total charge of others when she shouts, "Off with their heads!" For a child to become interested in the rules of a group, team or board game demonstrates the muscles to acknowledge the equal rights of others as separate people, tolerate waiting, and risk not winning the game.

In the five-year-old class the teacher began introducing more complex board games. One day, she brought a chess set to school. The teacher had tried introducing chess to the group the year before, teaching them the basic moves of each piece. At four, most of them could learn how the pieces moved, but they were much more interested in galloping to the other side of the board or having their knights knock the other pieces down.

Now at five or six, many of the children felt proud of having mastered the elaborate rules and enjoyed playing chess while others watched. One of the child observers said, "Your bishop doesn't move that way." "Oh thanks," said the player. "That's a hard move to remember." Most games never went to completion; it was enough fun to play by the rules and make the moves. The teacher reinforced the good feelings by commenting on how she could see they were enjoying playing by the real rules and not making up their own.

At the next parent group meeting, the family consultant mentioned her observation of the children playing chess in class. "Yes," said Dewon's dad, "it's a real change to see him sit down, move all the pieces correctly and watch me to make sure that I also move the pieces according to the rules. But he doesn't seem to want to keep playing until the game is over. I don't get it. Is he afraid of losing or something?"

"Hey," said another dad. "Your kid has learned to play by the rules. Do you know how big that is? The world is full of rules—how to relate to other people, how to drive a car, how to respect other people's property. I'm a lawyer and I spend my days around grown-ups who haven't learned what Dewon has learned."

A mother who was an elementary school teacher said, "We really have to appreciate what a momentous achievement it is for our kids to recognize that the world has rules, that it feels good to learn the rules and live by them. Soon, Dewon will be in elementary school, and I can tell you that half our work is helping the children learn the rules of behavior, the rules of their subjects like math or spelling or geometry, the rules of the playground, and hopefully the rules of living, like being fair, considerate, and loving. Many of the kids I see in my class of third graders have not accomplished what Dewon already has."

Dewon's dad said, "Well, you have all certainly made it clear. I was taking for granted something I should have celebrated and not staying with the current big step forward. He'll have plenty of time to learn about winning and losing at chess a little later."

- **PLAYING WITH WHOLEHEARTED PLEASURE**
  Play is essential to children's healthy growth.

Parents can promote this growth by

- **PLAYING WITHOUT GUILT OR RESENTMENT**
  It is no secret that children love to play. For many people, the old idea that children play and grown-ups work is still their working model of the main difference between adults and children. Grown-ups often aren't interested or feel they don't know how to play. Sometimes they push children away or ignore their play; other adults may overwhelm children with scary or overdemanding games. Increasingly, researchers and those who work with children have shown that play is not just a byproduct of immaturity but rather is essential to a child's physical, emotional, neurological, and social development.[76]

What is the role of adults in children's play? Without understanding the crucial support parents and teachers can give in structuring, elaborating, enriching, and expanding children's play and the important later positive impact of that experience, it is hard for grown-ups to think they should spend time and energy involving themselves. But once the distinction between real and pretend is firmly established, parents and children are liberated to truly enjoy play and grow from the shared experience. This is a challenge for most parents since many find it difficult to play without guilt or resentment.

Just as we addressed parental needs to enjoy adult pleasures without guilt, so too can parents reach for fun with their children without feeling guilty for wasting time, embarrassed for being silly, ashamed of goofing off, feeling bad about not knowing how to play.

Jodie's dad said he had a funny story for the parent group. He had set up the sprinkler for Jodie and her little brother Ted one hot summer day. He was watching when Ted slipped, sat down hard, and began to whimper. So he ran in and picked Ted up. Before he could move over to the side with Ted, the sprinkler came back around and sprayed him. Jodie gurgled with laughter and so did Ted. Their dad started to laugh too, and they all ran around getting totally soaked, falling down laughing. "My wife came home from the market and looked at us like we were crazy. For a minute I thought, 'What have I been doing?' and then she started to laugh too. I haven't had that much fun in years! She took a picture of us so we can put it in our album. It was great."

One of the moms smiled and said, "That sounds like a great scene. We might all enjoy it in this hot weather. But there are lots of times when the kids want to play stuff that seems pretty boring to me, and they like to repeat everything so many times even now that they are bigger. Don't you get tired of it sometimes?" Another mom said, "Yes, and then I feel bad for resenting the kids. I try to find some way to amuse myself when we go to the playground so I won't get so fed up."

Karen's dad said, "The other day, though, Karen grabbed my cell phone out of my hand when we were on a walk. She said, 'Play with *me*, Daddy!' I was mad at her since I wanted to check my messages, but now I'm wondering what to do with the conflict between her needs and mine." Jenny's mom agreed and said, "I find myself sitting there playing with her, but I want to look at my e-mail and the phone rings and the soup is on, and her play becomes just one more demand."

Sam's dad reminded the group of when they had talked about finding things to do together now that the kids are older. "But I still find that I really am not enjoying myself sitting on the floor, playing the same car game over and over. I'm relieved when the phone rings, which makes me feel I'm falling down on the job."

The family consultant noted that everyone seemed to be feeling disappointed in themselves, as if it should be natural to enjoy playing with children at their level. But parents might think about the reality that it is a difficult task to engage at a child's level. One suggestion is to start with small segments, just as you would with a new physical activity. One mom said, "That supplies the missing piece for me. I've found that it really works to tell myself that this is exclusively playtime with my child. I put away the cell phone and the computer and don't answer the phone. I give myself to the play and it feels great—a kind of Zen moment. But it's time limited. I don't expect myself to do it indefinitely, so I tell my daughter and myself that we will play until the big hand is on the five, and then I will start supper. I felt bad about limiting it, but this helps me see that it's okay to stop and build up the shared playing muscles gradually."

The family consultant remarked that children rarely need to learn to play as grown-ups do. But the grown-up effort to join in wholeheartedly offers an extra dimension of pleasure that comes from playing with a parent who enriches the game. It adds to and transforms the relationship. The message to children is that all their play has positive value, whether it's alone, with other children, or with their parents.

SYNTHESIS AND INTEGRATION

Putting together component emotional muscles leads to higher-order self-regulation

Parents can promote this growth by

- **ADMIRING PUTTING IT ALL TOGETHER**

The idea of emotional muscle is analogous to how we talk about physical muscles and the synthesis of component physical skills into a fluent physical performance. For instance, a child learning to ride a two-wheeled bike has to learn the following:

The safety rules like wearing her helmet, not riding in the street, stopping at driveways, looking and listening, pedaling and strengthening leg muscles, steering and braking, balancing on two wheels, and so forth. Each of these steps is an achievement, to be enjoyed as a mastery experience in its own right. Eventually all these skills are synthesized, put together so that the child becomes a smooth, competent bike rider who soon takes for granted just hopping on and going.

Given that parents and teachers break down tasks for mastery into manageable steps, they can also convey that putting all the bits together is a skill in itself. Synthesis and integration are considered higher-order mental functions, what scientists call executive functions. They rest on emotional muscles of patience, tolerance of frustration, hope and imagination.

Fiona's mother reported how proud she was of her child. They had traveled across the country to attend a large family celebration of her grandfather's birthday. There were many grown-ups and older children Fiona didn't know well, but she actively engaged them in conversation and play. She sat through a long, fancy meal without getting fidgety or silly. Her mom said, "I used to worry about taking her to family gatherings. My parents and older relatives expect children to be seen and not heard. I was afraid I would be embarrassed. But Fiona was an absolute delight and seemed to really enjoy herself. I think she felt good too about the whole trip."

All the parents basked in this mother's pleasure and recounted similar experiences of being pleasantly surprised at their children's competence and self-control. Then someone said, "But how did this happen? Not to make it an embarrassing memory, but I remember you carrying Fiona kicking and screaming out of John's third birthday party, and that was only a couple of years ago. Did they all just get older? Our pediatrician has one mantra—don't worry, he'll outgrow it."

Shawna's mother said, "My mama used to say all kids get older and bigger. It takes hard work to make them wiser." One of the dads, the former marine officer, said, "Think of all the muscles she's developed, plus clearly the muscle to put the skills together and become a child who is a joy to herself, to others, and to her parents. In basic training, we break down all the skills a soldier needs, and when they have mastered each one, we say, 'Now comes the hard part, putting them all together and testing them under fire.' I'm sorry to use military language, but that's my experience, and I think that Fiona went through years of basic training and then put it all together at the battle of Grandpa's birthday."

FLEXIBILITY

Meeting the challenge of novelty, differences, and the unexpected is an important life skill.

Parents can promote this growth by

* **INTRODUCING NEW EXPERIENCES**
From birth, children benefit from routines, needing predominantly the safety and comfort of usual foods, the same bedtime, predictable sequences, and so forth. They get anxious when they aren't prepared well in advance of changes. Five-year-olds still need routines, but they can also be introduced to new perspectives and possibilities. At the basic level of brain functioning, experience provides for a constant pruning of synapses throughout childhood and adolescence, allowing

for new connections to be laid down.[77] Thus both constancy and change are needed for optimal development.

Meeting the challenge of novelty, differences, and the unexpected is an important life skill. It demands flexibility and adaptability. This can range from trying a new food, to bravely going down the bigger slide, to sleeping at grandparents' house or learning a new way to cope with frustration. There are many methods for teachers and parents to foster this emotional muscle.

The teacher initiated a discussion at circle time about the things that kids were wary of trying. She said that she had been thinking about this on her way to school. She realized that she had always thought she didn't like coconut and so had never tried it. She stopped at the store and bought a coconut and looked in the school library for a book about tropical countries, where coconuts grow. After looking together at the book, the class worked to figure out how they were going to open the coconut, to taste it for snack. With the teacher, they went to get a screwdriver and hammer to crack it open.

Once it was open and the milk poured into a small pitcher, the teacher broke the coconut into pieces and passed them out to the children. Janey said, "Mrs. N., put a piece on your plate. You have to try it too." Mrs. N. laughed and agreed that she should be the first one to be brave and try something new even if she didn't know if she would like it. The kids watched as she tentatively took a little bite. "Mmmm," said Mrs. N. "This is sweet and tasty. Oh my, I like coconut after all. I'm so glad I tried it." Then the kids tried it. Some liked it and a few didn't, so they made a chart of how many people tried the new food, how many liked coconut milk, and how many liked coconut meat and how many didn't. Everyone was proud to tell their parents they had all tried the new food, even Mrs. N.!

Mrs. N. suggested that each child think about something they had never tried and everyone could talk about it the next day. In the morning, some of the kids talked about foods, but others talked about more complex challenges. Kyle said that his parents had planned for him to sleep over at his grandparents' one weekend, and he wasn't sure because this was the first time. After the coconut, he thought maybe he should try; maybe it would be fun. Mrs. N. asked the group what they thought. Jenny said, "Even if it isn't fun, it's good to try, and you'll feel proud." Sarah said she often went to her grandma's, and it was very special to do new things there that she didn't do at home. "It's fun, Kyle. I think you'll like it."

Mrs. N. suggested that one good way to prepare for new things was by pretending. "We could make a play about going to Grandma's. Sarah could tell us some things to put in the play, and everyone can join in with ideas. Then we can have one person be the grandma, and someone else be the kid, and others be the parents and other people, even the dog and the cat."

This teacher was offering an important tool. Now that the five-year-olds had a more solid foundation in distinguishing between real and pretend, the whole realm of pretend could open up as a way of using the imagination for working through experiences and preparing for new ones.

Danny's mother wanted to tell the parent group about a very good day. She reminded them that Danny had always struggled with frustration and disappointment and that she had often been discouraged when he couldn't seem to just accept things that she couldn't change. "We had a big family outing planned for last Saturday. My husband had been away on business all week, and we were going to go for a hike all together and then have a picnic in the woods. Danny and I made the sandwiches together the night before and wrapped everything up. He put his binoculars in his backpack to look for birds and everything.

"And then it was absolutely pouring rain when we woke up. I dreaded getting out of bed. I didn't want to face Danny because I was afraid he would pitch a fit. Eventually, I bit the bullet and got up. When I went into his room, Danny was standing, looking out the window with a really sad face. He said, 'Oh, Mommy, what shall we do? How can we have our hike? When will the sun come out?' I told him I was really sad too and frustrated that it was raining too hard. He started to look mad and said 'You mean we can't go at all?'"

One of the dads interjected, "Oh yeah, I've been here. This is where it can all go south." Danny's mom said, "That's what I thought too. But I said to Danny that the rain was in the bucket of what no one can control, so we would have to think of some other way to have a nice day together. We could use our disappointment to help us think really hard and imagine something else that would be fun." She described how Danny looked thoughtful for a minute, heaved a big sigh, and said, "I really wanted to go." They hugged and shared the feeling and then began to plan. When they had the idea for a picnic in the middle of the living room floor, Danny exclaimed, "But first let's hike all over the house, so it takes a long time to get there, just like in the woods." His dad, who had joined the conversation by that time, suggested that they draw some pictures of birds; he would hide them throughout the house, and they would all try to find them on their "hike." Danny's mom said it was one of their best family times; she would remember it forever. "And I will also remember that my big boy was able to be flexible and adapt to the new situation and make it into something really good."

ENJOYING COMPETENCE

Taking pleasure in effort and mastery.

Parents can promote this growth by

- **REINFORCING THE SATISFACTION OF EFFORT AND DOING IT WELL**
Research has demonstrated that competent preschoolers become capable schoolchildren who become successful adults.[78] This book is about building the emotional muscles that lead to and support competence. Pleasure is the essential ingredient in this process. We have found, though, that often only the accomplishment is stressed while the pleasure dimension is undervalued. There is a particular satisfaction from competence, which becomes the self-reinforcing motivator for acquiring and exercising skills effectively.

There is a complication in this picture, however, since pleasure does not generalize from one experience to another. In the brain and in our thoughts and feelings, pleasure is linked to the specific.[79] Negative feelings do generalize. When a child is afraid of one thing, he is likely to become afraid of anything connected to it. If a grown-up speaks harshly, it will take a number of positive interactions to erase the bad feeling.

Therefore, it is essential for adults to notice and underline with words and positive feelings the special pleasure of competence. The aim is to reinforce the satisfaction of effort and doing it well. This builds the emotional muscle of taking pleasure in mastery, which brain research shows is central to broaden, cultivate, and develop competent cognitive functioning.[80] As we mentioned in the three-year-old chapter, praise for being a hard worker has a positive impact, whereas praise for being smart has the opposite effect.

In a conversation about car trips at parent group, Mehdi's father remarked, "I feel as if we're spending a lot of time driving around these days. Mehdi is getting involved in activities. We go to soccer and music class, and we're thinking about Junior Cub Scouts." Genevieve's mother replied, "Genevieve told me she played soccer with Mehdi at outside time the other day. She said he kicked really far." Jim's dad joined in, "Sounds like Mehdi is pretty good at it. But I have such mixed feelings about formal activities at this age. Is it too much for them? I want him to have skills, but it seems really important for them to have fun. Does it push them too hard to have organized games and have to practice?" Mehdi's dad agreed that he wondered about that too and was thinking about how to make the judgment.

The family consultant described some of the research on the importance of pleasure and said that the parents seemed to be asking crucial questions. She noted that they had all been talking for years about the children's need to have parents encourage and admire their efforts and achievements, harking back to toilet mastery, managing to be in school without a parent, and so forth.

She continued, "We've talked before about how important it is that children not just get praised indiscriminately. They need specific feedback for their work and persistence in learning. By five, we are no longer talking only about specific skills. To that learning we are adding the further dimension that the children are now able to take inside not only the shared good feeling, but also the idea of it. They are learning the *idea* of having pleasure in learning a skill. This is what helps them generalize from one experience to the next and motivates them throughout life to use their pleasure in mastery to fuel ambition, persistence, and exploration."

Genevieve's mom said, "That makes sense, but I wonder how to do it." Sarah's dad suggested, "We've talked all along about each skill, but we haven't focused on the pleasure in the learning itself." Mehdi's father said, "That still sounds abstract. Maybe I can say to him when he rides his bike all the way to the corner—you have learned so many different steps to be able to ride your bike. It's not only fun to ride your bike, but you can also enjoy how much you have learned to do that. It was hard work, but it's fun to do that and learn."

Genevieve's mom exclaimed, "Now I get it! But can the kids understand?" The family consultant said, "Yes, they now have the cognitive capacity to understand general ideas about the workings of their own minds, to abstract and connect the particular experiences into a larger category. And they are busy taking things inside. So when you supply them with an idea, it makes sense of their experience and helps them to feel good at a new level. Over and above the enormous specific pleasures in mastering each skill, like kicking the soccer ball or scoring the goal, is the general idea that there is pleasure in learning, pleasure in mastery, pleasure in being able to do something that you couldn't do before. This could be a public event like scoring in the soccer game, but it is equally significant that they have learned to join in the family's work by setting the table or giving a toy to their younger brother when they have finished their full turn. Parents should not miss these opportunities to reinforce this emerging emotional muscle of pleasure in mastery."

Jim's dad said, "When I think of it, it's incredible how much they have learned in the last five years. It's so easy to be focused on the future and what they still have to master. But we have to savor their enjoyment in the learning process they have worked through to get there. It's pretty satisfying for me as a parent to look back and see their own pleasure as the motivation to master new things."

SEEKING THE SOURCE OF PAINFUL FEELINGS

Regulation of aggression and unhappiness gives children the opportunity to enhance good feelings and break out of negative vicious circles.

Parents can promote this growth by

- **ENSURING THAT CHILDREN TRY TO IDENTIFY THE SOURCE OF ANGER, FRUSTRATION, OR DISAPPOINTMENT**
  In contrast to the particularity of the connection between pleasure and achievement, all people, as a matter of self-protection, are prone to generalize painful experiences beyond the specific instance. "I woke up on the wrong side of the bed" expresses the common knowledge that a moment of bad feeling in the morning can generalize to the whole day. Unlike our description above of the necessary effort to spread the sense of pleasure beyond particular skills, parents and teachers have to do the opposite for negative feelings. The goal is to inhibit the spread and focus attention on the particular source of the anger, frustration, disappointment, resentment, rivalry, and so forth.

Aggressive behavior in early childhood does not disappear but continues to affect children in every area of functioning throughout their lives.[81] Children don't automatically outgrow difficulty in managing anger and hostility. We have described earlier the self-defeating circle of anger in preschoolers. There is a window of opportunity before elementary school when parents and teachers can make sure that children have learned to master their aggressive feelings and impulses and developed the emotional muscles they need to resolve conflict and regulate their feelings. One method is to ensure that children learn to accurately pinpoint the source of their anger, frustration, or disappointment.

Addressing aggression has been important at every age. What is new for the five-year-olds is their capacity to use their minds actively to regulate their internal experience. We can legitimately demand that they take responsibility to identify the source of the trouble. Parents are part of this effort and have to learn to face the issues honestly. "He's tired" is no longer an adequate explanation.

Joanna's mother enlisted the group to brainstorm with her about Joanna's difficulty in shifting her feelings about her little sister once she got going. "I know we've talked about how their moods can vary, just like ours, but this feels like she starts herself down a hill of negative feelings and then just keeps going, and everything bothers her and makes her angry." Taylor's mother agreed, "It gets confusing since I don't want to stop his feelings, but it doesn't feel right to just let them go on and on." Miranda's father, a doctor, said that it is well-known that anger affects all systems, like the heart and immune systems, but he had just read a study about how anger over time affects lung functioning, even in young adults, so it seems really important to get a handle on this issue. It can affect basic health as well as relationships."[82]

The family consultant agreed that parents and teachers have a new task at this age, encouraging and expecting the children to enlist their already-developed muscles of making feelings into signals, controlling impulses, and using their minds to problem solve. He noted, "It's like you can now say, 'You can't just stay angry. Your anger has helped you notice something's bothering you. You can feel really good about using your anger as a signal. Now your job is to figure out what started it, so you can go past the anger, fix the problem, and move on. I'll help you if you need me.' So Joanna can be called on her mood sooner rather than later. The more we can link anger to its specific trigger and evoke pleasure at figuring it out, the more we can limit the spread and the development of a habit of anger, which can have such serious later effects."[83] He called this the new emotional muscle of responsibility for seeking the source of the feeling.

Joanna's mother thought this would be really helpful but wondered where to go next when Joanna says her sister is the source of the trouble. "That's the difference now that they're five," said the family consultant. "You can help Joanna get more precise, narrowing down what specifically is bothering her. The more concretely she can define the issue, the easier it is to find a solution. You can ask Joanna to pinpoint what her sister did or what about her sister made her angry."

Joanna's mom said, "Well, we might get down to her objecting to her sister's existence!" "If that's really her issue," said another mom, "then we're back to the three buckets. She is going to have to accept her sister's presence and work with you to learn more ways to get along. She can't do anything about her sister's existence, but she can do something about her sister taking her markers."

The family consultant added, "Maybe our point here is that no one should be allowed to inflict their anger on everyone else because that is an aggressive action in itself. We can help them find alternatives and, equally important, get pleasure from finding an alternative."

KNOWING HOW TO HAVE A GOOD GOOD-BYE

Develop the strength to bear sadness.

Parents can promote this growth by

- **TEACHING THAT SADNESS COMES FROM LOVING**
Life is filled with helloes and good-byes.[84] From the beginning of the school experience both children and their parents have developed a series of emotional muscles to deal with separation. They have learned to differentiate separation from traumatic abandonment and permanent loss. They have learned that growing independence is not a loss. Instead it's an opportunity for closeness at a new level.

In the same light, they have learned that assertion is not aggression and that independence does not imply angry rejection or failure. Children manage without their parents at preschool, not because they hate their parents but because of the positive, secure foundation parents have provided.

At six years old, children and parents are ready to say good-bye to Allen Creek, their teachers and the family consultants they may have worked with since early toddlerhood or even pregnancy.[85] Everyone feels sad; the final separation muscle to develop is to have the strength to bear the sadness. Without work on this muscle, there can be a bad good-bye, which can have lasting negative effect, causing the other muscles related to separateness and separation to wither and atrophy.

We have repeatedly seen that by January or February of the graduating year, parents turn their thoughts to the future, talking about the new school for the following September. Their anxieties, hopes, and daydreams center on the future. At parent group meetings, they exchange notes on various schools and worriedly ask the family consultant if their children will be able to meet the academic criteria of government testing mandates. They pester teachers to offer more lessons or different lessons. The children also become anxious. Like the parents, they start talking about next year and which school they will be going to.

The teacher of the graduating class reminded the parents and children that there were still nine months to go before they started big school. She said that nine months is a lifetime to a young child, so right now we are going to focus on where we are now and how we got here. The teacher began a memory project. All the children were asked to bring photos of earlier times. The teacher made sure that the request was workable for children in biological and adoptive families, checking with each parent about how they wanted to talk about it with their children. Each child would have a scrapbook of pictures, stories, and memories of how they were and what they did before. The children loved this project and shared photos with each other of the time before they could talk or walk or still pooped in their diapers.

At a parent meeting, some parents expressed puzzlement about the memory project. "Why go over old times and talk about old teachers or old friends or our dog who died? This will only make the children sad and upset." Another parent said that she had been excited and energized thinking about big school. This memory project was bringing her down, making her feel sad and realize how much she would miss Allen Creek.

"What's wrong with sad?" asked the family consultant. There was a silence, then one parent said, "Sad is like depressed. I was really depressed when I was a teenager, and I don't want to go through that again." Most parents nodded in agreement, and some added other personal experiences of being sad or depressed after the death of a parent or a miscarriage or the death of a pet.

The family consultant, who happened to be an eminent researcher in the field of depression, said, "Okay, time for me to be authoritative. This is from the horse's mouth since this is my area of professional expertise. Sadness and depression are often thought to be the same, but they are totally different phenomena. Modern neuroscience demonstrates that sadness and depression light up different parts of the brain on scans.

"Depression is a complex experience related to rage, helplessness, and sometimes abuse. Sadness has to do with love. The breakup of a long unsatisfactory love affair may trigger a depression. The death of a loved parent will probably leave you feeling intensely sad. When you finish a novel you really love, you may feel sad because a loving experience has ended. You're not feeling used, abused, abandoned, or angry, which is what triggers a depression. In your sadness at the end of the novel, you may recall favorite scenes, you may search for another novel by the same author or anticipate the publication of the next one. You may decide to reread the book. Sadness, if managed, will be growth enhancing. Depression is rage-filled self-destruction. If you confuse sadness and depression, as many people do, you can turn a loving and hence sad good-bye into an angry depressive reaction."

There was a long silence. After a few moments, the family consultant said, "I'm sorry, I didn't mean to come on so strong, but this is an important distinction. In order to help your child have a growth-enhancing good good-bye, you have to be able to stick with your own sadness and support your children bearing their sadness."

The children seemed to be ahead of the adults. While the children were enjoying recalling and taking inside their loving memories, their parents were still focused on the future. At the next parent meeting, the family consultants started by describing their observations of how the children were working on their memory project. They didn't seem upset at all. Perhaps there was something important to learn from the kids. The family consultants noted that this was a big good-bye for the family consultants too. They had worked together with many in the group for five years, so perhaps it was a good time to recall together and consolidate what had been learned over that time.

Some of the parents became tearful as each shared what they felt they had learned over the years and how much they would miss the warmth of the group and the usually gentle nudges of the family consultants. "If it was such a good experience, we don't actually have to lose it," said one parent. "Over these last months, we can do what our children are doing, bear the pain of sadness in order to remember, and consolidate what we have learned and gained." Another parent said, "We feel safe with each other. It may sound sappy, but we now have the muscle to bear the sadness and admit that we love each other."

USING STRATEGIES

*Knowing they can find a strategy gives children
confidence to face challenges.*

When parents teach children a repertoire of strategies, children can grow up learning that they will always be able to think of a plan.

Parents can promote this growth by

- **TEACHING ANTICIPATION AND PREPARATION**
The role of anticipation and preparation has been largely the responsibility of parents, caregivers, and teachers. In infancy and toddlerhood, adults anticipated changes out loud and made sure they were gradual. For young children, changes, especially separations, were presented in manageable steps to support mastery and a sense of predictability. Parents used their own words and taught children words to make sense of what was ahead. Five-year-olds are more self-aware and more self-sufficient. From a consolidated position of partnership with children, adults can increasingly hand over responsibility for utilizing strategies.

Joan had a difficult beginning, born with a neurological problem that affected the use of one arm and one leg. She suffered many early losses in her country of origin and was adopted just before she was three. When she first joined the junior preschool class, she had little language, few social skills, and difficulty in motor activities. She progressed very quickly, with her devoted and active adoptive parents working together with Allen Creek staff and other professionals to address her various developmental needs.

By five, Joan had full receptive and expressive language, was well liked by her classmates, and could participate in all the curricular and physical activities. Joan actually showed greater persistence, focus, and capacity to start and finish a project than many of the others. She had developed the emotional muscle to accept and compensate for her physical limitations and was able to experience pleasure in her own accomplishments without comparing herself to others.

At certain times, however, seemingly for no apparent reason, Joan would deliberately ignore her teachers, disrupt group activities, be physically pushy and verbally bossy and aggressive. She seemed to lose her new academic achievements, such as writing her letters or listening to and understanding chapter books being read by her teacher. The teachers were puzzled; appeals to Joan's inside helper had no effect.

At their weekly meeting with their class family consultants, the teachers said that Joan was like two different girls, one bossy, controlling of others, and angry with no "stopping muscles." The other was pleasant, engaged, joyful, empathic, loving, and competent. The family consultant noted that they were vividly describing Joan functioning sometimes in the closed system and sometimes in the open system, both aimed at making herself feel safe. There must be something that felt really frightening and potentially overwhelming to Joan if her emotional muscles couldn't help her feel strong enough to sustain good functioning and stay in the open system. We should work out what the triggers may be so that we will be able to help Joan develop strategies for putting aside this unhelpful way of feeling safe.

The following week, Joan's favorite teacher was out sick for two days. On her return, Joan wouldn't look at her and soon started the bossy, out-of-control behavior. This was the "aha! moment" for the team as they realized that separation was the trigger for overwhelming Joan's competent emotional muscles and reinstating closed-system power dynamics in an effort to protect herself from panic. This insight enabled the teachers and Joan's parents to better prepare her for impending separations and work more specifically with her on tolerating unexpected events. Over the next period, they talked more explicitly with Joan about thinking and planning ahead. Soon, Joan began to look ahead herself. She talked from the beginning of December about the upcoming winter holidays. Her bossy behavior faded away. It seemed she was no longer experiencing every separation as a catastrophic surprise. The strategies of anticipation and preparation are an emotional equivalent of the essential warm-ups for effective use of physical muscles.

Over time, with much effort and repetition at home and school, Joan developed the muscle to deal with separations more adaptively. She herself began to talk ahead of time about sad and missing feelings, of holding absent people in mind, and her feeling that her parents and teachers kept her in mind when they were away. At graduation from Allen Creek, six-year-old Joan hugged her teacher and said, "I'll miss you, but I'll always remember you, and I know you'll always remember me."

• **TEACHING AND MODELING SELF-TALK AND TALKING WITH OTHERS**
We have suggested that parents use words with children from birth on, naming, explaining, anticipating, and making sense of experience. Words are a powerful tool. Allen Creek parents, teachers, and children have all experienced the usefulness of words as a strategy to help them contain and modulate feelings.

It was a cold winter day. During outside playtime, Danny realized that the sandpit had a thick, icy surface. He first tried to chop at the ice but then discovered that he could run, flop down, and slide across the ice on his tummy. All the children wanted to try, and they spontaneously formed a line, waiting with excitement for their turns. George was at the end of the line and wanted to cut in. All the children stopped him, and one child said, "You can wait for your turn. It won't take long."

George got angry, looked sulky, and stomped off to sit alone on the steps of the climbing structure. His teacher heard him muttering to himself, "Waiting muscles." George sat there for no more than two minutes, then stood up, took a deep breath, squared his shoulders, then began to laugh with pleasure as he ran to the end of the line. The sliding game went on for a long time with all the children having fun. The teacher never had to intervene. When it was time to go indoors, the teacher praised the whole group for inventing a fun activity, doing it safely, and taking turns so that everyone had a good time. She then whispered to George how strong he was to use talking to himself to get over his anger so quickly so that he could then join the fun. George smiled broadly and said, "It sure was fun. Did you see how far I slided?"

George was using a very important emotional muscle, the capacity to recover on his own. Recently, psychologists have focused on the capacity to bounce back as one of the major components of resilience.[86] George bounced back by using the strategy of talking to himself. This strategy will be helpful to George throughout his life.

Even younger children show empathy and help each other out at hard times. A new feature with five-year-olds is their capacity to remind each other to use strategies to help themselves.

Gloria's mother had a serious illness with many ups and downs. Whenever her mother was particularly unwell, Gloria's school behavior deteriorated. She did things that she knew were against the rules, like trying to go out the main door to the parking lot or running into the second playground without permission. When her teachers stopped her and remonstrated, Gloria collapsed into floods of angry tears, unable to listen or talk at first, and alarming the other children with the intensity of her feelings. The individual moments were dealt with in various ways, but the teacher wanted to make a wider learning opportunity for the whole class.

When Gloria was in a good period in school, the teacher started a general discussion in circle about big feelings and all the ways the kids know how to help themselves manage them so the feelings wouldn't feel too big. The teacher went over the learning steps from when they were very young, reminiscing about how they used to pretend to squeeze those too-big feelings down until they were small enough to fit into one hand.

The teacher was using talking in the group as a strategy to help the children remember to use the muscles they had already developed. Over time, the teachers saw that the strategy of talking something through with others became a major problem-solving tool and an effective calming strategy for all the children.

- **ENLISTING PHYSICAL STRATEGIES**

As part of the regular curriculum at Allen Creek, the classroom teacher and the creative arts specialist do dance, movement, physical education, and yoga with the children. In the context of those lessons, the adults explicitly include the idea that there are things to do with one's body that can help manage feelings and impulses. Parents are also helped to learn these strategies and support their children in applying them.

The next time Gloria had a bad day, two of her friends suggested that they all take some deep breaths. The three girls stood together at the side of the classroom and began to count breaths. Gloria participated with pleasure in this shared activity and calmed down noticeably. "That feels better," she exclaimed.

During the year, the children learned many techniques, like lying flat on the floor, breathing through the left nostril (a yoga technique), taking time by themselves or asking for time with the teacher, turning on music and making a dance with the feeling, counting to ten forward and backward.

During parent group, Max's dad laughed and said he was surprised and delighted at what happened when he came home from work one day in a crabby mood. Max took one look at him and advised him to take eleven breaths through his left nostril. They did it together, "and it worked! Besides I was so pleased that he was wise and helpful."

- **MAKING A "TOO BIG" FEELING INTO A "JUST RIGHT SIZE" FEELING**

The five-year-olds were working with clay. There was a big mound in the middle of the table and the children were taking off pieces of different sizes to make animals for a farm. Sam remarked, "We had this big, messy blob and now I just made a statue of a cow." The teacher said, "That reminds me of the way we found to help with feelings that were too big when you were younger. Remember how you used to squeeze those too big, messy feelings down into a little ball you could hold in your hand so you could look at it and figure out what it was about? Sam took a big, blobby piece from the mound and made a cow, and Jenny just made a cat for the barn."

A few days later, John came into school upset. He threw his backpack under his hook and grunted good-bye to his dad. The teacher looked at him inquiringly. John went over to her and said, "I think I need to squeeze your finger to help myself get these feelings smaller. It was too hard this morning." His teacher said, "When you squeeze my finger that helps you remember that you know how to get your feelings down to the right size. Next time you can try to do it yourself and I'll be here too."

- **FINDING AND IMPLEMENTING PLEASURABLE POSSIBILITIES DESPITE ADVERSITY**

Sometimes, there is nothing a person can do when times are tough. Then the best response is to draw upon internal and external resources to find pleasure.

Stanley's mother talked in parent group about an experience that she felt was important. She reminded the group that her husband has had to go out of state for work. So they are only seeing him intermittently. Stanley was being stubborn and defiant the week before, and she was feeling pretty impatient. Then she realized what was going on. She sat down with him and said, "I think we are both missing Daddy a lot, and we're dealing with it by getting cranky with each other." Stanley burst into tears and hugged her. She went on to say, "So I said to him that we had to find a way to both feel better. What can we do?"

She said she recalled what the group had learned about sadness and missing; she suggested to Stanley that instead of only having angry feelings about missing Daddy, they could think about the fun they have when they are together. Stanley brightened up and talked about how his daddy was missing the snow since he was in Texas; last winter, they built snowmen together. The mom described how she said they could build a snowman together, take a picture, and send it to Daddy. Stanley was excited, his mood changed, and he began planning what the snowman would be like; how pleased Daddy would be to get the picture!

In the group, she emphasized that focusing on pleasurable possibilities with Stanley made her more aware of how she felt stuck in resentment about her family's predicament, and she hadn't tried to be more imaginative about addressing the situation. After her talk with Stanley, she decided to investigate ways to talk to her husband by video on the computer, which would also make his daddy much more present for Stanley.

The family consultant said, "I really appreciate how much parents help each other and teach me. You've taught us something important tonight. Hard feelings need to be actively addressed and alternatives sought. Stanley's and your anger, understandable, even though you know rationally that your husband's absence is for the whole family, has to be recognized and not denied. But it is crucial to take the next step, to go beyond the anger to the sadness and the love it represents. Finding pleasure beyond that situation is a powerful tool for dealing with life."

"The best part of the story," said Stanley's mom, "is that when I told him how we could talk with Daddy on the computer, Stanley said, 'I'm going to read him a story so he will have a nice bedtime and he will know that I am learning to read.'"

- **PROMOTING DRAMATIC PLAY**

Parents and teachers have been working for years to establish and reinforce the distinctions between real and pretend, thought and action, feelings and reality. By the time the children turn five, they have a fairly sturdy base, especially in school, where the pretend is never allowed to become overwhelming or scary. Strategies can be acted out in a play or story, which reinforces the skills for the children and gives them the opportunity to test options without real consequences. [87]

Stanley had told his friends in circle that his dad was in Texas for work. His teacher knew that Stanley would benefit from some intellectual scaffolding for understanding what was going on and thinking about his feelings. She knew that all the other children could expand their repertoire of strategies from what would help Stanley by making a play of his particular story. She suggested that the children think of who the people are in the story. "Who will be the Daddy who has to go far away for work? Who will be the big and little brothers who are left at home? Who will be the mommy missing her husband? Who will help the mommy when she doesn't have daddy around?"

The children eagerly became engaged, throwing out ideas for scenarios and situations. Stanley was the expert since he knew what it was like. He was named the director. The kids asked him about Texas and all went to find it on the map. A whole week was spent canvassing the options for dealing with an absent father. All the possible feelings and situations could be safely explored in the pretend world of the play.

- **ENCOURAGING ASKING FOR HELP TO PROBLEM SOLVE**

In the above discussion of teaching strategies to children, we have emphasized the goal of the children internalizing responsibility and taking the initiative in finding solutions. But part of taking responsibility for realistic assessment of the situation is knowing when you need help and being brave enough to ask for it, partnering with another to solve the problem.

As the children selected parts for the play about a daddy in Texas, Gerry went off by himself. His teacher went over and said that the class was trying something pretty new. Even grown-ups sometimes find it hard to do something different. Grown-ups learn they can ask for help. It's not babyish; it actually takes very strong muscles. She left him and returned to the group. At one point she said, "We need someone to pretend to be the engineer who drives the train to Texas. Is there anyone who can do that?" She could see that Gerry was interested but still held back.

The teacher asked if anyone had ever been in a train. Ella talked about her trip to Chicago. The teacher asked if anyone had ever driven a train. No one had. "So," she said, "whoever takes this part will have to be brave enough to ask for help to learn how to drive a train. Maybe I'll go the library after school today and ask the librarian to help me find books abut driving trains." At the end of the day, Gerry approached the teacher and said, "I think I would like to learn how to pretend to be the train driver."

- **INTRODUCING THE CONCEPT OF STRATEGY**

This can occur at any point in the year, depending on the child. But sooner or later, parents and teachers can introduce the general or abstract concept of having strategies and how the very idea can give you confidence to figure out what to do. Adults are models of people who use strategies all the time.

One day in class, when the teacher had planned to serve melon for snack, she discovered that it was overripe and couldn't be used. Momentarily dismayed, she exclaimed, "Oh dear, I'm not sure what to do!" Then she said out loud, "Wait a minute, when I feel this way, I remind myself that I know a lot of strategies." She went to ask the teacher in another class if they had any extra fruit; the children happily tried pomegranates for snack instead even though they had been anticipating trying the melon. The teacher complimented their flexibility and reminded them of how she had felt momentarily helpless.

In a conversation during snack, she continued, "Do you remember all the things we have talked about doing when our feelings get too big or we have a problem to solve?" Joanna said, "I make a plan." Best friends Isaac and George laughed and said, "We help each other." Dan suggested, "Sometimes I look at a book for a few minutes or I talk to my mom."

"Those are such helpful ideas," said the teacher. "They are called strategies," and she got up to write the word on the whiteboard. "Even before you have figured out exactly what to do, you can remind yourself that you know so many strategies that you will be able to solve the problem."

In a parent group, Peter's father described his surprise the evening before. Talking at supper about an upcoming car trip to grandparents for Easter, he had said, "I'll have to plan our route." Peter piped up, "That's a strategy, Daddy." His father said, "I was blown away that he knew that word and that concept. When I asked him about it, he said Mrs. N. had been telling them the idea." Peter had said, "Mrs. N. told us to remember that we already know a whole lot of strategies." His dad said he was realizing that he should bring Peter in on his thinking about things. "I can tell Peter that I am looking for what strategy to use when I have a problem to solve. So we are going to look at the map and plan our trip together. We'll also talk about how different things are at Grandma and Grandpa's so we know how to deal with that."

The family consultant agreed this represented a big step forward and said, "Now they are old enough for us to step it up another level. Five- and six-year-olds are getting sophisticated in their thinking. They can use abstract concepts as tools. We can teach them not only the various strategies we've been talking about all year, but also the *idea* of strategy. Whenever we address a situation, we can now add, 'We were planning ahead. That's called a strategy. When we think of a strategy, it helps us use our waiting muscles, our imagination, and our skills.'"

Isaac's mother had been listening quietly and then said, "I want to tell you a story because I think we are talking about something that can be really important for our children. When I was six, I learned in school about the Holocaust in World War II. They told us how many people died and how there was nothing anyone could do. I found this very frightening. I began to have all kinds of nightmares. My parents were worried about me. Then it happened that there was an exhibit about Raoul Wallenberg at the museum.

"My parents took me to see the exhibit and told me the story of how Raoul Wallenberg, who was a Swedish diplomat in Hungary in 1944, was very upset at what he saw happening to the Jews, so he decided he had to think of a way to save them. My mother said that he thought and thought and came up with a plan to fool the bad Nazis and help Jews escape. He saved many, many lives. I had no more nightmares that night or after. I think now as we talk about offering our children the reassurance that they can trust themselves to find a plan because they have the very idea of a strategy, that we are giving them what my parents gave me. They showed me that people don't have to feel helpless and hopeless."

- **HOW PARENTS HELP BUILD THE EMOTIONAL MUSCLES OF**

USING EMOTIONAL MUSCLES
Parents help by
• HELPING CHILDREN REMEMBER THE MUSCLES THEY HAVE

PLAYING COOPERATIVELY
Parents help by
• EXPECTING AND ALLOWING CHILDREN TO INDEPENDENTLY INITIATE, SUSTAIN, AND ENJOY COOPERATIVE GROUP PLAY

WITHSTANDING INTERNAL AND EXTERNAL PRESSURES TO BLUR THE DISTINCTION BETWEEN REAL AND PRETEND
Parents help by
• INSISTING ON REALITY-BASED SOLUTIONS

RESTRAINT
Parents help by
• EXPLAINING, DEMONSTRATING, AND COACHING RESTRAINT

EMBRACING THE RULES OF REALITY
Parents help by
• REINFORCING YOUR CHILD'S PLEASURE IN MASTERY OF REALITY RULES

PLAYING WITH WHOLEHEARTED PLEASURE
Parents help by
• PLAYING WITHOUT GUILT OR RESENTMENT

SYNTHESIS AND INTEGRATION
Parents help by
• ADMIRING PUTTING IT ALL TOGETHER

FLEXIBILITY
Parents help by
• INTRODUCING NEW EXPERIENCES

ENJOYING COMPETENCE
Parents help by
• REINFORCING THE SATISFACTION OF EFFORT AND DOING IT WELL

SEEKING THE SOURCE OF PAINFUL FEELINGS
Parents help by
• ENSURING THAT CHILDREN LEARN TO TRY TO IDENTIFY THE SOURCE OF ANGER, FRUSTRATION, OR DISAPPOINTMENT

KNOWING HOW TO HAVE A GOOD GOOD-BYE
Parents help by
• TEACHING THAT SADNESS COMES FROM LOVING

USING STRATEGIES
Parents help by
• TEACHING ANTICIPATION AND PREPARATION • TEACHING AND MODELING SELF-TALK AND TALKING WITH OTHERS • ENLISTING PHYSICAL STRATEGIES • MAKING A "TOO BIG FEELING" INTO A "JUST RIGHT SIZE FEELING" • FINDING AND IMPLEMENTING PLEASURABLE POSSIBILITIES DESPITE ADVERSITY • PROMOTING DRAMATIC PLAY • ENCOURAGING ASKING FOR HELP TO PROBLEM SOLVE • INTRODUCING THE CONCEPT OF STRATEGY

EMOTIONAL MUSCLES IN CHILDREN 0-5

THEME AGE	FEELINGS	MASTERY/ AUTONOMY	MANAGING NEGATIVE FEELINGS	REALITY	RELATIONSHIPS	EXECUTIVE FUNCTIONS
5's	Enjoying competence; Playing with pleasure Connecting love & sadness; Good good-byes	Flexibility	Restraint; Seek source of painful feeling	Rules of reality; Maintaining real vs. pretend	Play cooperatively	Using emotional muscles; Synthesis and integration; Using strategies
4's		Worries as a spur to mastery	Generating internal controls; Regulating aggression	Living in real world; Internalizing realistic standards	Form group conscience	Integrate emotional muscles
3's	Learning emotional cause and effect	Persistence and commitment to goal; Assertion & exploration	Tolerating frustration in play; Anger as signal	Making choices; Distinguishing real and pretend	Pleasure in sharing experiences	
2's	Contain love & hate; Name feelings	Striving for mastery; Bravery	Making feelings "just right" size	Accepting realistic power and limits		
1's	Tolerate mixed feelings; Empathy; Respond positively to challenges	Agency & responsibility	Self-control; Self-awareness	Making meaning of experience		
Babies	Trust	Initiative; Focus; Flexibility; Anticipation; Cause and effect; Dependability; Competence	Understanding consequences;			

EMOTIONAL MUSCLES IN PARENTS

THEME AGE	RETAINING POSITIVE FEELINGS	SEPARATENESS	MANAGING NEGATIVE FEELINGS	REALITY OF YOUR CHILD	ATTUNEMENT/ RELATIONSHIP	PARENTHOOD
5's			Exercise judgment about emotional responsibility		Understanding misbehavior as an attempted solution	Stamina; Maintaining self-esteem; Satisfying adult needs
4's	Finding positive and assertive in child's wishes		Accepting reality limitations; Differentiate authoritative & authoritarian	Honest appraisal of child; Engage with issue of aggression	Partnering with your child; Creating a support network; Revitalizing adult partnership	
3's	Taking pleasure in child's new capacities	Integrate love and separateness; Respect child's privacy; Holding love through separations; Sharing child's love with others	Competence, not dominance			Feeling good in role as parent; Self-reflection
2's	Holding on to love	Tolerating different pleasure needs of child and adult	Differentiate assertion & aggression	Embrace individuality of child; Engage with reality of aggression	Empathy	Including social consequences; Advocating for your child
1's	Finding positive in activity; Enjoying steps along the way	Transforming relationship; Retaining mastery and autonomy as goal	Tolerating own sadness		Working to stay in tune; Crediting power of language	Responsibility for safety; Setting realistic limits; Accepting role as model
Babies	Holding on to love; Creating a positive cycle; Keeping joy and love in the picture	Separation vs. separateness	Bearing uncertainty & facing unknown; Bearing own intense feelings; Living through beby's distress	Opening self to reality of baby's emotions; Recognizing when to seek help	Making alliance with baby; Creating supportive partnerships	

ENDNOTES

1   For a more comprehensive, professional discussion of the theoretical underpinnings of the idea of emotional muscle, please see our paper "Building Emotional Muscle in Children and Parents," in Psychoanalytic Study of the Child, vol.65, 2011. Emotional muscle is a part of the open system in our developmental model of self-regulation. The idea of two systems of self-regulation is a thread through our writings, starting in 1970 and first published as such in 1991. A more recent summary of these ideas may be found in Novick, J. and Novick, K. K. (2001), Two systems of self-regulation, Journal of Psychoanalytic Social Work 8: 95-122, and in our later books *Working With Parents Makes Therapy Work* (2005) and *Good Goodbyes: Knowing How to End in Psychotherapy and Psychoanalysis* (2006).

2   For more details on Allen Creek Preschool, please visit the website at www.allencreek.org. Allen Creek Preschool is a founding member and an accredited psychoanalytic school of the national nonprofit Alliance for Psychoanalytic Schools.

Babies and Their Parents

3   Markova, G. A. and Legerstee, M. (2008). How infants come to learn about the minds of others. Zero to Three 28: No. 5, 26-31. In this study, the authors offer a framework to explain that infants understand the thoughts and feelings of others through sharing emotions with their caregivers. They note that infants are born with three predispositions: (1) the ability to recognize people as similar to themselves, (2) awareness of their own and others' emotions, (3) recognition of the caregivers' attunement.
    Salo, F. T. (2007). Recognizing the infant as subject in infant-parent psychotherapy. International Journal of Psycho-Analysis 88: 961-79. This clinical study confirms the accuracy and efficacy of relating to babies

as subjects in their own experience, even in extremely serious clinical conditions like failure to thrive.

4   Trevarthen (1979). Communication and cooperation in early infancy: a description of primary intersubjectivity. In: M. M. Bullowa (Ed.) Before Speech: The Beginning of Interpersonal Communication (pp. 321-347). New York: Cambridge University Press.

5   Thompson, R. A. (2008). The psychologist in the baby. Zero to Three. 28: No. 5, 5-12.

6   Markova, G. A. and Legerstee, M. (2008). How infants come to learn about the minds of others. Zero to Three. 28: No. 5, 26-31

7   There is a very useful and sobering summary of recent research on sleep patterns in children and their short and long-term effects in children and adolescents in *NurtureShock: New Thinking about Children*, by Po Bronson and Ashley Merryman (2009), Twelve Hachette Book Group, New York. He reports that changes in preschoolers' routines, for instance, on weekends if they go to bed later and sleep later, have been shown to affect IQ adversely.

8   Tronick, E. Z. and Gianino, A. (1986). Interactive mismatch and repair. Zero to Three. 6: 1-6. Novick, K. K. and Novick, J. (1987). The essence of masochism. Psychoanal. Study Child 42: 353-384.

9   Novick, J. and Novick, K. K. (2001). Two systems of self-regulation: psychoanalytic approaches to the treatment of children and adolescents. J. of Psa. Social Work 8: 95-122.

10   Doidge, N. (2007). *The Brain That Changes Itself*. New York: Viking Press.

11   Panksepp, J. (2001). The long-term psychobiological consequences of infant emotions: prescriptions for the twenty-first century. Infant Mental Health Journal 22: 132-173.

     Researchers have systematically studied infants' emotions for only the past forty years. Parents, nurses, and some pediatricians already knew that babies are full of feelings, the same as the rest of us. What has emerged, however, is a gradually enriched picture of the breadth, depth and complexity of infant emotions, with clear evidence of how early they come into play. See, for example, the pioneering work of S. Tomkins (1991). Affect, Imagery, Consciousness. Volume 3: The Negative Affects: Anger and Fear. New York: Springer. And Tomkins, S. (1992). Affect, Imagery, Consciousness. Volume 4: Cognition: Duplication and Transformation of Information. New York: Springer. Paul Holinger's book with K. Doner, *What Babies Say Before They Can Talk* (2003), New York: Simon and Schuster, offers a good summary of the general thinking.

Warren et al (2008), The emotional foundations of social understanding, Zero to Three: 28, No. 5: 32-39, describe the nuanced unfolding of the sequence of predominant emotions in the first year.

12 There is a powerful and pervasive Anglo-American tradition that children's growth takes place via separation from parents rather than through the development and support of their separateness as autonomous individuals. This has ramifications lifelong. For discussions of this issue at later ages, see, for instance, DeVito, E., Novick, J. and Novick, K. K. (2000) Cultural interferences with listening to adolescents. Journal of Infant, Child and Adolescent Psychotherapy 1: 77-95. See also Palombo, J. (2011 in press), Executive function disorders and self-deficits. In: Mental Health and Social Problems: A Social Work Perspective, Alex Gitterman and Nina Heller, Eds. New York: Routledge.

13 Allen Creek Preschool and other schools in the Alliance for Psychoanalytic Schools have various outreach programs for consultation to day cares and preschools. Many examples in this book are drawn from that work. We are grateful to colleagues from the APS for sharing material.

14 Henderson, A.M.E., Gerson, S., and Woodward, A. L. (2008). The birth of social intelligence. Zero to Three 28, no. 5: 13-20 (p.19).

15 Bauer, P. J. (2009). The life I once remembered: the waxing and waning of early memories. Zero to Three 30: No. 2, 14-21.

16 ibid.

17 Researchers describe this play as "proto-conversation." Markova, G. A. and Legerstee, M. (2008). How infants come to learn about the minds of others. Zero to Three 28, No. 5, 26-31.

18 Panksepp, J. (1998). Affective Neuroscience: The Foundations of Human and Animal Emotions. New York: Oxford University Press.
Panksepp, J. (2001). The long-term psychobiological consequences of infant emotions: prescriptions for the 21st century. Infant Mental Health Journal 22: 132-173.

19 Novick, J. and Novick, K. K. ([1987, 1991], 2007). Fearful Symmetry: the Development and Treatment of Sadomasochism. New Jersey: Jason Aronson

One-Year-Olds and Their Parents

20 Tomasello, M. (1999). Social cognition before the revolution. In: P. Rochat (Ed.) Early social Cognition. Mahwah, NJ: Erlbaum. Pp. 301-314. The 9-month revolution refers to a nodal point in brain development and social-cognitive functioning.

21 Novick, J. and Novick, K. K. (2007). Fearful Symmetry. Aronson: New Jersey, Chapter "Talking with toddlers;" Katan, A. (1961). Some thoughts about the role of verbalization in early childhood. Psychoanal. Study Child 16: 184-188. New York: International Universities Press; Bruner, J. (1983). Child's Talk. New York: Norton Press; Salo, F. T. (2007). Recognizing the infant as subject in infant-parent psychotherapy. Int. J. Psycho-Anal. 88: 961-979.

22 Thompson, R. A. (2008). The psychologist in the baby. Zero to Three 28, No. 5, 5-12.

23 Satter, Ellyn (2000). Child of Mine: Feeding with Love and Good Sense. Boulder, Bull Publishing Company.

24 National Research Council and Institute of Medicine (2000) From Neurons to Neighborhoods: The Science of Early Development, J. P. Shonkoff and D. A. Phillips (Eds.). Washington, DC: National Academy Press.

25 There is a demonstrated relationship between acceptance of realistic limitations and later resilience. Haglund, M.E.M., Nestadt, P. S., Cooper, N. S., Southwick, S. M., and Charney, D. S. (2007). Psychobiological mechanisms of resilience: relevance to prevention and treatment of stress-related psychopathology. Development and Psychopathology 19: 889-920.

26 This Allen Creek technique of the "whole turn or "full turn" has proven useful in homes and schools in many places.

Two-Year-Olds and Their Parents

27 Thompson, R. A. (2008). The psychologist in the baby. Zero to Three, 28, No.5, p.7

28 The research evidence for these findings is based on work with mammals. The suggestion is that this also applies to humans. See the work of Freeman, cited in Doidge, N. (2007). The Brain That Changes Itself. New York: Viking Press p.118

29 Warren et. al. (see endnote to chapter on one-year-olds).
30 Furman, E. (1985). On fusion, integration, and feeling good. Psychoanalytic Study of the Child 40: 81-110.
31 Haglund, M.E.M., Nestadt, P. S., Cooper, N. S., Outhwick, S. M. and Charney, D. S. (2007). Psychobiological mechanisms of resilience: relevance to prevention and treatment of stress-related psychopathology. Development and Psychopathology 19: 889-920. "Acceptance is an adaptive coping strategy commonly found among people who are able to tolerate extreme and uncontrollable stress . . . Acceptance involves recognizing the uncontrollable aspects of certain stressors, reappraising the stressor in light of that information, changing expectations about outcome and control of outcome, based on reality, and focusing on controllable aspects of the stressor. Acceptance is not to be confused with resignation, which is giving up or coping passively" (p.910).
32 Toilet mastery is a concept coined by Robert Furman, from work at the Hanna Perkins Center for Child Development, a founder school of the Alliance for Psychoanalytic Schools. More discussion can be found in Furman, R. A. (1991). On toilet mastery. Child Analysis 2: 98-110.

Three-Year-Olds and Their Parents

33 Attachment is the term used to describe the bond that grows between infants and their parents, particularly their mothers. It includes biological and psychological components, interacting from the beginning, affecting and affected by complex aspects of each person and their environment. Early attachment patterns persist powerfully into later relationships.
34 Adoption is a challenge to biological parents, adoptive parents, and adopted children. The many successful adoptions rely on clear-sighted understanding that adoption is a meaningful factor for all parties in most aspects of development. It can, however, be a negative loading, burdening a child's development when it is denied. When the impact of adoption is not denied, parents can take steps to address, for instance, their own and their children's attachment needs.
35 The concept of the unconscious parts of the mind is a cornerstone of the general psychoanalytic theory of normal and pathological mental functioning. For a vivid description of the operation of unconscious

factors in normal and pathological parent-child relationships, we suggest Fraiberg, S., Adelson, E. and Shapiro, V. (1975). Ghosts in the nursery: a psychoanalytic approach to the problems of impaired mother-child relationships. Journal of the American Academy of Child Psychiatry 14: 387-421.

36 For more explanation about "mirror neurons," we suggest Doidge, N. (cited in an endnote in the chapter on two-year-olds).
The "mirror neuron was discovered by neuroscientists in the mid-1990s (Gallese, V., Fadiga, L., Fogassi, L., and Rizzolatti, G. [1996]). Action recognition in the premotor cortex. Brain 119: 593-609. The mirror neuron fires both when a monkey engages in a specific activity and when the monkey observes another engaged in a similar activity. The lead author of the study applied his monkey findings to humans, suggesting that mirror neurons enable an automatic, direct and accurate simulation of the other's experience. Some authors question this application, citing the need for further studies to prove the impact of mirror neurons on human functioning.

37 For more detailed discussion of issues of transference and externalization between parents and children, please see Novick, K. K. and Novick, J. (2005), Working with Parents Makes Therapy Work, Aronson, New York.

38 Siebert, A. (1996). The Survivor Personality: Why some people are stronger, smarter and more skilled at handling life's difficulties . . . and how you can be, too. New York: Berkeley Publishing Group.

39 Dweck, C. (2007). The perils and promise of praise. Educational Leadership 65:34-39.

40 "Two-way feelings" is a term coined at the Hanna Perkins Center in Cleveland, Ohio, a founder and accredited member of the Alliance for Psychoanalytic Schools.

41 Putting a feeling or characteristic outside to get rid of anxiety, shame, discomfort, or conflict is a psychological mechanism called externalization. Novick, J. and Novick, K. K. (2007 [1970]). Projection and externalization. In: Fearful Symmetry: The Development and Treatment of Sadomasochism. Aronson, Rowman and Littlefield: Lanham, Maryland.

Four-Year-Olds and Their Parents

42 Bushman, B. J., Baumeister, R. F., and Stack, A. D. (1999). Catharsis,
    aggression, and persuasive influence: Self-fulfilling or self-defeating
    prophecies? *Journal of Personality and Social Psychology*, 76, 367-376.

43 The best predictor of sibling relationships is how older children get along
    with their best friends. Preschool friendships predict future competence
    in other sorts of relationships and in aspects of personal well-being. This
    study found that the quality of preschool friendships was a stronger
    predictor than the mother-child bond. Kramer, L. and Kowal, A. (2006,
    January 26). Study Links Early Friendships with High-Quality Sibling
    Relationships. *ScienceDaily*.

44 *NurtureShock: New Thinking about Children*, by Po Bronson and Ashley
    Merryman (2009), Twelve Hachette Book Group, New York.

45 There is a long-standing literature in psychoanalysis concerning
    the development of conscience, or "superego." The term "inside
    helper" was coined by Erna Furman at the Hanna Perkins Center,
    Cleveland, Ohio, an accredited psychoanalytic school in the Alliance for
    Psychoanalytic Schools.

46 Birch, S.A.J., Vauthier, S. A., and Bloom, P. (2008). Three- and
    four-year-olds spontaneously use others' past performance to guide
    their learning. Cognition, 107: 1,018-1,034

47 Rimm-Kaufman, S. E., Pianta, R. C., and Cox, M. J. (2000). Teachers'
    judgments of problems in the transition to kindergarten. *Early Childhood
    Research Quarterly*, 15(2), 147-166.

48 For many years, Allen Creek Preschool has offered regular consultation
    to area preschools and daycares through its Early Childhood Outreach
    (ECO) program and its Early Childhood Training Initiative (ECTI). These
    effective community efforts have developed the Graduated Intervention
    Program (GrIP), a stepwise assessment and intervention model.

49 These ideas refer to our model of two systems of self-regulation, in
    which individuals choose at points of developmental challenge to
    respond in either an open-system, realistic way or a closed-system,
    magical way.

50 This newly developing pattern of relationships arises out of the
    many aspects of the child's growth that are going on simultaneously.
    Psychoanalysts have traditionally described this constellation of feelings
    and relationships as the Oedipus complex. More modern ideas include a
    different description for girls, the Persephone complex.

51 Emerson, Ralph Waldo. Essays, 1st Series. New England Reformers.

52 Straus, M. (2008). Science Daily. Spanking Kids Increase Risk of Sexual Problems as Adults. http://www.sciencedaily.com/releases/2008/02/080228220451.htm

53 Taylor, C. A., Manganello, J. A., Shawna, J. L. and Rice, J. C. (2010). Mothers' spanking of three-year-old children and subsequent risk of children's aggressive behavior. Pediatrics 2010; 125: e1057-e1065.

54 Keller, P. (1970). A Shepherd Looks at Psalm 23. Zondervan, Grand Rapids.

55 Good ideas may be found in Sears, W. and Sears, M. (1995). The Discipline Book: How to Have a Better-Behaved Child from Birth to Age Ten. Little, Brown and Company. The section on 10 Reasons Not to Hit Your Child covers many aspects of this topic.

56 The best predictor of sibling relationships is how older children get along with their best friends. Preschool friendships predict future competence in other sorts of relationships and in aspects of personal well-being. This study found that the quality of preschool friendships was a stronger predictor than the mother-child bond. Kramer, L. and Kowal, A. (2006, January 26). Study Links Early Friendships With High-Quality Sibling Relationships. *ScienceDaily*.

57 Getting rid of an unwanted or undesirable aspect of oneself by putting it psychologically outside, attributing it to someone else, is called externalization.

58 The Alliance for Psychoanalytic Schools is an international nonprofit organization dedicated to supporting the formation of more schools that integrate modern psychoanalytic developmental ideas with best practices in early childhood education.

59 Denham, S. (1998). Emotional Development in Young Children. New York: Guilford Press

60 ibid.

61 Goodman, M. and Tomasello, M. (2008). Baby steps on the road to society: shared intentionality in the second year of life. Zero to Three 28: No.5, 21-25.

62 Siebert, A. (1996). The Survivor Personality: Why some people are stronger, smarter and more skilled at handling life's difficulties . . . and how you can be, too. New York: Berkeley Publishing Group.

63 The phrase "good enough" was first coined by D. W. Winnicott, a British pediatrician and psychoanalyst who wrote about children's development being nurtured by "good enough mothering.

Five-Year-Olds and Their Parents

64 Thompson, R. A. (2009). Doing what doesn't come naturally: the development of self-regulation. Zero to Three 30: 33-38.

65 Thompson, ibid. p.34

66 For discussion of the historical psychological traditions in our culture surrounding growing up and going away, see DeVito E., Novick, J. and Novick, K. K. (2000). Cultural interferences with listening to adolescents. JICAP 1: 77-95.

67 For extensive and clear description of these issues, see Bronson, P. and Merriman, A. (2009). *NurtureShock: New Thinking about Children*. Hachette Book Group: New York.

68 Mischel's pioneering work on frustration tolerance and capacity to delay gratification in four-year-olds demonstrated how young children can be asked to be in charge of themselves.

69 See the more detailed discussion of stretch versus stress in the chapter on three-year-olds.

70 At Allen Creek and other APS schools, there are regular evening offerings for the community, with lectures and discussions about topics of child development and parenting. The format varies, but the common aim is to foster "thoughtful parenting." The shared underlying assumption is that parents can make a tremendous difference if they reflect on themselves, think through their reactions, values and decisions, and realize that their warm, loving involvement is the delivery system for growth enhancement in their children. "Stated simply, relationships are the active ingredients of the environment's influence on healthy human development" (National Research Council and Institute of Medicine (2000). From Neurons to Neighborhoods: The Science of Early Development. Jack P. Shonkoff and Deborah A. Phillips, eds., Washington DC, National Academy Press.)

71 For a significant discussion of the dangers of a "quick fix" from medication, see Whittaker, R. (2010), Anatomy of an Epidemic, Random House, New York, especially chapters 11 and 12 about children and adolescents.

72 See earlier references to Heckman; Thompson; and Novick and Novick.

73 Diamond, A. (2002). Normal development of prefrontal cortex from birth to young adulthood: cognitive functions, anatomy, and biochemistry. In: D. T. Stuss and R. T. Knight (Eds.) Principles of Frontal Lobe Function (pp.466-503). New York: Oxford University Press.

74 Erna Furman (199) describes four steps to independent functioning. At first parents do for the child; next they do with the child; then they stand by to admire. This third step is crucial in setting the conditions for the child to take inside the parent's pleasure in her own good feelings of accomplishment. Then the inside helper will be a source of internal praise and motivation for further good feelings. Only after consolidation of these three steps is the child ready to do something independently.

75 Gopnick, A. and Seiver, E. (2009). Reading Minds: How infants come to understand others. Zero to Three 30: 28-32.

76 Panksepp, J. (2001). The long-term psychobiological consequences of infant emotions: prescriptions for the twenty-first century. Infant Mental Health Journal 22: 132-173.

77 Tierney, A. L. and Nelson, C. A. (2009). Brain development and the role of experience in the early years. Zero to Three 30: 9-13.

78 Leong, D. J. (2006). Developing self-regulation: the Vygotskian view. Academic Exchange Quarterly. Dec. 2006
    All scientists now agree that early competence predicts later success, but this paper presents a strong view on the possibility of *learning* self-regulation as we propose in this book.

79 Walker, M. P. and Stickgold, R. (2004). Sleep-dependent learning and memory consolidation. Neuron 44: 121-133. Walker, M. P. and Stickgold, R. (2006). Sleep, memory and plasticity. Annual Review of Psychology, 57: 139-166.

80 Panksepp, J. (2001). The long-term psychobiological consequences of infant emotions: prescriptions for the twenty-first century. Infant Mental Health Journal 22: 132-173.

81 Novick, K. K and Novick, J. (2011). Ibid.

82 Jackson, B., Kubzansky, L. D., Cohen, S., Jacobs, D. R., Wright, R. J. (2007). Does harboring hostility hurt? Associations between hostility and pulmonary function in the Coronary Artery Risk Development in Young Adults Study. Health Psychology 26: 333-40.

83 The family consultant was drawing on studies that have identified the amygdala as the part of the brain that registers negative feelings while the hippocampus processes pleasure. When a person is tired or stressed, the activity of the hippocampus is diminished and the negative feelings of the amygdala can more easily hold sway. This finding underscores the importance of getting to the source of negative feelings, then reactivating pleasure in the effort and the relief of return to a happy state. Walker, M. P. and Stickgold, R. (2004). Sleep-dependent

learning and memory consolidation. Neuron 44: 121-133. Walker, M. P. and Stickgold, R. (2006). Sleep, memory and plasticity. Annual Review of Psychology, 57: 139-166.

84 Novick, J. and Novick, K. K. (2006). Good Goodbyes: Knowing How to End in Psychotherapy and Psychoanalysis. New York: Jason Aronson; Rowman and Littlefield.

85 Allen Creek offers discussion groups for pregnant parents and potential adoptive parents. Many of these families return to join parent-infant group soon after birth or adoption. Thus many families are involved with Allen Creek for up to seven years.

86 See Fredrickson, B. L. (2004). Resilient individuals use positive emotions to bounce back from negative emotional experiences. J. of Personality and Social Psychology 86: 320-333; and Novick and Novick (2011).

87 The power of dramatic play is codified in the "Tools of the Mind" curriculum for preschools. See Bedrova, E. and Leung, P. (2006). Tools of The Mind: A Vygotskian Approach to Early Childhood Education, 2nd Edition. New York, Prentice Hall.

INDEX

ABOUT THE AUTHORS

Kerry Kelly Novick and Jack Novick, PhD have been working with children and families for over 45 years. Psychoanalysts and psychologists, they bring their broad and deep knowledge of development in accessible words and concepts to parents, teachers, pediatricians, nurses, and the wider community through newspaper articles, a popular weekly online parenting column (annarbor.com), talks, papers in professional journals and three earlier professional books, translated into several languages.

Kerry Kelly Novick received degrees in Comparative Literature from the University of California at Berkeley and Psychology from University College, London. Kerry is a past President of the international Association for Child Psychoanalysis.

Jack Novick received a degree in Literature and Mathematics from McGill University in Montreal, his MA in Experimental Psychology from the New School for Social Research in New York, and his PhD in Clinical Psychology from New York University. Among his many positions, he was Co-Director of Research at the Jewish Board of Guardians in New York City and Chief Psychologist for Youth Services at the University of Michigan Children's Psychiatric Hospital.

They both trained as child psychoanalysts with Anna Freud in London, England. Jack went on to do adult training at the British Psycho-Analytic Institute and Kerry at the New York Freudian Society. Long associated with the University of Michigan Medical School, they are both in clinical practice with families, children, adolescents and adults in Ann Arbor, Michigan. They are founders of the innovative, award-winning Allen Creek Preschool in Ann Arbor and the international Alliance for Psychoanalytic Schools. In addition to their consultations in schools, they have also worked in many different settings with children of all ages, like directing summer camps for normal and autistic children and free walk-in clinics for teenagers. Internationally-recognized authorities on child and adolescent development, they teach at universities and training centers throughout the world.

Jack and Kerry have three children and four grandchildren.

Visit their website at buildemotionalmuscle.com
&
EVERYDAY PARENTING QUESTIONS FOR KERRY at annarbor.com
&
Allen Creek Preschool at allencreek.org

Jack and Kerry are available for selected speaking engagements and interviews.

Praise for their earlier books—
"They give us a landmark work. This book will prove indispensable to mental health professionals." Leonard Shengold, M.D. on *Fearful Symmetry*

"Their clarity of thought and clinical focus make their book a joy to read." Robert L. Tyson, M.D., F.R.C.Psych. on *Fearful Symmetry*

"*Working With Parents Makes Therapy Work* is an extraordinarily important contribution. Their work underscores the inevitable ongoing interaction between parent functioning and child development." Leon Hoffman, M.D., Director, Pacella Parent-Child Center

"This book offers further elaboration and new applications of the Novicks' earlier research on the 'two-systems model.' It is so well-written . . . it represents a bold new vision of the role of parents in the psychoanalytic treatment of child and adolescent patients." Jerrold R. Brandell, Wayne State University School of Social Work on *Working With Parents*

"Through vivid and compelling vignettes . . . they demonstrate that . . . a patient's system of self-regulation can be transformed from one that is joyless, constricted and closed to one that is healthy, alive and open." William B. Meyer, MSW, BCD, Duke University Medical Center on *Good Goodbyes*